UNCOMMON HERO

The John Seagraves Story

David Seagraves

Oxnard
A division of Pro Planning Corporation

Copyright © 2012 by David Seagraves
All rights reserved.

All photos reprinted by permission

Cover design by Bill Walker
Editing by Barbara Hunter
Interior layout by Zuzana Urbanek

No part of this book may be reproduced in any form or by any electronic or mechanical means including information storage and retrieval systems, without permission in writing from the author. The only exception is by a reviewer, who may quote short excerpts in a review.

Printed in the United States of America

Library of Congress Cataloging-in-Publication Data

Seagraves, David
    Uncommon hero: the John Seagraves story / David Seagraves
    LCCN 2012907115
    ISBN-10 0985055502
    ISBN-13 978-0985055509
    1. Biography. 2. History of America.

DEDICATION

To Dad,
who found his passion
and shared it with the world.

Acknowledgements

Writing a book is one wonderful challenge after another, so I am grateful for the help and support of many people. First and foremost, thanks to my beloved wife and best friend Tanja, along with our precious four-legged daughter Belinda, for your loving energy, support, and encouragement during these two-and-one-half years while I labored through the many facets of writing this book.

To my dad, John, for a compelling story that needed to be told, remembering so much after 65 years, and living a life worth living. I hope this book makes you proud, both for the work that went into it and the many inspiring messages conveyed to others. To my mom, Mildred, for your love, encouragement, and support for this project, the important edits, suggestions, and research. To Pat, for wanting to make a contribution somehow, though we ran out of time, and to Linda, who always wanted me to tell the best story possible.

Many thanks to Kim Robinson Sincox, Museum Services Director, and Mary Ames Booker, Curator of Collections, Battleship NORTH CAROLINA, for assisting my parents throughout the 2009 Reunion, showing interest in my father's story which sparked the inception of this book, and providing relevant photos, documents, official references, support materials, and needed advice to further authenticate this book.

To my good friend Anthony Sarno for being my brother all these years and helping me implement our Internet marketing strategy. To Peggy McColl for extraordinary training on what makes a book a bestseller. To Steve Harrison, Geoffrey Berwind, and Raia King for providing critical promotional training at the right time, contributing outstanding insights, and recategorizing the future of a brand. To Bill Walker for doing a great job designing an eye-catching book cover and helping me think through the marketing priorities of the book.

To my editing team members from the Southeast, starting with Barbara Hunter for your passion for correctness with the printed and spoken word, doing an outstanding job polishing and refining the final draft of the manuscript. To Zuzana Urbanek for going above and beyond with edits, finishing touches toward a beautiful page layout, and final steps to self-publishing the book. Many thanks to the multitalented Randy Drew for mentoring me through the first several drafts as writing coach, military history buff, reference source, and copyeditor. To Maryann Webb for your copyediting expertise, coaching, and writing tips to vastly improve my manuscript. To Captain David R. Scheu, Sr., Former Director, Battleship NORTH CAROLINA for your feedback and encouragement with the military chapters. To Bobby Long for providing an important first round edit to steer the book in the right direction.

To Steve Drew and Sgt. Brad Drew, USMC, for assisting my parents throughout the Reunion, showing an interest in my father's story, and ushering my parents to Randy. To Richard Fitzhugh for editing our family photographs. To Battleship NORTH CAROLINA former crew members and their families for helping my father realize he is part of a unique, noteworthy family.

And thank you to my supporters who have purchased and/or promoted this book. May you, the reader, enjoy the many lessons the book reveals while following my father's inspiring journey. I am honored by your interest.

Table of Contents

Foreword ix
CHAPTER 1: Dirt Poor 1
CHAPTER 2: Early Burden 11
CHAPTER 3: Fork in the Road 25
CHAPTER 4: The Promise 39
CHAPTER 5: Enterprising Youth 53
CHAPTER 6: Graham Jackson 67
CHAPTER 7: Naval Boot Camp 75
CHAPTER 8: St. Simons Island 91
CHAPTER 9: On the Move 101
CHAPTER 10: The South Pacific 117
CHAPTER 11: The Showboat 129
CHAPTER 12: Life Onboard 147
CHAPTER 13: Taste of War 163
CHAPTER 14: Shore Leave 175
CHAPTER 15: Gunner Shot 195
CHAPTER 16: Tipping Point 205
CHAPTER 17: Defining Moment 217
CHAPTER 18: Price of Freedom 229
CHAPTER 19: Bittersweet Homecoming 243
CHAPTER 20: New Family Influences 255
CHAPTER 21: Building an Empire 271

CHAPTER 22: The New South	283
CHAPTER 23: Tested	293
CHAPTER 24: World Traveler	303
CHAPTER 25: Reunion	313
Epilogue	321
Afterword	325
About the Author	329
Bibliography	331
Endnotes	337

Foreword

How can poverty make a man rich? The simple answer lies in an equation I once heard in a personal development workshop: E + R = O. Experience plus Response equals Outcome. Experience is what happens in any person's life, for better or worse. Many times we have no control over that. It is absolutely true that we put ourselves in a position to succeed. But no matter what we have done to help or hurt our chances of success, things will happen. What we *can* control is our response to that experience. How we respond is the difference between receiving a short list of ideal outcomes and a plethora of imperfect ones.

Experience is created by history, the status quo, and the perceived entitlements of the day. That which prevailed during the 1930s (Senior generation) would not resemble the 1950s (Baby Boomer generation), or the 1970s (Gen X), or 1990s (Gen Y). The truth is that every generation has its challenges with layers of complexity. Each age group wrestled with grueling choices based on the cards they were dealt. For this reason we should not trivialize what others before us have gone through, what we will most certainly endure during our time, and what our children will face as a result of us, both good and bad.

People raised during the Great Depression traversed a difficult landscape of historical significance as perhaps the worst time in American history to grow up. Subsequent generations habitually write off reflections and methods of the past as old fashioned or as unimportant events that have little impact on their daily lives today. Herein lies the first big mistake of every culture – not solely because history has a tendency to repeat itself, but more because we completely ignore what lifetimes that came before us can teach us to improve our lives today.

We covet our opinions, short cuts, and inventions. We want to believe that we are in control and we don't need people telling us how to live, what to do, what to say. As we grew up, we showed tendencies toward rebellion and that we had a better way. Every generation saw new breakthroughs in technology and efficiencies that made their elders outmoded and outdated. Thus, it is natural to assume that we know better than those who came before us as if we were actually smarter – the second big mistake.

We can stop making the same big mistakes with every new generation if we recognize that change is the only constant, and challenge is never far behind, no matter what our lot in life. In fact, no matter where we come from, no matter what our circumstances might be, no matter what we own, no matter what anyone says about us, it is not permanent. We hold on to elements of life like a closet full of clothing we no longer wear. The day we decide to clean out the closet, we have an idea, a vision for what might replace the discarded garments. Even if we don't have it yet, we make room for it. We can reconstruct our lives this way as well.

My father was unlucky enough to be born a few years before the Great Depression, but he never let it affect him. He came into a world already impoverished, so he had nothing more to lose. Some say it is harder to start with nothing, while others argue that to lose everything and rebuild it is much harder. To a young man who had very little from the beginning, he did not know any differently and only sought to succeed, with absolutely no idea what that might look like, what it would take, and, with everyone in the same soup, no one to ask.

Without much education, he learned to adapt, to shed one skin to acquire another. If nothing else, he recognized where he was and he lived his life in search of the next opportunity, however it presented itself. The U.S. Navy opened a door to a vast new world, and he recognized that fact right away. His military experiences do not make this book a military book. Other books have been written with far greater detail than this. What's important is how he responded at every turn.

Tom Brokaw once referred to the World War II generation as "The Greatest Generation" because of the circumstances they had to overcome to redefine themselves collectively as a world leader. Cultural problems hardly made the United States an expert in domestic or foreign relations. However, my father typified his generation because he refused to give up. His entire generation loved work because that insured that they and their families would not go without shelter, clothing, food, the first most basic necessities of Maslow's hierarchy of needs. And his generation earned their way through life. Work – hard work – became the Senior generation's formula for success.

Again, more recent generations believed they had found a better idea. Work was passé. Leisure and conspicuous consumption defined them. Such decisions have shown a consistent path toward indulgence, addiction, and self-destruction. While every living human being has the right to choose their lot in life, they also should know they have a choice, like every generation did before them, exactly how they respond to their origins, their current state of affairs, and their future.

I'm going to make a bold statement about the cycle of generations. I believe that drinking the "Greed is good" Kool-aid proclaimed by Michael Douglas' character Gordon Gecko in the movie *Wall Street* during the 1980s has finally run its course. The dot-com bust told us that technology can bringing wealth and luxury fast, but in order to be sustainable, adaptability, new ideas, and leadership are the keys to the modern-day kingdom. The founding fathers of contemporary commerce work harder than ever to stay on top of their industries, leading to the reality that hard work has become the new fashion.

I wrote this book because my father had a fascinating story to tell. As I delved deeper into his past, I identified patterns in my father's 85 year history. Six drafts of inquiries showed me an important fact about him. Poverty taught him key survival skills and how to perform under pressure, testing his character and determination, regardless of his lack of education or a silver spoon in his mouth. Sure, people can argue the definition of "what is rich," but that is irrelevant. The man has earned respect by climbing out of dirt poor conditions, with no hope except the love of his mother and siblings, found a connection between passion and commerce, and used his tireless work ethic like a fountain of youth to get what he wanted from life.

He has since owned many homes and businesses, he has traveled the world multiple times, and in his mid-80s continues to live a happy, vibrant life with my mother… *after* triple bypass heart surgery. To meet him casually, he might be wearing his Navy cap with great pride. That alone speaks to a time forgotten, when men like him were not allowed to do many things. My father had to fight history – American history, African-American history, and Navy history – to make history during the war. Defining moments in a man's life can crystallize his place in the hearts and minds of others. He never let anything stop him. He never let anyone steal his dreams. He never quit on himself.

John Seagraves receives appreciation as a hero to each generation that meets him. Not just for his deeds, but for how he lives. Love a craft, master that profession, and make thousands of believers, as he did. I contend that if you do this simple thing, you will change everything.

CHAPTER 1

DIRT POOR

*"Dreams come in a size too big so that
we may grow into them."*

Josie Bisset

Independence Day 1926 was not worthy of celebration to most residents of Griffin, Georgia. Nobody had enough money to honor the nation's holiday, and the July afternoon sun forced even the most enthusiastic of children to play in the shade. Adults up and down the street could only sit on porches, swat flies, watch after their children, and wait until nightfall for relief. In the distance, a terse discussion between a man and his wife carried through the neighborhood. The woman complained that it was too hot to cook.

For Rhunette it was impossible to celebrate. The tin roof under which she sweltered did little more than shield direct sunlight. Her worn-out nightgown covered her plump body, sticking to her sweat-drenched skin. She constantly repositioned her back to support a belly so full it threatened to burst any minute from a long pregnancy. As the sun set, all she could do was fan herself and wait in preparation for her first child to be born. Meanwhile, Bud, the father of Rhunette's child, toiled in vain behind the house to make something grow, listening for a sign to call the midwife down the street.

    Their relationship was complicated. Bud and Rhunette had never married. Her circumstances had been forced upon her when Bud chose to mate with the 14-year-old girl. He owned a café and lived across the street from his business in the tin-covered shack she now called home.

    Initially she took a liking to Bud when he wanted her to work for him. Her father Johnny Johnson had suspicions about the man but said openly very little. Her more outspoken parent was her mother Lizzy, who regarded employment to be a rare opportunity and encouraged her to pursue it. Rhunette inevitably felt privileged by the prospects and flattered that an older man spoke kindly to her. He flirted with her until one day his harmless overtures turned. She resisted. But he forced himself upon her, changing their lives forever.

    Just after her 15th birthday, Rhunette showed signs of pregnancy. When it was confirmed, Lizzy did everything she could to keep the older man away from her daughter, to no avail. Lizzy felt partially responsible, never imagining that Bud would take advantage of a girl so young. Confrontation between them revealed Bud's forceful nature, and Rhunette's parents relented.

Pregnancy made Rhunette feel grown up. She wanted to be an adult, insisting she was capable of making her own decisions.

The morning following Independence Day, Rhunette's baby wasted no time getting started. The sun had not yet risen as she calmly suggested that Bud retrieve the midwife. She slowly stood up and deliberately made her way toward the bed. Characteristic of the women of her day, she demonstrated a strong will to survive, regardless of the conditions. It took every ounce of energy she could muster to position her otherwise strong, resilient frame to deliver this child. Too poor for a sedative and too repulsed to drink from the bottle of grain alcohol Bud left by the side of the bed, she did what she could to prevent her baby from coming before help arrived. When the midwife knocked at the door, Bud let her in and went back outside. He wasn't overly interested in the whole affair as the women went to work to bring his first child into the world.

Without any complications, on July 5 at 8:30 a.m., John Edward Seagraves was born. Rhunette named her son after her father Johnny. Lizzy defiantly insisted on calling him William. The issue would not be resolved until the day John became old enough to answer to his name. Bud didn't care either way. He'd grown distinctly bitter beyond the war.

World War I proved a brutal engagement of men battling the strength of wills and nature. For Bud's opponents, unfortunately, the power in his hands had equaled his desire to live, which had made him a lethal foe in hand-to-hand combat. During battle, any Allied soldier lucky enough to have survived being stabbed, shot, or blown up by the Germans had either lost limbs to the surgeons or had been poisoned with mustard gas. Bud Seagraves had been fortunate enough to walk off the battlefield with his limbs intact, but his lungs would never be the same.

Bud had been an obedient and reliable infantryman in the United States Army, yet he was an ill-tempered and angry civilian. Every burning breath he took reminded him of how life had changed upon his return to America. The First World War had been a desegregated affair. In contrast, making the long thankless trip back to Georgia from Europe, he had no choice in the deep American South but to accept segregated social conditions subsequent to the war's conclusion. Back home was a world that hated him more than the Germans had, a world that routinely lynched black men – especially those wearing the U.S. Army uniform. Death in war made sense to him; death at home did not. Bud's lungs burned badly this time of year, but he refused to complain. He got his revenge holding it in and hating the world instead.

For the first two years after John's birth, the Seagraves household was an unhappy place. Bud was not an educated man, but he was smart. In his mind, he knew he was right and the world was wrong. Deep down he had no use for a hollering son who kept him up at night. John's father became less and less able to provide for his family as the country approached the Great Depression. With little food or resources, Rhunette was unable to improve conditions for her newborn, her husband, or herself.

When Rhunette became pregnant again, her parents fought back anger. More starving children made no sense. Johnny had had enough of this pedophile and went after Bud with a gun. The two had words. Witnesses thought

Rhunette's father would shoot Bud dead in the street, but Lizzy and Rhunette jumped between them and stopped him. No shots were fired.

Shortly after John's second birthday, Rhunette provided her son with a baby sister named Virginia. John sometimes observed his little sister with curiosity. He wondered what she was so upset about, realizing the noise seemed to increasingly upset his father. Prone to fits of rage, Bud stormed out of the house, causing John to gravitate toward his mother. She tried everything to sooth Virginia's troubled spirit. Nothing worked.

John instinctively stayed close to his mother's maternal warmth. Bud showed no genuine interest in family matters. Lack of money was always his main concern. Sometimes he went days without customers, and when he made a few dollars, Bud found new ways to squander his money. Playing cards, drinking, and carousing helped him forget the family he left behind.

Some of John's earliest memories were about the three-room shack in which he was born. It was here that he began to notice the world around him, taking in his surroundings in greater detail. There wasn't much to look at, but he didn't know any better. He walked around where he once crawled in the small kitchen, bedroom, and living room which doubled as a second bedroom. Not a single flat surface could be found in the house. Everything drooped. Rain or shine, the weather took its toll on this house.

Clearly, the weather was least kind during heavy rain. The broken-down hovel was made of wood appearing grayish-brown, with a porch that sagged and two small wooden steps in need of repair. The house stood on cinder blocks to keep the floor from saturating during torrential rains. With the slight slope the house was built on, even the cinder blocks did not keep the floor from touching the ground. Georgia soil was made of red clay, hard enough to repel water. At a glance there was nothing to prevent the house from simply washing away. The tin roof overhead was often so loud during heavy rain it both frightened Virginia and drowned out her wailing.

Bud wasn't much of a repairman and frequently argued with Rhunette over maintenance issues. John watched as his father hung old newspaper on the walls to cover leaking cracks. John was too young to know that paper was neither waterproof nor stain resistant. Inadequate was the best Bud could do, or perhaps as much as he could afford. He complained to Rhunette that she didn't understand what he had been through. In his struggle for money and respect, he concluded that if it didn't involve either, it was women's work.

Everyone was dirt poor. Poverty wasn't personal. Yet for Bud, it was very personal. Overall, black people experienced especially great hardships in an attempt to live a decent life. Bud could plainly see that everyone needed to eat. They just could not pay for it. Many of his customers were black sharecroppers who had lost their cash crops in cotton to barren soil, faulty methods, erosion, boll weevils, and declining prices.

Then on October 29, 1929, "Black Tuesday" capped a momentous downturn in the New York Stock Exchange. The Stock Market Crash of 1929 brought industry and banking to a halt. Whatever had kept the slow-moving southern economy going faltered, practically shutting down agriculture completely. The Great Depression immediately followed.

Bud stood by as families migrated away from the rural South to urban centers or northern industrial communities in search of unskilled work.[1]

In need of additional help, Bud told Rhunette if John was old enough to work that Bud would make him get a job. She was not amused.

Rhunette was not one to entertain feelings of hopelessness. Still, she struggled to maintain a positive outlook for her children, but Bud's dark moods weighed heavily upon her. His abusive behavior further provoked her misery. Often at night, when she thought everyone was asleep, John could hear his mother crying. He laid there quietly, without moving, listening with great sadness and suffering along with her. At his young age, he would have done anything if he knew what or how. In the morning, he carried her suffering with him and stuck by her side, watching for any signs that things were better. For now, hope would not be forthcoming.

With the full support of her parents, Rhunette accepted the necessity to leave Bud. She could not tolerate his fierce temper nor endure any more mistreatment. What forced her decision, however, was the fear that staying with Bud might put the children in danger. She had to make a change for herself and her children. With her father's declining health contributing to her parents' financial struggles, they collaborated like many other families and decided to relocate to the city, excluding Bud. Rhunette sent a telegram to her brother James Johnson.

To Rhunette and her children, Uncle James was more than her babies' uncle; he was a savior to them all. James was a very tall, slender, loving man all too willing to dote over his niece and nephew. A hard-working professional, he was a gentleman married to a respectable woman. He had proven consistently to be very dependable. James knew that Bud was volatile. He also knew that one day he would have to remove Rhunette from that explosive environment. A God-fearing man, James was leery of Bud but not afraid of him. His sturdy countenance and values illogically intimidated Bud, who was largely relieved to see the family go.

James responded to the requests of his parents and Rhunette with a date to help them and the children move. He found them a new home, paid the rental down payment, and then moved everyone forty miles north to Atlanta from Griffin. John was three years old, his sister Virginia only one. They relocated from a downtrodden shack in the country to the biggest city in the Southeast. Deliverance looked like a little three-room house on West Street off Oliver Street.[2]

Shortly after moving to Atlanta, Rhunette's father Johnny fell extremely ill. The benefit of a black hospital could not reverse his condition. Before long, he passed away. Symptoms indicated he died of prostate cancer in his forties.

Were it not for Uncle James, John would have been influenced solely by two grown women and an infant sister. Sadly, his mother and grandmother continued to argue over naming rights. Rhunette and Lizzy presented John with a very strange conundrum. First, they both asked him to acknowledge them as his mother. In a confusing obligation to satisfy the women, John called his mother "Rhunette," while referring to his Grandmother

Lizzy as "Mom." Second, with no end in sight, the time had finally come to address the name dispute.

Rhunette and Lizzy had continued to clash over his birth name. Rhunette chose the name John and her decision was final, citing that she brought him into this world and that was the name she decided he should have. Lizzy loved him so much she felt she had naming rights, too, and she favored the name William, actually "Bill" for short.

Willful as she was, Lizzy and the rest of the family remained stuck on calling John "Bill" despite Rhunette's objections. Lizzy's argument was that she had few pleasures in life, specifically two – her beloved grandson and a pinch of Brutton snuff. She would not be denied her desired role in John's life. She derived great pleasure in saying, "Billy! God sure gave 'Nette that boy. But that's 'my' boy!" If only to keep peace, Rhunette gave up, figuring it would do no harm.

The bond between Rhunette and John was built on continuity and trust. This mother's love may have been short on resources, but not on purpose. She knew her son was smart and only needed encouragement and support, something that had been sadly lacking from his own father. She knew her brother James was a good influence on him. She would be quite pleased if John followed James' example.

With a three-year-old son whose father refused to nurture him, Rhunette decided she needed to do whatever she could to help John find his place in the world. She felt that she should spend as much time with him as he wanted to spend with her. Instinctively, a mother knows what interests her child, and Rhunette knew John enjoyed cooking. In her heart she was happy to have something to offer him besides nourishment, clothing, and shelter. Not only was she very good at cooking but she also made it look easy as she glided effortlessly around the kitchen. He watched every move she made with great curiosity. She enjoyed watching him learn with the leftover piecrust and some extra filling. He rolled out the crust and copied her to make his own sweet potato pie. "That's quite an accomplishment," she kept saying to herself.

CHAPTER 2

EARLY BURDEN

*"Just go out there and
do what you've got to do."*
　　　　　　　　　Martina Navrátilová

After moving to Atlanta, Rhunette met a man and finally married him. His name was Robert King. James questioned his sister's choice. He loved her and her children, but he spoke candidly about her haste and lack of judgment. She didn't know King very long or well, and dead-beat husbands were all too common.

Rhunette confided her need for a partner to comfort her loneliness, share the expenses, and be a father to her son. James studied King and saw the drinker and most likely the gambler in him, but nothing particularly threatening. Later he gave her his blessings, sincerely hoping it would work out for everyone involved, particularly John. James never told his sister how much of a fuss his wife Fannie had made about him taking care of his family. Normally accommodating with his wife, James had made it very clear to Fannie that he would never turn his back on his blood, no matter what, and demanded her understanding.

King was a man of slight build and average height. In contrast, Rhunette was tall and sturdy. He worked as a stonemason engraving tombstones. John assumed his new stepfather was skilled in his craft, or at least that he worked very hard, because King was never around. Always respectful toward adults, John called him "Mr. King." Even if John had few expectations of the new man of the house, he secretly hoped King would be the man his father had refused to be. Maybe King would take an interest in raising him. If that didn't happen, John's faith was still in his mother, the source of all his love and hope.

King didn't mind fathering Rhunette's children but he wanted one or two of his own and wasted little time getting started. By late October 1930, almost one year after the start of the Great Depression, Rhunette and King had a daughter named Helen, and a year later another daughter named Doris.

To his elders, John seemed to be growing like a weed during the summer of '31. Lizzy teased him adoringly about how big he had gotten as they readied themselves for another relocation, this time to Rock Street. Rhunette and Lizzy made a game of moving with John. Privately they hoped he would not start asking questions about why his family moved so much. Neither of them wanted to tell him a lie or attempt to explain their financial problems to a five-year-old boy. As they pulled away from the curb in a horse-drawn cart, John looked back with fond memories of baking pies and bonding with his mother. He knew he'd he never forget the little house on West Street.

In 1933 time passed quickly. Having baby stepsisters Helen (3) and Doris (2) to care for, John kept busy around the house helping Rhunette whenever she needed him. He was a good boy and a good son.

One afternoon Rhunette slowly swayed in her rocking chair, repairing one of her tattered house dresses with a needle and thread. Little Doris puttered around the house getting into things. Rhunette told her to go to bed and she resisted. Doris wasn't one to cry but something troubled her. Rhunette attributed her daughter's growing independence without sufficient language skills to defiance and tantrums like any two year old. After lingering a little bit longer, Doris reluctantly walked into the other room, quietly going to sleep.

A couple hours later, Rhunette asked John to go check on his sister and wake her up to prevent her from staying awake all night. When he entered the bedroom, Doris lay motionless and cold with a white substance on her mouth. John turned to tell his mother she would not respond.

Rhunette walked into the room. Inspecting her youngest baby, she tried talking Doris into waking up, noticing her pale skin and the dried residue on her lips. Without a response from her little girl, Rhunette became consumed with fear. Her grip on reality slipped. She could no longer see clearly as she wrestled with panic. Holding Doris in her arms and rocking her lifeless body, Rhunette could do nothing as tears streamed down her cheeks. John stood there helplessly looking at both of them as his mother shook her head no, looking around the room, searching for a cause, a solution, anything. By that time she knew it was too late to get Doris to a hospital. For a mother to outlive her child was tragic; being too impoverished to know the reason planted a seed of incomparable suffering.

Grieving nearly suffocated Rhunette. Accepting Doris' death tormented her. King finagled a makeshift baby casket, and the family held a small service in the Rock Street house. Friends and family came to pay their respects. Rhunette sat in her bedroom with baby Doris until the child was buried. Dressed in her Easter outfit, Doris' peaceful body rested amid the tortured living who felt her loss most. As visitors passed by gazing at her little girl, Rhunette relived the hours before her death, scrutinizing her actions in every detail. Her inability to identify what she missed left a broken heart and an open a wound.

In the end, no one knew why she died. With barely enough money for a casket and no money for a headstone, King never marked the grave where she'd been buried. Like the cobbler whose kids went without shoes, King could not afford a gravestone for his own child. He rejected the idea of a "cheap" piece of wood for a headstone, preferring instead to one day return with an engraved headstone. As time passed, that never happened. Eventually it became clear no one knew exactly where she was buried.

Lizzy attempted to comfort her daughter without success. Everyone felt strongly that Lizzy should stay with the family and address bereavement issues with Rhunette, John, Virginia, and Helen. Beset with dreadful memories, Rhunette had no choice but to move away from Rock Street. Everyone was ready for a change, with Lizzy there to help start again.

John was approaching six years of age, and the time had come to consider his education. King found a little house on Paynes Avenue a half mile away from a school. That seemed far for a six-year-old by some standards, but the neighborhood was decent. Soon thereafter Rhunette enrolled John in first grade. On his first day she proudly walked her son to the school, and Lizzy was there in the afternoon to see him home. All the attention on John's first days in school served as a distraction. Emotions ran high with the rest of his family.

King's sadness about the loss of Doris surfaced as he drank away his sorrows without any care for the needs of John, Virginia, and Helen. Rhunette apparently misinterpreted King's silence for indifference and disregarded his suffering. King's demons lured him into numerous drinking and gambling joints on the way home, presenting fresh opportunities to escape the wrath of Rhunette. Weakened by his sorrow, he walked in the house long enough to receive his verbal punishment and walk back out with what little money he still had in his pockets.

For the time being, Rhunette and King welcomed Lizzy into their new Paynes Avenue house to provide support. But Lizzy kept insisting on calling John "Bill," which rubbed Rhunette the wrong way. After Rhunette lost Doris, she became easily agitated by Lizzy's insensitivity to the situation. In the past, Rhunette had tolerated the name charade. No longer. Rhunette reiterated to Lizzy in a heated discussion that these were her children, not Lizzy's, and to respect her wishes. The commotion had originally begun over who would walk John to school on his first day. With raw nerves around the house, the conflict between Rhunette and Lizzy escalated. King didn't have much to say about it since John wasn't his blood, but he wanted the rankling to stop. Days later, Lizzy moved back to live with Uncle James and Aunt Fannie in another part of Atlanta. John was sad to see Lizzy go. He knew his grandmother loved him, his sisters, and his mother, despite the arguments.

After Lizzy left, frequent arguments flared up between Rhunette and King. King could not do anything right. Among the many items on Rhunette's list were losing track of Doris' burial site, never putting a headstone on her grave, not being there when she needed him most, not bringing the money home on payday, and a host of other offenses she wanted to hold against him. Wearing her pain as she did made her vulnerable to emotional breakdown at any time. John didn't know what the arguments were about, but he knew the word – money. King did not bring home enough to pay the rent. With all the tension around the house, John was happy to leave the house and go to school.

School became John's sanctuary. Learning gave him a chance to prove himself and please his mother. Rhunette helped him with his homework, preferring that over another dispute with King.

Rhunette blamed city life for her predicament with King. She complained to Lizzy he had too many options, not enough discipline. Following first grade and barely a few weeks into seven years of age, John was about to endure another move. It was Rhunette's idea to move away from the city. This time the family relocated to a community on the rural outskirts of Atlanta called Armour.

Armour wasn't far from the city, but far enough. Rhunette's primary goal was to make King bring home his pay. She reasoned if King came straight home from work without stopping for a drink, their finances would be fine. If he stopped, then he would have difficulty getting home before dark. If he didn't make it home before dark, he would never find his way home because there were no street lights along the roads. Without street lights like in Atlanta, King would have to sleep in a ditch. Rhunette's punishment for King's drinking and gambling habit was that he'd have to sleep in a ditch on the side of the road if his bad habits were more important than his family.

Despite her deterrents, Rhunette had to overcome a far bigger and very real issue, specifically the new house and the neighborhood. The house had no utilities at all. This was the price Rhunette was willing to pay to save money and break King of his bad habits. They had no running water, no electricity. They called the toilet a backhouse, which was affectionately referred to as "the little house."

The neighborhood had several characteristics of forgettable uniqueness. Families relied on well water at the end of the block. Far worse than no running water or electricity was the air. Immediately after they arrived, John noticed a putrid, nauseating smell in the air. When he asked his mother about it, she refused to discuss the matter. It didn't take long to find out that a crematorium nearby burned road kill in a giant furnace and converted the byproduct to fertilizer.

Not too far away was the train depot, where hobos jumped trains going in and coming out of Atlanta. One day, one of the hobos lost his footing while jumping between train cars, slipped, and fell between two cars while they were pulling out of the loading docks. One of the train cars ran over his head, splattering his brains all over. Without much information about the unknown man, many wondered whether his body ended up at the crematorium.

Ultimately, Rhunette's plan failed. King took his pay and disappeared drinking and gambling for days, leaving the family without any support. The family was starving, King wouldn't bring home any money, and Rhunette was pregnant again.

John's stepsister Marjorie was born in 1933 when the family already had too many mouths to feed on too little money. King was nowhere to be found, as if having children was as simple as spilling a glass of milk he didn't care to clean up.

John struggled to reconcile the emotions around him. His siblings cried out of frustration, a consequence of empty, aching bellies due to lack of water and nutrition. His mother had reached the end of her patience. King showed no remorse in leaving his family behind. John had seen his mother upset before, and he felt her pain as if it were his. John worried about his mother so much that he had difficulty concentrating in school.

Daily lunches for grade school children typically consisted of sandwiches and cocoa. John knew his mother was upset about not having enough to eat, so one afternoon he put half of his sandwich in his pocket and brought it home to her. When he pulled the half sandwich out of his pocket, it hardly resembled his original lunch, all crumpled and balled up. He tried to spread it out and refashion something edible from the remains. The gesture brought tears to his mother's eyes.

In their neighborhood, all the houses on their side of the street lined up in a row very close together. One evening a kitchen fire broke out. The burning property sat at the far end of the block on the same side of the street as the house where Rhunette, King, and the children lived. The first old wooden house started burning, and the fire spread to the next house and the next. In a desperate attempt at solidarity, all of the neighbors and their children tried to control the flames by any means necessary, waving blankets, flinging dirt, throwing water they had in their houses or well water. Unfortunately, they just could not procure enough well water fast enough. They filled up buckets one at a time and threw the water against the sides of the houses, hoping the fire would not spread. As the fire approached the final remaining house – John's house – everyone ran to the house and did what they could to save it. Thankfully, they were able to stop the fire in time.

King returned home just before daybreak the following morning. He had been out drinking and gambling again, although he won some money. As he entered the back entrance, the sun was just beginning to illuminate the landscape around the house. A drink of water would help reduce his headache in the morning, he thought, so he stood there sipping from his glass while glancing out a rear side window. Against the rising sun, he could not believe his eyes when he saw every other house burned to the ground.

Weeks later, and up to that point, the community well had performed adequately as the only source of drinking water. But something peculiar was happening. An unknown blockage caused everyone to draw less and less water. Not only was less water available, but a noxious odor also seemed to be rising from the well. Community elders declared the well inoperable until further notice and called the police.

Three police officers arrived and recognized the smell. They insisted the children step back while the chief and a deputy inspected the well, and another police officer began questioning adults about strange behavior in the area. As an older crowd gathered, the anticipation mounted. The parents told their children to return home and behave. The deputy whispered a few words to the chief. The police chief decided to reveal the mystery blockage at the bottom of the well. It was a dead man. Several people gasped, as the news sparked questions about who it was and how he got there. The police estimated the dead man had been down there for several days and likely contaminated the water. It was a miracle no one got seriously ill. The fact was that only the day before a number of children had started complaining of nausea.

Lizzy was back living with the family again and it was just as well. King was completely unreliable to help around the house and Rhunette needed all the support she could get. When Lizzy heard the news, and her grandchildren complained of stomach aches, she went into the woods behind the house to pick what looked like a handful of common leaves and roots. She threw the roughage in a pot of boiling water and made a tea that tasted bitter. All her grandchildren took turns drinking the brew. A little while later they felt much better.

With little or no money, elders preserved their strange medicinal mixtures like indigenous cultures passing on generations of "magic" potions through oral histories. No one ever wrote anything down. They just put odd ingredients together and called them "home remedies."

Sometimes Lizzy made tea out of pig's hoofs or toenails. If any of the children were very sick, she gave them a teaspoon of sugar with a few drops of kerosene lamp oil. While it was impossible to determine whether any of her recipes served any true medicinal purpose, several witnesses could verify that they worked.

Lizzy had another gift, one only the good Lord could explain. Worrying about his mother, John developed a nerve disorder causing his head to shake uncontrollably. After a day of this, Lizzy said to John, "Come over here, boy. What's wrong with you?" She inspected his head and neck and pulled him away from the table where she sat. Behind a door, she held his head firmly within her grasp and began to pray. John had no idea what was happening, but as soon as she released him his nervous tick went away. He was cured. He walked away from her dumbfounded as she grinned at him. She could heal her grandchildren in the strangest of ways, yet her legs always seemed to have open sores or bandages covering them. That his grandmother's magic worked for her grandchildren but did not work for her puzzled him.

The resulting calamities from the ill-fated decision to move to Armour grew to such an extent that Rhunette quit trying to correct her husband's behavior. She looked Lizzy in the eyes and confessed that her plan backfired. The plain truth was obvious. A dead man poisoned the only source of water on the street, there was no plumbing or electricity, backhouses were used for toilets, and a crematorium was polluting the air. All the houses on her side of the street except hers were burned to the ground. King was no longer a regular part of the family. She failed…again. The time had come to leave Armour and return to the city.

Rhunette and Lizzy consulted James for suggestions, and he recommended a small house on Pelham Street. Staying closer to Uncle James and Aunt Fannie easily beat living in the boondocks to manipulate King's behavior. At least now the family could return to civilization, with electricity, running water, and toilet facilities again. King relished the notion of moving back to town even though he was not included in any of the decisions. Eight-year-old John could attend a school closer to home, and sanity could be restored.

Despite relocation improvements, King didn't care for continually being told what to do or being out-voted by Rhunette and Lizzy. Lizzy was a domineering woman who spoke her mind, and that caused problems between her and King, sometimes between her and Rhunette as well. Tension continued to build between Lizzy and King until he told Rhunette one of them had to leave. King asserted his influence, since he was still the primary breadwinner of the family, and finally put his foot down. Rhunette reluctantly had to ship Lizzy back to stay with Uncle James and Aunt Fannie. To keep peace and a roof over her head, Rhunette accepted Lizzy's departure. No one ever explained to John or his siblings the reason why Lizzy went back and forth so often.

Uncle James had married Aunt Fannie, a woman from an upper-crust family. She was culturally refined and educated. Aunt Fannie kept company with the likes of Martin King. She did not care for Lizzy. She described her mother-in-law as "too loud and country." The two women could not have a discussion without it ending in an argument. Thus, the revolving door for Lizzy between Uncle James and Rhunette seemed inevitable.

John bore witness to his grandmother going back and forth on a regular basis. As his grandmother's health declined, Uncle James moved her back in with him to keep an eye on her over Aunt Fannie's objections. James knew his mother had poor circulation in her legs, making it increasingly difficult for her to walk. John protested every time Lizzy headed back to Aunt Fannie and Uncle James's house hoping to stop her from leaving, and this time was especially difficult. Rhunette had another baby on the way.

CHAPTER 3

FORK IN THE ROAD

"Action springs not from thought, but from a readiness for responsibility."
— Dietrich Bonhoeffer

Before Rhunette left home for the hospital in 1935, she turned to John and told him she would bring him another little brother. In the meantime, John was in charge. She knew King probably would not return to help out with the children for very long, if at all. John, however, had plenty of experience watching over his siblings, and his mother had confidence in him. Rhunette's friend Sheehee hung around the house waiting for Rhunette to say her goodbyes to the children. Rhunette didn't have many friends because her children, chores, and financial concerns occupied all her time. When Lizzy wasn't around and King did his disappearing act, Rhunette relied on Sheehee for adult conversation.

Rhunette bid Sheehee farewell with instructions as they stood next to the horse-and-buggy taxi. At the last minute, Rhunette remembered to leave money for John. She gave Sheehee 25 cents with a request to pass the money on to John to buy food. Rhunette and John had already discussed what he needed to do, including buying food at Bronner's General Store. She told him to get greens, grits, and anything else he needed with the money. John had done everything before. He knew what dry goods were stored in which barrels and what increments of one- or two-cent portions stretched his money.

As the horse and buggy circled around and headed back up the street, Sheehee waved at Rhunette, watching the buggy slowly ascend the hill and pass its peak. When Rhunette was out of sight, Sheehee looked at the front door where the children stood. She smiled and waved at them, then started walking down the street, slipping the twenty-five cents in her pocket. She never looked back, leaving nine-year-old John to fend for Virginia, Helen, Marjorie, and himself with no food in the house.

Later that day, and without knowing that Sheehee walked away with his food money, John and the others began to get hungry. One by one, they chimed in, becoming a chorus of complaints. The idea struck him that a man up the street had a vegetable garden and the vegetables were ripe. Without knowing what else to do, he walked up the street to the man's garden in the middle of a September Saturday afternoon and started digging up sweet potatoes with his hands, along with picking collard greens. His stomach ached so much he didn't think to ask the man who owned the vegetables.

Once he got as many vegetables as he could carry, he returned to the house, added some wood and coal to the burning stove, and put the collard greens on to boil. Then he buried the sweet potatoes in the cinders of the fireplace. His brother and sisters gathered and watched his every move in hopes of a meal sometime soon. He didn't really know what he was going to do with the potatoes because he could not remember the sweet potato pie recipe, but he figured he should peel them anyway. All of a sudden, there was a knock at the door. Startled and frightened for a moment, the children turned to the door and then to John for guidance.

When John opened the door, a tall white man stood there. John looked up at the man who spoke in a menacing tone, "Boy, did I just see you up there stealing my vegetables?" John flinched. "No sir!" Exasperated by the wrong answer, the man pushed the door open, walked in and demanded, "Where's your momma?" John told him, "She went to the hospital to bring me back a little brother." The man walked into the kitchen and looked around, automatically eyeing the row of babies looking up at him. Standing behind the man, John looked up at him and said, "We're hungry." Quickly assessing the situation, the lanky fellow recognized dire need and became filled with compassion. He took a breath, turned to John, and replied, "I want you to come up to the house and get some food. And one thing you won't ever do again is to steal and then lie about it! Do you understand?"

Embarrassed, and with a sheepish tone, John accepted the man's terms, then looked at his siblings and told them everything would be all right. He instructed Virginia to watch the smaller children, and he walked to the house as the man told him. The benevolent neighbor and his wife gave him all kinds of vegetables, including black-eyed peas, even cooked foods, and then they volunteered to help him carry the food back to his house.

When John and the couple arrived with food, the little ones became very excited, smiling from ear to ear. Looking for places to put the food, the man's wife peeked around the small house to inspect the conditions the children were living in. Her husband told her the children's mother went to the hospital today to bring them back a brother. She looked back at her husband, knowing they had to help. Between them, they decided to watch over the four young children while Rhunette recovered from childbirth in the hospital. She was gone five or six days.

When Rhunette returned home, instead of the brother she promised John, she brought him twin sisters. John informed her of what the neighbors had done to help in her absence, which explained the unexpected surplus of food. Rhunette knew very well that 25 cents didn't buy that much food. She was so grateful for the kindness of neighbors she did not know that words escaped her for a moment. When Rhunette asked John about the money Sheehee was supposed to give him, he responded that he never received any money. She became so infuriated she choked words back and instead thanked John for doing such a good job. She was not surprised that King never showed up the whole time she was in the hospital but she was still disgusted with him, and as for her so-called friend Sheehee, well, she had a few choice words for both of them.

The next day there was a knock at the door. She hoped the kind neighbors had come calling so she could thank them personally for taking care of her children. Opening the door with a gracious smile, Rhunette stood facing the sheriff. He proceeded to tell her she was past due on the rent and he and his deputies were going to put their things out on the street. "That triflin' man!" she shouted aloud. They were two months behind on a seven-dollar monthly rent payment.

Rhunette's only request of King had involved settling the delinquency. Instead, he got the bright idea to solve two problems with the same money. All he had to do was stretch his pay by winning at craps and poker to cover the back rent, and he could have some money left over. In fact, the plan almost worked. His winnings had put him up enough to cover the back rent after a hard luck streak, except he had gotten greedy looking for extra play money. Naturally, he had lost all of his winnings. Too ashamed to come home empty-handed, he didn't come home.

The sheriff ordered two young deputies to empty the house. There wasn't much to move as the authorities put everything on the sidewalk – an old familiar mattress made of feathers and squeaky springs, a makeshift dresser, a broken-down table, and mismatched chairs. Rhunette, with two screaming infants and four terrified small children, was extremely upset about where they could go to live. Delivering a child seemed to her enough work for one week. Looking to Rhunette for hope, John cried because she cried.

Through his tears, John told his mother that he would get a job and help out. He began to tell her about a white man who had offered him a job selling vegetables, not the neighbor, but another man. His mother turned to him and said, "Boy, I want you to keep going to school." John worried that he could not go to school anymore because he was the oldest. Trying to think of a solution, he decided to go find Uncle James and tell him what was happening. Uncle James would know what to do. Without hesitation, John spun around and took off in a full sprint to fulfill his mission. He ran for miles and, as always, he remembered the way.

James worked at the Biltmore Hotel, one of the most exclusive hotels in Atlanta. He had a respectable, good-paying job as a waiter serving wealthy guests who stayed in the hotel. Late that afternoon, James came to rescue Rhunette and her children with a friend who had a horse and a wagon. With little to move, James and his friend stacked all his sister's worldly possessions onto the back of the horse-driven wagon in one load.

Uncle James went up to Lindsey Street and rented an apartment for his sister, nieces, and nephew. His friend took the haul over to the apartment, which had no heat or electricity. While this was nothing new to them, at least the new apartment had an icebox. It wasn't much, prompting James to send his friend, Rhunette, and John to get oil for heat and lamps and ice for the icebox while he watched the children. Sitting down in a chair to play with the children, James secretly thought it wise for John to observe the process in case he must take James' place one day.

Despite the frequent relocations, distractions, and interruptions, John was a fine student in school. His teacher always told him he was a smart child, encouraging him regardless of his environment. He learned fast and was able to do the reading and math lessons as well or better than many other fourth graders. When his teacher asked him what he wanted to be some day, he replied proudly, "I want to be a doctor!" Perhaps he said this in hopes of helping his mother pay for her visits to the doctor's office with the children.

An observer could plainly see that John was so busy parenting or assisting his mother that he would never find time to become a doctor. By the time he was ten years old, he had five sisters. His sister Virginia was eight, Helen was five, and Marjorie was three. His twin stepsisters Miriam and Marian were one year old. Had Doris not died when she was two, John would have had six sisters. He knew he needed to do more.

Once the family moved to Lindsey Street, John found himself at a fork in the road. His family needed money. John elected to quit school and find work. In his spare time, he could be found sitting and reading whatever he could find—a newspaper, magazine, book, even a dictionary—whatever he came across. He learned and absorbed new vocabulary by listening and asking questions. He had already grasped arithmetic by going grocery shopping for Rhunette. A great deal of his self-esteem came from early responsibilities and his sense of independence choosing work over school. John committed himself to helping his mother and the family. He knew if King stayed around the house more often, John could return to school and study to become that doctor some day. But he was not counting on it.

One afternoon, John told his mother he'd find work and disappeared. He walked to the house of a man named Mr. Roberts. John reminded Mr. Roberts of the job he had offered and asked if he could have it. The man seemed surprised at his initiative and amused that the youngster of ten years knew what he wanted. They discussed the work and hours of operation, deciding John could start the next morning. John shook Mr. Roberts' hand in agreement before starting the job. Uncle James had taught him this was how men conducted business.

The small business owner marshaled his mule-drawn vegetable cart every harvest season and rode through the neighborhood selling his fruits and vegetables. John became his "runner," riding on the tail end of the cart. Mr. Roberts sang a little ditty to let people know he was coming: "Watermelon man – Red to the rind – Ain't nobody got none just like mine…" Customers came to the street and picked what they wanted, and the runner carried their produce to their front door. John earned twenty cents a day helping Mr. Roberts sell his inventory. Upon delivery, customers paid him for their purchase plus a tip for delivery service, usually a penny or more. By day's end, John took home as much as fifty cents.

As time passed, Mr. Roberts came to trust John. He spoke of being a cousin of Eugene Talmadge, the segregationist Georgia governor. "Critics denounced [Talmadge] as a dictator, a demagogue, and a threat to the tranquility of the state, but his supporters considered him a friend of the common man and one of the state's outstanding governors… [Talmadge] unsuccessfully ran for the U.S. Senate against the incumbent Richard Russell…" later that year.[3] While Mr. Roberts didn't always agree with his cousin's politics, he regarded Eugene as a good man. He went on to explain why he offered John the job.

The last boy he hired attempted to steal some of the money he had collected for vegetables by claiming that some customers did not pay him. To confirm his story, the vendor had returned to each customer, verifying what had happened. After he learned that the boy was filching money and telling lies, Mr. Roberts got his money back from the boy and subsequently fired him on the spot, telling him to never come back. He told John he would not tolerate dishonesty and made sure John understood the primary conditions of employment – "No lying and no stealing!" A youngster of few words, John had learned his lesson about stealing other people's property the previous year when he promised to never steal and lie about it again to his neighbor. His word was his bond, another of Uncle James' teachings.

    Sitting on the back of the cart day after day, John accepted a responsibility he should not have had to take on at his age. He knew he was not alone in making the sacrifice. He saw other kids hustling to get money for their families, too. What troubled him, however, was not that he had to sacrifice his schooling, but that no one from the school inquired about his absence. He quickly let the disturbance pass and he remained focused on supporting his family.

    Mr. Roberts often stopped by Bronner's General Store for one thing or another. He particularly liked Brown Mule Chewing Tobacco and constantly spat out tobacco juice. After a good day of tips, John gave his mother his earnings and she asked him to run down to Bronner's to pick up a few items for dinner before it got too dark. As he approached the store, the owner, "Peg Leg Bronner," asked him if he wanted to make some extra money.

Bronner spoke like a gravel-throated old goat, red from too much Georgia sun. He'd seen John in his store many times and knew the boy worked very hard for the vegetable cart vendor. Bronner told John a friend needed some help and asked, "You want to make fifty cents tonight? Come back at seven o'clock p.m." Curious, John looked him squarely in the eyes and said, "Fifty cents?" Having taken a liking to John, Bronner nodded in acknowledgement. Without hesitation, John responded enthusiastically, "Yes sir."

At 7 p.m. sharp John walked toward the front of Bronner's General Store. The owner stood there waiting, leaning against the front door with a blade of grass between his teeth. Bronner's friend sat in the driver's seat of an old Tin Lizzie, a front-crank Model T Ford. The unknown man glanced at Bronner with a nod, then looked at John and told him to get in the back and lie down on the floor. The man didn't want to be seen with a little black boy riding around with him where they were going. John hesitated, not certain how to react to the stranger's peculiar directive. John asked the man, "Why?" Bronner was amused by the precocious ten year old and, satisfied that they had found the right kid for the job, looked down at John and said, "Don't worry, no harm will come to you, boy." John accepted Bronner's word and did what the man said, hiding under a blanket on the floor between the front and back seats.

Their first stop was deep in the woods. The man picked up 15 or 20 cans of liquid and put it on the front seats, back seats, and around the floor board with just enough room for John to keep hiding. They drove in and out of different neighborhoods with John hiding on the floor behind him. When they entered the black neighborhoods, the stranger told John to jump out and drop off brown paper bags with cans in them to one man after another in exchange for lighter-weight paper bags. Older black men carrying shotguns, pick axes, cane blades, and various homemade weapons greeted the enterprising little fellow. Mr. Bronner's friend ran a clandestine bootlegging operation and he needed help conducting routine deliveries. John's job was to deliver the goods and collect the money, just like on the vegetable cart.

Once John understood his role in the enterprise, he knew the night was still young with many more deliveries to be made, given the number of cans strewn around the car. Some of the bootlegger's customers were Ku Klux Klan members. John had never been so close to Klan members before, distinguishing them by how they spoke. Knowing these people were just outside the door of the car, John was scared to death. His only option was to hide quietly and refuse to move until the man told him it was safe.

Nearly three hours later they arrived back at Bronner's, having completed the runs. Bronner sat in a rocking chair on the front porch of the general store awaiting their return. When Bronner's friend told him to, John climbed out of the back and exited the car. He felt grateful to be back in safe territory. The bootlegger paid him 50 cents as agreed and John headed home, quite pleased with himself.

The moment John walked in his front door, though, he had to answer to a very angry mother. Rhunette and Lizzy worried all evening, wondering what had happened to their pride and joy. Lizzy waved her hands in the air, shouting, "Oh, Lord! Thank you, Lord, for bringing that boy home safe!" Rhunette was so worked up that she grabbed her favorite switch. Long willow tree branches hurt the most. John's mother grabbed him by the arm, spun him around, and started whipping him across the backs of his legs with the willow branch for coming home so late. She said, "You have no reason to be out this late at night at your age!" John told her he helped a man who paid him 50 cents. She didn't care one iota.

Even with a beating, John was happy to be home. Reflecting on the day's events, he reasoned that riding around delivering liquor was dangerous and he had no desire to do it again. His vegetable cart work was much easier and safer, even though the hours were longer for less money.

In retrospect, he acknowledged an important quality about Mr. Roberts: his spirituality and respect for everyone. He once told John, "I take people as they are and I don't discriminate." He always addressed John's mother and others as, "Yes, Sir, Yes, Ma'am," unlike the local insurance salesman who had no respect at all. This salesman had a reputation as a moronic street hustler. Stopping by the house to collect a five- or ten-cent premium, he irreverently called John's mother "Nette" or "girl." John fumed about that man, never once realizing his developing sense of professionalism had already set boundaries for right and wrong.

The average ten year old would not attempt to make sense of society's most perplexing dichotomies, but John tried. Contradictions divided him, surrounding him but not consuming him. What with conflicts of race and the moral dilemmas of good and evil people, the diligent versus the slothful, the kindness of others compared to terrible cruelty, some generosity juxtaposed against rampant greed, he observed without judgment. He appreciated the lesson plan and how it incorporated teachings about business, having regard for others, and honest behavior. John more than anything valued his special bond with Mr. Roberts, considering the older man to be far more than an employer, more like a teacher and mentor.

Apparently the feelings were mutual. Mr. Roberts in turn grew fond of his courageous young protégé, coaching and encouraging John to make ethical decisions in his life. The cart vendor taught John to carry himself with dignity and never let anyone talk down to him. Those profound messages reminded him of his Uncle James, fair and honest in contrast to a world full of hate and anger.

By his 11th birthday, John had left his childhood behind in exchange for the finer aspects of breadwinning. In a new kind of school he happily paid his dues. Many questions challenged him, but they remained largely unspoken. John embraced his responsibility to feed his family and he proudly pursued that single-minded goal. His growing reputation as an achiever set him apart from children and adults alike at a time when few honorable choices existed.

CHAPTER 4

THE PROMISE

"Character is the total of thousands of small daily strivings to live up to the best that is in us."
— A. G. Trudeau

From the back of that cart, John had learned much about who he was becoming. As fall led to winter, vegetable crops withered with the season. Even while his tenure under Mr. Roberts' guidance came to an end, he knew the memories of this turning point in his life would stick with him forever. In forging his own path, the independent 11-year-old had more heart and determination than opportunity.

Without paid work, John wanted to prove his resourcefulness in self-employment. His first attempts to create money resulted in him picking up scrap iron from along the railroad tracks or selling rags, anything that had value. His initial efforts yielded low returns. If nothing else, he embraced the freedom to create new adventures, expand his horizons, and take the next step somehow.

John may not have known what to do yet, but his mother and grandmother supported his efforts regardless. Meanwhile, newborn stepbrother Calvin came along, prompting Lizzy's return. She provided meaningful emotional support for Rhunette and the children, applauding John's initiative in bringing much-needed money into the household.

King viewed his son Calvin's arrival from a distance, coming and going freely with little or no accountability to the family. His general negligence did little to ingratiate himself with anyone. He tolerated John with mixed feelings, not that anyone cared what he thought. Moreover, King resented the implication that Rhunette and Lizzy considered his 11 year old stepson to be the man of the house, a direct affront to him.

John didn't compete with anyone nor did he have to. It was easy to forget he was just a child at a time when everyone grew up fast. His contributions counted like anyone else's, his motivation sparked by his devotion to his mother. In his world, King did not exist. John's success put pressure on King to clean up his act or look bad in his own home. As far as anyone in the house was concerned, the harsh criticism King received was well deserved.

King took offense at being regarded as the bad guy, compelling him to stay away. Making matters worse, John was another man's son. In King's mind, the boy wouldn't be anything were it not for King being around to feed him and put clothing on his back. King's self-pity served him and him alone.

As John got older, bigger, and more confident, King saw an opportunity to take respect from John. John did his best to avoid King in the house. Ironically, this fueled King's desire to seize his chance and straighten the boy out. John had embarrassed King, who was so blinded by rage that he was determined to teach John a lesson about who was the boss. One day, without provocation, King attacked John, kicking and beating him. Suddenly the assailant felt an abrupt thud behind his right ear.

King blinked his eyes several times, attempting to see clearly again. He was shocked to find himself on the floor, his head bleeding. King looked up at John and Rhunette, sharp pain ripping through his skull. At the top of her lungs Rhunette hollered, "Don't you ever touch my son again, you good-for-nothing heathen!" The infuriated, powerful mother leaned over the abusive stepfather, still holding the baseball bat she had used on his head. King never entertained the idea of ambushing her son again.

A few days following the attack, John ended a long day of scavenging and returned home with a few pennies in his pocket. It had not been a particularly productive day, but he planned to go back out again the next day hoping for better results. His mother sat him down after dinner to tell him she had received a letter from his father Bud. The letter said he wanted John to return to Griffin and help him in his café. A father wanted his son to come work with him and learn the business.

The request offered some chance for reconciliation, even advancement between father and son. Rhunette had observed John's struggles. She explained to John what a good opportunity this was for him to get to know his father and maybe start a new chapter for both of them.

She continued to hatch a plan that might resolve their differences. Rhunette speculated that at least John could learn some new skills in the restaurant business.

John struggled with his father's request. His mother wanted what was best for her eldest son and genuinely believed this was the best course. John disagreed. Rhunette urged him to go and he resisted. John didn't want another job, and he certainly had no interest in leaving his mother. His memories of his father yelling and screaming at his mother made him angry and turned his stomach. The man was a stranger to him.

Realizing that rummaging was not successful, John weighed the growing burden of finding anything of value against the possibility of working with his estranged father and learning restaurant skills. He didn't know what to expect. As time passed, he recognized that his father was his flesh and blood. Could his father be any worse to be around than King? John reluctantly considered the bright side of the proposition. The idea grew on him. Besides, Griffin would be an adventure, and he wanted more adventure.

When John arrived in Griffin, he officially met Sara, his new stepmother and Bud's second wife. As nice as she was, John's chest tightened as vaguely unpleasant memories surfaced about his early childhood. Not much had changed in the years since Uncle James had moved the family forty miles north to the city. Looking around the area, John saw nothing but dirt roads, dense thicket, huge trees, unkempt shrubs, and withering shacks. Sara attempted to make small talk, but John had suddenly become withdrawn and regretful that he had come to Griffin. He feared boredom more than anything. The very next day, he learned that boredom would be only one of many issues.

The instructions John received were brief. Each day started the same way. Every morning John got up with the roosters and went outside to clean "chitlins," short for chitterlings, otherwise known as pigs' intestines. He also had to clean pigs' stomachs, which were called hogmaws, along with ribs, ears, feet and tails, and tripe, the more common term for cow's stomachs. Handling chitlins was the worst because they were so slimy and far more nauseating. The smell of pigs' guts was so bad he had to breathe through his mouth to keep from vomiting. He got used to the rest of the work, but he was certain he would never get used to the chitlin smell. If he was nothing, John was honorable about keeping his word by making an effort to work with and get to know his father. Instincts told him nothing had changed.

After early-morning food preparations for the restaurant, he returned home to clean the house, take out the trash, empty the "slopjaw" (toilet bucket), then run back to the restaurant to wash the pots and pans. When he was done there, John walked four miles to town every day to buy supplies for the restaurant and carry them back. He did what he was told and watched his father work once his errands were completed. Bud was a man of few words, making their time together awkward. In many ways, Bud didn't know what to say to his own son. He knew John was smart. The core issue was that Bud could not decide whether to treat his son as family, as an unpaid employee, or as a personal servant.

Bud's restaurant sold breakfast, sandwiches, and meals. The small café had four tables, though most food was takeout. Tired of being broke and with little else to do, Bud worked all the time and expected John to do the same. The house sat next to the restaurant, eliminating any recreational alternatives. Bud's menu selection favored pork products because a pig or pig parts were easy to get cheap. The only beef product he sold was tripe.

Croaker and chicken were also on the menu. Both required more work than pork or tripe. A croaker was similar to a perch, a small, bony whitefish that tasted good. John had to clean the fish, but he learned to leave the bones in the croaker because it was too much work to get all the bones out and in doing so he just tore up the meat. The ordeal to make a chicken meal was a whole other story.

First he had to boil some water and catch a chicken, easier said than done. Then, to kill it, he had to wring the chicken's neck by grabbing the chicken below the head and swinging it around until the neck broke or the head came off, rendering the chicken incapable of escape. The chicken danced around until it finally died. After that, they grabbed the chicken by its feet and dipped it into the pot of boiling water to loosen up the feathers for removal. Plucking the feathers was no easy task either.

After all the hard work prepping the chicken, a bounty of parts produced several different meals at very low cost. Legs, wings, breasts, and thighs were the obvious parts. Chicken lovers also ate livers, gizzards, even the feet. John pulled the skin off the feet to be fried along with everything else. Necks made good chicken stock. Only the head and knees went into the trash. Every chicken John killed diminished his appetite for any kind of chicken dish, no matter how popular.

The Menu

Eggs and Grits	10 ¢
w/fatback or sausage	15 ¢
w/Salmon	15 ¢
Pig Ear Sandwiches	5 ¢
Salmon Croquette Sandwich	5 ¢
Tripe Sandwich	5 ¢
Chili Dogs	5 ¢
Pulled Pork Sandwich	10 ¢
Croaker Sandwich	10 ¢
Brunswick Stew	15 ¢
Fried Chicken with Potato Salad	20 ¢
Fried Chicken's Feet with Potato Salad	15 ¢
Fried Gizzards or Livers with Potato Salad	15 ¢
BBQ ribs	25 ¢

An elementary school sat across the street and down a bit, close enough for John and some of the school's students to be startled at the sight of each other the first time. John could see and hear them at recess, laughing and running. As kids do, they eventually invited John to come play with them, but he never had time to play. The chores seemed endless.

After some time they asked him if he could go to school with them. With great desire to join them, he asked his father one day, "Dad, can I go to school? It's right across the street." Bud flatly replied, "You got no need to go to school!"

John cursed the day he came to Griffin. Every day, time slipped away. Life seemed to be passing John by. The boredom led him to equate his condition with that of slave labor. John felt like a prisoner, a plantation slave. He visualized how slaves must have felt with no rights and no choices. He had heard stories about them in the old South but had never thought much about their lives until now.

One of the kids told him a new movie called *Each Dawn I Die*, featuring James Cagney, had come to town. A bunch of the kids were planning to go, and he wanted to go to the movie with them. He asked his father if he could go. His father told him without hesitation, "No!" The excuse was that Sara did not feel well, while Bobby, his two-year-old stepbrother, ran around the house unrestrained. Sara was pregnant with their second child, leaving John with no choice but to stay home and help her around the house. John felt sympathy for Sara. He could see that his father had hit her more than once even though she was always nice to him. John struggled to accept his father's behavior, whispering adamantly to himself, "Hitting a woman isn't right!"

Defiance began to pump through John's veins. After dinner, he cleaned up the dishes and pots. Fed up with indentured servitude, John wanted to see the movie and decided he was going no matter what the consequences. With Bobby asleep and Sara as comfortable as she could be, he waited for the right moment to slip out the back door.

Later, the credits rolled and the lights came up after the Cagney film ended. What a movie! Something about the adventure stirred his imagination. For the short time that John sat in the theater, he reached the pinnacle of excitement. The character that Cagney played was bold, brave, and fearless. This character made John want to see the world firsthand. Walking back home, he relived the scenes and situations, inspiring him to mimic the dashing hero defeating the villain. If only he could do that in real life.

He approached the house planning to quietly sneak in the back door and go to sleep. As soon as he opened the back door and walked inside, he could see his father sitting there, waiting for him with his old army belt. Bud immediately laid into John, rambling and cursing, beating him with the belt. All the turmoil woke Sara, but there was nothing she could say or do. She too had been on the wrong side of Bud's wrath and felt for John. While Bud whipped John with the belt, he also accused his son of stealing his corn liquor from behind the house. Apparently, Bud had a special hiding place for it and intended to sell it. His private stash disappeared while John was at the movies.

Naturally, John could not think clearly when he was getting whipped with an army belt. Thinking back, John remembered that he and his friend were retrieving wood in the yard when they witnessed his father hiding a bottle under the back of the house. John tried to explain that his friend must have taken the liquor or his daddy put him up to it. Bud didn't care what came out of John's mouth. John was guilty because Bud said so, escalating his reeling spiral of fury.

This proved to be the first of many episodes of accusations and beatings. Resentment built up sharply within John toward his father. He no longer wanted the obligation of being Bud's son, nor working in his business like a slave, nor tending to his house like a servant. He had had enough of not being permitted to go to school and no money to get back home to his mother.

At that point, John had been with his father for nearly three months. During this time, John found a hole inside himself that could not be filled, as if his father was taking something profound away from him. It wasn't just having a little fun that he missed so much. John realized it was his childhood. He unwittingly traded his education and childhood away to be his father's mule.

Rhunette kept in touch with her son by mail, encouraging him to work hard and telling him he was doing the right thing by helping his father. Without enough money for the train and knowing his father would not let him go, much less give him money for a ticket, John began plotting his escape.

Another letter came from home. Bud asked John, "What's your mother saying?" Before he could second-guess himself and without hesitation, John told him, "It said that momma wants me to come home. She's not feeling very good." Bud could count money without a problem and knew John could, too, but he could not read or write. It was Sara who wrote the original letter for John to come to Griffin and Sara again who wrote the menu board at the restaurant. She didn't even ask to read the letter. In the spur of the moment, John's plan needed her cooperation, if not her support, to work. Sara looked at John, letting her eyes silently answer his plea for help.

John's father seemed to be ignoring his appeal completely because Bud had not said a word about it. A day went by, then another. John grew restless and irritable like a caged animal. Dull eyes of resignation reflected his overwhelming sadness as John began to believe he would spend the rest of his life there. He thought about running away, knowing King would be much easier to put up with. For that matter, working all day not knowing where his next meal came from would prove gratifying compared to this. He could just vanish and see the world like in the movies. But the movies always made things look easy. He considered every option while waiting for an answer. Every day lasted forever to a youngster eager to leave.

On the third day, Bud approached John while he was cleaning fish. He gave his son change to pay the train fare back to Atlanta. He never bothered to ask Sara what she thought he should do. Even Bud could see the boy was miserable and did not belong in Griffin. While he was satisfied that he taught his son a few useful things about running a business, the restaurant was not John's responsibility. Bud wished he could say something before his son returned to his mother, but he did not know what to say or how to say it. He could only watch as his son boarded the train.

All the way back to Atlanta, John was both relieved and grateful for the chance to live again. Studying the blurring landscape as it raced past his window, a critical thought came to him. John made a promise to himself that would set a course for the rest of his life. The promise was if he had a chance to do something significant, he would do it. He had escaped the worst situation imaginable and he wanted more from life than being trapped or told what to do all the time. He wanted the chance to see the world, learn new things, meet new people. Who knew when he'd get that chance, but this was his new goal in life.

John was so happy to be home with his mother and grandmother again he was completely beside himself. The two doting mothers smothered him with affection at the kitchen table and implored him to share tales of Griffin. He had nothing good to say about his father, but shared that Sara was nice and that little Bobby was a terror. They laughed heartily. Then he told them about his countless chores, and Rhunette, saddened by his tale, poured affection over him and teased him lovingly. After what he'd been through, he was overdue for a few laughs. Lizzy told him that he had become a young man after that ordeal. And Rhunette had been right. John had received a crash course in restaurant operations, food preparation, restaurant shopping, cleaning, and maintenance from his father. In the big city, that meant he could find a legitimate job opportunity.

Soon after he settled back into his Atlanta home, Sara wrote to John through Rhunette. The letter stated that his father was in the hospital and he wanted John to return to Griffin because Sara needed his help running the restaurant. Hearing his father's request, he considered what would happen to Sara and little Bobby if he did not return. John liked Sara and appreciated what she did to help him leave that terrible place, but he also treasured the promise he had made to himself on the way home. Considering both sides, he told his mother, "No, I won't go. I'll never go back there!" John didn't know whether his mother responded to the letter or not and he didn't care. His mind was made up.

A week or so later, when he thought the matter was behind him, John's mother received another letter, this time more urgent. His father was still in the hospital and Sara begged him to come back. The predicament hit him hard because he knew Sara suffered an untenable situation with her pregnancy, raising little Bobby, and carrying out all the duties of running that restaurant. Still, he refused to go back to Griffin for anything.

A couple of weeks later, Rhunette notified her son that his father had passed away. She asked him if he wanted to attend the funeral. John not only wanted nothing to do with the funeral, he had no regrets for never going back. He reasoned his father had nothing to say to him and treated him badly. Whatever happened between them didn't matter anymore.

But it did matter. Regardless of the circumstances, John's three months of hard labor translated into restaurant experience. Few 11 year olds could say that with resolve. Actual restaurant training was like gold, the leg up he needed, and John had every intention of using it.

CHAPTER 5

ENTERPRISING YOUTH

*"Few things can help an individual
more than to place responsibility on him, and to let him know
that you trust him."*

Booker T. Washington

John's training in Griffin and his promise to himself set him on a mission. A well-known restaurant named the "Ship Ahoy" on Lucky Street near Fairline hired John on the spot. He helped the Chinese chef peel onions, potatoes, and shrimp. John also helped the chef cook food, wash dishes, and whatever else the chef needed him to do. Whenever people left a steak or a good-sized portion of other meat on their plates, he washed it off and took it home to eat. He brought a bag of food home every night. His household had so much meat that Rhunette started giving it away to the neighbors before it spoiled. John and his family ate like never before.

To see the confident 11-year-old boy find his way brought great satisfaction to Rhunette. Her pride and joy exceeded all her expectations in helping the family during difficult times. He seemed so focused and determined that she worried about him growing up too fast. She kept her concerns to herself in hopes that nothing would change for her son, saying a prayer daily for his safe passage.

On his 12th birthday, John celebrated with a long shift at the Ship Ahoy. He followed his normal route home, taking the trolley at Ashby and North Avenue. From the trolley station he continued walking alone on a poorly-lit street. Within a block of his home, he noticed a car pulling up behind him. He turned and saw two police officers riding in the car. Having pulled up next to him, the officer on the passenger's side rolled his window down and told John to stop. He asked John what he was doing out that late at night. John replied he was coming from work. The cop accused him of lying, climbed out of the squad car, and badgered him about his story. Then he slapped John across the face, knocking him down. He cursed at John, telling him to get up and run.[4]

After being accosted for no reason, John got up angry and did not comply with the officer's order. He refused to run. Incensed by his defiance, the cop picked up a double-fist-sized rock and threw it at the back of John's head. John felt the vibration as the rock whizzed by his right ear. He ran home.

When Rhunette heard what happened, she knew her fear became real. She felt so powerless to protect her son that she began to pray, asking the Lord to protect John. The ordeal left her unnerved for weeks. John did not change his routine and refused to be affected.

Several months passed before she paid a visit to Reverend Devonport down at the Twelfth Street Baptist Church. She shared her fears with him. In his opinion, the predicament she described had but one solution.

The entire family gathered at the church on a cold winter Sunday for a formal occasion. Rhunette and Reverend Devonport had strongly believed that John should get right with God. Reverend Devonport commenced with the baptism of John Edward Seagraves, performed indoors, though John literally broke a thin top layer of ice as he was lowered to immersion in a pool of wintry-cold water.

Around that time, a lot of talk surrounded a new movie coming out called *Gone With The Wind.* John had been told the author of the story was a local celebrity. Late one afternoon, prior to the premiere, the cast from *Gone With The Wind* came into the Ship Ahoy to eat dinner. As it turned out, the Ship Ahoy was only two blocks away from the famous Loew's Grand Theatre located at the corner of Peachtree and Forsyth streets in downtown Atlanta. The theatre became an instant landmark the night it hosted the premiere of *Gone With The Wind* on December 15, 1939.[5]

The Ship Ahoy was a popular restaurant, and John had certainly done well providing for his family, but management saw fit to work him half to death. After working long hours for a seven-day stretch, he was too exhausted to continue, and one night he just walked out. After almost two years, right or wrong, he chose not to return. However, he was an enterprising youth determined to find his way.

Hanging around Peachtree Street, John met a fellow named Joe Battle. Joe was a year older than John and worked several jobs around the area. John found him to be a good-natured fellow. One thing about Joe that tickled John was his love for "chili pig ear" sandwiches. He bought them from a little Jewish-owned café on Peachtree Street that sold food to black people. Having lost interest in restaurant work, John accepted Joe's offer to help him get a job at Liggett's Drug Store. The owner hired John to make deliveries.

For the first two weeks the job seemed honest and easy. Then one day John delivered an order to a customer who suddenly made a sexual advance toward him and grabbed him inappropriately. He was so shocked and bothered by the offense that he immediately returned to notify his boss. John was angry that a customer had violated him, but he didn't know what he expected his boss to do. After hearing what happened, the employer dismissed the incident and walked away, leaving John completely disturbed. He swore he would quit before he delivered anything to that house again. True to his word, John refused the next time the perverted man requested a delivery. His employer promptly fired him.

John found himself getting up to go to work with nowhere to go. Not sure what he wanted to do for employment, he decided to relax for a few days. John really enjoyed going to the "81 Theater" by himself, usually eating sandwiches and watching movies or shows. Sometimes the theater ran a double feature and a cartoon for ten cents. For five cents more he could add a stage show like Silas Green dancing and singing, or for ten cents extra he could see Snake Review clowning around telling jokes.

One afternoon a fortune teller and her front man gave psychic readings randomly to the audience, working their way around the room. They approached John sitting by himself in an aisle seat. The front man put his hand over John's head and said to the lady fortune teller on stage, "Tell me something about this young man." She responded, "He has two dimes in his pocket, will experience many things, and will live a long life." As it happened, John had two dimes in his pocket, and his experiences had already far exceeded his peers. He looked at her in amazement. As they proceeded to the next kid, he wondered whether it was a sign that his wish to see the world would come true. The psychic demonstration made an impression on him he could not forget.

John walked away from the theater pondering his past work history and starting to think about his future. With qualified work experience, he knew he could try new and different opportunities for employment. Because John was tall for his age, he never had any problems finding work or convincing people to hire him. Hard work challenged him in a positive way. By developing a solid work ethic, he sought greater responsibility. John reflected on his role models, knowing he could distinguish right from wrong. He did everything he could to help his family and gave his mother most of his earnings.

As a young man of 14, he had become more and more independent. Since he did not work every day, he was happy to run errands for his mother, like shopping for food or going down to city hall to pay the water bill. Temperatures in the South often leaned toward hot, causing him to build up a thirst. The public water fountain provided separate bubblers marked "white" and "colored."

One could very well have called him rebellious because his moral compass defied segregation whenever the opportunity presented itself. He remembered what Mr. Roberts told him about treating everyone with equal respect, and he followed that philosophy by drinking from the "white" bubbler. He admittedly didn't know the penalty for getting caught and didn't care. John was surprisingly objective about his circumstances. Taking pride in himself and standing up for his right to choose the quality of his life compelled him to take chances.

John studied his work experience further. He concluded that working for one employer took away his freedom to find better options. The more he looked around, the clearer he saw an opportunity to start his own business. Investing in an old push lawn mower and sickle, John began to cut grass and work odd jobs to keep cash flowing and allow him the independence he coveted.

George Washington High School's football team practiced every weekday afternoon in preparation for Friday games. During the fall, the days had cooled a bit, making the afternoons quite pleasant for watching the older kids do agility drills and run plays. Envy tugged at John's heartstrings as he observed them, but he reminded himself that he had decided he could not help his mother if he attended school. In some ways, self-employment gave him a head start in life over school kids. At the very least, he was free to come and go as he pleased.

He walked away from the school grounds pulling the lawn mower behind him on a little wagon. Before he got very far, a man named Graham Jackson, a musician of some renown who had seen the industrious youngster before, approached him. He asked John what he would charge to cut his lawn and run errands for him. John assessed the lawn, thought about a fair price, and responded. Mr. Jackson accepted and they shook hands.

With just a few odd jobs, business was not brisk. However, John placed his autonomy ahead of money for a very special reason. Freedom wasn't something he thought much about until he had been old enough to work for his father. The experience taught him that he didn't know what he had until someone took it away. Working for his father had made him feel trapped. Sure, he had learned a great deal from his father's crash course in restaurant operations, yet entrapment had stolen any joy he might have experienced in his return to Griffin.

He also knew that freedom came with a price. He had to get up and look for new opportunities every day. In the end, that was fine by him. He wanted it that way.

Not everyone agreed with his outlook. Many older men reluctantly accepted their circumstances and had limited choices. Some men broke under the pressure of their responsibilities to feed their families. They usually had to do what they were told. Some were clearly afraid to speak out and claim what they wanted from life. Maybe that made John different. While he was not the only young man seeking to provide for his family, he felt empowered by taking it upon himself to help his family, unlike King, who shirked his responsibilities, and Bud, who hated everything and everybody. John's stepfather and deceased father had provided him with as much direction on how not to live as Uncle James and Mr. Roberts had taught him how to live.

At a young age, John developed a philosophy to do what he thought was right and ignore what other people said. He did not have all the answers, but he rejected being a flunky. If he ran errands, he did so on his own terms. John was confident that eventually he would figure things out and be successful. Despite his enthusiasm, there were times he missed just being a kid.

A year went by. John had plenty of time to evaluate the cost of freedom. Having little to show for his efforts, he tired of lugging lawn equipment around in search of his next meal. With a basis for comparison, John discovered he could always find a meal working in restaurants, just like his father before him.

A buddy of his named George Johnson recommended that John come to work with him at the Northside Delicatessen. George, who was a couple of years older than John, told him that the Jewish fellow who owned the restaurant near 10th and Peachtree paid $10 per week. Compared to sometimes earning a few pennies a day, he decided that $10 a week for washing dishes, pots, and pans would be a welcome respite. The deli owner didn't allow the staff to eat anything more than chicken's feet and necks, but John could handle that. Originally he thought he couldn't stomach chicken, but food was food when his stomach was empty.

John knew his job and enjoyed himself again. He made his job look effortless in so many ways that the owner wanted to know his secret, wishing he had five more employees like John. One day his employer overheard John discussing his previous work history and responsibilities in past jobs. Eavesdropping discreetly, his boss found the discussion intriguing. John had done deliveries before, leading the owner to consider food delivery. Subsequently, the opportunistic Jewish fellow modified John's job description.

John needed a bike for the job, therefore his boss told him, "Go to the bike shop down the street, pick out a bike, and we'll deduct 50 cents a week from your pay." John picked out a bike priced at $10. Not long afterward, he got a flat tire and needed it repaired. John pushed the bike to the place where he bought it and asked the owner to fix the flat. The bike shop owner said he wanted to repossess the bike, claiming that John's employer had never made any payments. John didn't believe a word the man said, riding the bike away on one good tire.

After John reported the dispute to his boss, the feisty Jewish man told John to go back down to the bike shop owner and get the tire fixed, insisting the bike shop owner was lying and deli deliveries were piling up. John didn't know who to believe, but someone was lying. Weighing the bike against the job and running the numbers in his head, he crafted a solution: Leave the Northside Delicatessen, keep the bike, and abandon his final week's pay to cover the cost of the bike.

John felt the satisfaction of resolving a difficult business dispute. He was happy to trade the job for a bike, viewing transportation as an important asset to a broader employment search, and he figured out how to fix the flat tire himself.

Occasionally John had a taste for crème-filled Krispy Kreme doughnuts and he paid a visit to the popular hangout on the corner of Peachtree and 11th Street. It served black people only from a rear window. As John noshed on sugar-sweet glazed doughnuts, a man about 25 years old stood in line to buy some as well. Sharing a common pleasure, they started talking. The older man told John he was going into the service. More interesting was the part about him leaving his job at the Peachtree Theatre as the cleaning and maintenance man. He told John his pay was $25 per week and recommended that John go apply for the job.

The unemployed opportunist with new transportation thought he had won a prize! Twenty-five dollars was more than double John's salary at the Northside Delicatessen. For a 15-year-old, that was a lot of money. The next day John applied for the job and received a salary offer of $17 per week.

Accepting the offer, John felt his life take a positive turn. He felt he had come into his own at the right time. Uncle James had accepted an offer of a prestigious position as a Pullman Porter for the New Haven Railroad so that he and Aunt Fannie had to relocate to Boston. In turn, Lizzy moved in permanently to help Rhunette raise the children. A peculiar consequence of John finding good steady work resulted in King hanging around the house more. With John out of the house most of the time, and Rhunette and Lizzy preoccupied with the kids, King could relinquish all his demands as head of the house. For the first time the house became peaceful.

The Peachtree Theatre was only two blocks away from the Northside Delicatessen on Peachtree near 13th Street. John's job description included pretty much every task required to operate the theater except handling money. He changed the marquee outside, replaced all the framed poster boards in the lobby, cleaned and maintained the lobby and viewing areas, and helped where needed at the concessions. Originally he assisted an older man picking up film from the distributors on Ivy Street until he knew the routine himself. Once he delivered the film to the projection room, he learned the science behind on-screen film projection and splicing the film.

The latest projector technology in 1941 was a Peerless enclosure that used carbon to telegraph the light from the movie onto the background and project it. The machine was a Simplex, with four reels per container. When the film transferred to a companion reel at a certain point, a tab inserted in the film would drop off and made a "ping" noise striking the floor, letting the projectionist know the time to change film machines was approaching. After that he stood next to the other machine and stepped on the pedal when he was ready to switch from one machine to the other. When the second light came up on the screen, he pressed the button and the reels would switch.

One afternoon John was sitting in the back of the theater watching a movie. He saw the dot flash in the upper-right corner, giving the operator one minute. Knowing the process by heart, John knew the ping sound was next. As expected, the second dot showed up in the upper-right corner of the screen giving the signal to step on the pedal and switch reels. Uncharacteristically, the screen turned white. The reels didn't switch. John jumped out of his seat, ran up to the projection room, and found the operator, reeking of alcohol, unconscious in a chair. John calmly switched the reels and the film continued.

The setting sun cast shadows across the street from the theater one day when John left work. Before heading home, he stopped to watch some kids playing craps in front of the theater on the Peachtree Street sidewalk. A police cruiser pulled over and parked. Two officers stepped out to break up the gathering. Having seen John around town, the officers prejudged him to be a young hustler erring toward wrong-doing and presumed he was teaching the young delinquents how to play. Against his protests of innocence, the officers shoved John into the back of the squad car.

As they argued with him, two white women saw the whole thing and intervened, giving the officers a piece of their mind. The women owned the boarding house across the street where one of their employees, a nice black lady, often fed John biscuits. The two women defended John, telling the officers that he worked at the theater and he had done nothing wrong. Further, if they wanted to take John, they had to take all the kids. The officers released John with a warning and dispersed the children.

John and his family enjoyed a stable quality of life thanks to his determination. No one seemed surprised that he celebrated his 16th birthday working a normal day at the theater. Compared to slogging through pots and pans in some sweatbox restaurant kitchen, he barely broke a sweat working in the theater. His weekly salary provided him a decent living with the promise of earning the same $25-a-week salary his predecessor had made. He visualized himself being a projectionist one day, and that paid even more money.

Being able to see movies every day seemed like a dream come true to John, even though seeing the same ones over and over got boring at times. Still this was the easiest job he had ever had. He achieved a level of contentment that inspired confidence every day. The sum total of his experiences added up to this. Management trusted him so much that he got his long-time buddy Sam Walker a job at the theater, too. Having an employer wasn't so bad after all.

Coming out of the Peachtree Theatre one late afternoon, John ran into Graham Jackson again. He had neither worked for nor seen Mr. Graham in some time. Jackson inquired about his well-being and his current occupation. After John proudly detailed his promising situation, Jackson asked him, "Are you interested in joining the Navy?" John shrugged, cracking a smile.

Truth be told, he never considered enlisting in the service, but the idea intrigued him. His friend George had shipped out for the Great Lakes installation in North Chicago a year before. Great Lakes enlistees trained as "Naval Seabees," a clever nickname for the Navy's Construction Battalion. John assumed the Navy shipped George to Illinois to teach him the construction trade. Paid training struck him as a smart move. Jackson wanted John to meet with him in the Federal Building to give him all the details.

With a bright future as a projectionist on the horizon, John found himself on the horns of a dilemma, weighing the pros and cons. He figured if he stayed in Atlanta, the projectionist job could be the limit of his future. This was his first big opportunity to do something special. It could be the chance he had been waiting for.

The U.S. military called, and brave men answered. He wanted to see the world, fly to exotic lands. He imagined fighting for his country. He could meet up with his friend George and they could explore the world together. Remembering what the fortune teller said, he got excited: he "… will experience many things, and will live a long life."

John visualized himself living his own James Cagney movie.

CHAPTER 6

GRAHAM JACKSON

"With courage you will dare to take risks, have the strength to be compassionate, and the wisdom to be humble. Courage is the foundation of integrity."
Keshavan Nair

As a black accordion player in the 1930s and 1940s, Graham Jackson was President Franklin D. Roosevelt's favorite entertainer.[6] FDR frequented the Warm Springs Foundation Hospital where he received a series of specialized medical treatments for a debilitating and incurable case of polio. Quite often Jackson accompanied FDR to the President's second home in Warm Springs, Georgia, as his personal guest.

John recollected the day he witnessed President Roosevelt's motorcade making its way down Chestnut Street where Uncle James and Aunt Fannie lived. The President was in an open convertible, smiling with his trademark cigarette holder between his teeth. Secret Service agents drove the vehicle and sat in the front passenger side seat and in the back seat, flanking him from either side. John heard all the noise from the motorcycles and the sirens blaring without knowing what was going on. He was among the fortunate few who caught a glimpse of the president and architect of a new America.

Apparently, FDR had passed through the neighborhood to pick up his friend Graham Jackson. No one could explain any other reason for FDR to be riding through a black neighborhood in Atlanta. Jackson lived off Hunter Street, directly across the street from George Washington High School. Later, as a gift for Mr. Jackson's loyalty, President Roosevelt built a small white house for him, designed to replicate the White House in Washington, D.C.

On April 11, 1945, FDR watched Jackson rehearse a few songs for a minstrel show in the president's honor the next day at the Warm Springs Foundation Hospital. The event had been dedicated to the treatment of polio victims. Just after 1 pm on April 12, President Roosevelt was posing in a seated position for a watercolor portrait when he fell to the floor. Graham Jackson, warming up and getting his makeup done for the show, heard the news and ran to FDR's side. At 3:30 pm that afternoon the president was pronounced dead. Jackson played for Roosevelt 23 times during FDR's tenure as the nation's leader. *Life* magazine's April 23, 1945, issue showing the famous photograph of Jackson mourning the death of his friend would eternally link the two men.

Graham Jackson had asked John to pay him a visit at the Federal Building to discuss joining the Navy. John accepted the invitation, thinking why not? John had never been recruited before and felt privileged. The potential for heroic adventure fueled his curiosity and excitement. Besides, Sam had thanked him for getting him a job at the theater and signed up with the Army. The Army had already shipped George to a northern suburb of Chicago to trains as a Seabee, John's assignment choice. Little by little, the U.S. military fit into his bigger vision.

On the sunny warm morning of June 26, 1943, John entered the federal building, a stark, austere building with big doors, long halls, and an air of formality that demanded respect. The office was on the first floor, hidden behind a maze of turns as he searched for the back of the building. He had seen the building from the outside plenty of times but knew nothing about what went on inside. John, feeling something special was happening for him to be there, found Mr. Jackson's office easily enough to know deep down he was ready to punch his ticket and go wherever fate led him.

Graham Jackson struck John as medium height, medium weight, medium vocal tone, and even moderate disposition, just an average person. He had a folksy, southern quality about him. Jackson greeted John wearing a Chief's uniform and called him "Bill." He asked John where the name Bill came from. John did his best to explain the peculiar dispute between his mother and grandmother. Jackson chuckled, then instantly changed his expression, getting straight to the point. He wanted John to join the Navy.

"The Navy needs black sailors," he blurted out. John told him, "If I go, I want to go to Great Lakes." Jackson reacted, "No problem." Jackson's response came out so clearly that John never doubted his request had been granted. What really swayed John was Graham Jackson's confident deliberation. He told John how the Navy would pay for his education when he completed his obligations in case he still wanted to finish school, a hot button that Jackson recalled.

Times had changed considerably since Jackson had first observed that same entrepreneurial kid one afternoon when John took a break from pulling his lawn care equipment to watch George Washington High School students at football practice. Jackson continued to explain the benefits of getting the GI Bill, medical coverage, and other perks of military service. The list of bonuses sounded more like winning a prize. No one had ever made anything sound so good before.

One thing concerned John. He asked, "How old do I have to be?" When Jackson answered, "17," John tried to contain his disappointment, worried that he was too young to receive the best thing ever offered to him. He painfully confessed, "But, I'm not 17."

A straight shooter, John confronted his only barrier to seeing the world. Without hesitation Jackson dismissed his concern. "Put the date of your age back to June 5 rather than July 5," he said with a smile. John balked. His first impression of the idea struck him as dishonest.

Every fiber of his being wanted to utter the word that would change everything. He hesitated, taking inventory of his journey and his readiness for the next step. The moment he heard himself say, "Okay," his mind went blank. He just made the biggest decision of his life.

Graham Jackson sold John on joining the United States Navy and they both knew it. Jackson did his job. John wanted to go. But John could not lie to himself; he respected the uniform, purpose, and dignity exclusive to enlistment. And he could not resist. All he had to do was sign on the dotted line, no need for a birth certificate or identification. Since John's family residential history appeared consistently inconsistent, he filled out the paperwork using Aunt Fannie's sister Thelma's address. Jackson had John sign the paperwork, then told him, "Raise your right hand to be sworn in and repeat after me…."

Jackson followed with, "You be here at 7:30 a.m. tomorrow morning. We'll get you where you need to go and get you situated right away." Jackson told John, "You're going to go through your induction in Jacksonville, Florida, then go to Great Lakes." John protested, "Florida? Why Florida?" Jackson assured him, "They'll transfer you once you get there. Are you interested in serving on an exotic island somewhere in the Pacific?" John chirped heartily with a huge smile, "Sounds good to me!" John acknowledged Jackson's authority by accepting the logistics. After all, he was a personal friend of the President of the United States.

The day after John's enrollment into the U.S. Navy, he boarded a train and shipped out for Naval Boot Camp. On his way to Florida, John had plenty of time to think about what happened. Even though everything materialized so quickly, he had no regrets except one. It didn't bother him that he signed up and left his family the next day. Deep down John dreamed that something like this would happen. What bothered him was why Jackson insisted on him signing up in such a hurry. Why the rush?

Talk of depression and war had not reached John. From the late '20s to the early '40s, he grew up knowing nothing else but the Great Depression. The 12-year-old boy who emerged from Griffin promising to make the most of his life if he got the chance struggled like anyone else, yet found work in Atlanta when others didn't. For blacks and whites alike, employment opportunities were understandably scarce. Millions of Americans nationwide searched hopelessly for work. The service offered starving, displaced Americans hot meals, new clothing, and the chance to fight for their country.

No one told him the U.S. Navy had labor issues in the midst of the war effort and they needed black enlisted men to replace Filipinos in their steward's ranks. Another omission indicated "[t]he Chief of Naval Personnel, Rear Adm. Randall Jacobs, was surprised at the small number of volunteers, a figure far below the planners' expectations, and his surprise turned to concern in the next months as the 17-year-old volunteer inductees, the primary target of the armed forces recruiters, continued to choose the Army over the Navy at a ratio of 10 to 1. The Navy's personnel officials agreed that they had to attract their proper share of intelligent and able Negroes but seemed unable to isolate the cause of the disinterest...

Only when the Navy began assigning black recruiting specialists to the numerous naval districts and using black chief petty officers, reservists from World War I general service, at recruiting centers to explain the new opportunities for Negroes in the Navy was the bureau able to overcome some of the young men's natural reluctance to volunteer. By 1 February 1943 the Navy had 26,909 Negroes (still 2 percent of the total enlisted): 6,662 in the general service; 2,020 in the Seabees, and 19,227, over two-thirds of the total, in the Steward's Branch."[7]

John would have been equally blind to Graham Jackson's driving motivation to meet the opportunity and obligations to his friend President Roosevelt to recruit as many men as he could find who were capable of serving the nation's agendas abroad.

No doubt, Jackson did his job effectively as a black recruiter persuading black men to join the service. He was not obligated to explain initiative details, war status updates, the dangers of defending their country, or proving their worth to their white counterparts. To serve a man's country was an honor and a privilege. In the end, the U.S. Navy cared little about Jackson's methods.

Jackson was not the enemy; he was a pawn being brokered to use his influence. War and a volatile culture struggled to put divisive values aside for a cause. America's war machine anticipated needs in Europe and in the Pacific, citing black personnel as challenged but convenient. Little did the collective body of military wisdom realize the importance of courage, bravery, and sacrifice in this same class of men many Navy blue-bloods deemed below them.

John's complaint amounted to being recruited on a need-to-know basis. How his services would be allocated was not optional. Many black volunteers added significant meaning to their aimless forgettable pasts and conditional futures… futures determined by their willingness to endure a two-class system at home and abroad. The Navy needed bodies to win a war against tyranny and fascism. Any differences between blacks and whites would have to wait. Social resolutions were always secondary.

The chain of command demanded that all enlisted men follow orders. For any man willing to fight and die for his country, accurate or fictitious birth records did not matter. Special requests, thoughts, or feelings did not matter. Northern or southern boot camp training did not matter. Messman or Seabee did not matter. At all cost, winning the war mattered.

CHAPTER 7

NAVAL BOOT CAMP

"Man is so made that when anything fires his soul, impossibilities vanish."
                                        Jean de La Fontaine

Instead of being sent north to the Great Lakes Training Center, John rode the train further south to the Jacksonville Receiving Station for Basic Training. Heading south disappointed him, but Mr. Jackson told him he would be transferred after he got there so he was not worried. On Monday, June 28, 1943, he entered a United States Naval Facility for the very first time. Two days earlier, on a sunny Saturday, he had discussed joining the Navy with Graham Jackson. The day before, the Navy had put him on a train. John kept thinking how things happened fast in the service.

At the Jacksonville train station, John followed instructions and located a bus full of black enlistees going to boot camp as well. Everyone rode the bus in silent apprehension. Finally at the receiving station, he climbed off the bus and approached the first person of authority. The chief watched them disembark with a look of disdain. The white instructor in his late thirties showed little patience for the black volunteers. John ignored his demeanor and approached him, expecting simple instructions to be redirected to the Great Lakes Facility north of Chicago. He tried to explain what Mr. Jackson told him.

A boot camp instructor well-versed at breaking and molding men into disciplined Navy men, the chief stood fast amid his well-heeled look of indifference. One glance at John and he barked, "You aren't going anywhere but where we put you!" That was the beginning. John knew right away that his new commitment would test him. He quickly found out he left civilian life to become U.S. Navy property, no more or less significant than a sea bag or a weapon. Either he did what he was told or he got court-martialed.

John had suspected Mr. Jackson lied to him, and at once he knew. For a few moments he cursed his stupidity for believing Jackson. All his complaints swirled around in his head. He wanted to be a Seabee and see the world with his buddy. He thought he would have gotten by at the Peachtree Theater had he stayed. But then he replayed his promise to himself. Making the most of his life could not include Georgia. He wanted to see the world, not just raise his siblings. The noise in his head quieted down, freeing him to focus on the tasks before him.

Naval Boot Camp

As soon as the young men disembarked the bus and fell into some semblance of order, they followed orders and walked to the disbursement building to get their gear. From there they proceeded to their sleeping quarters to get organized. The barracks was a two-story building located in a segregated part of the base. Separate lodging in boot camp was no different than anywhere in America, one of the few characteristics shared between civilian and military life. The implication was that black volunteers should be right at home with segregation despite the military culture. About 40 black sailors received bunk assignments, including John who landed on the second floor.

As soon as the recruits dropped their gear, the chief came into the barracks and began to bark orders. This man behaved as if someone had stolen something from him and he was mad as hell about it. He was a southerner with a rotten attitude, mostly toward black people. The chief told his latest group of misfits he was accustomed to commanding young white sailors but he was given the task of being the drill instructor to an entire barracks of black enlistees. He wasn't sure which he hated more, black people in general or his assignment to whip them into shape. The opinionated trainer didn't like it one bit and spoke his mind openly.

The chief told the recruits to form two lines and then he started pacing, yelling at them one by one. After getting the attention of each man individually, he stepped back in front of them, eyeballed them and griped, "I don't like working with negrahs! You men are here to do Basic Training. For six weeks, I will tell you when to move and each and every move you must make. First, you will go to sick bay and get your shots. Reveille is 0600, breakfast is 0700, and training starts at 0800. Do not be late or it will cost you!"

When he commanded the men to "fall out," there was fear in many of them. John could see most everyone else was like him, feeling awkward and out of their comfort zone. Lining up at the infirmary, many never had shots before. Oversized needles for tetanus, malaria, and other necessary immunizations shook up both large and small men alike. Except for standing in line to get their gear, shots, and meals, nearly everybody kept to themselves, not knowing what to expect.

The next morning the men stood at attention as instructed. The chief insisted the motley mob do things the right way, starting with how to march, "Left, right, attention! Left, right, attention! Halt." As a group, their sloppy cadence persisted to the chief's disdain. Several recruits came from the country with minimal schooling; they didn't know their left from their right.

Dissatisfied with formation spacing and posture, the chief roared, "You men fall in line. Press arms and hands against shoulders to the person next to you, arms length from the person in front of you. Attention. Now march. Hup-two-hup-two-hup-two!" The perfectionist drill instructor seemed content to march the recruits either until they found a rhythm or their legs fell off. He did not care which. They marched for about a half hour more. Then the chief commanded, "Men halt! Take five."

Any drill instructor worth his stripes knew how to "break him to make him." In the U.S. military, the job called for deconstructing civilians and rebuilding them to become fighting material. Only then could a sailor or soldier become a credit to the uniform. Newbies always walked in with baggage, civilian issues that needed to be neutralized. By the time the chief finished with them, they walked out proud representatives of the U.S. military. That was his plan for this bunch like any other, but he honestly did not know how this "experiment" would work out.

Because the Navy maintained its fleet on water, all Navy facilities, including inland bases, accessed huge bodies of water. That meant wet conditions and well-fed bugs. Jacksonville, Florida, in July was hotter and more humid than Georgia, particularly in uniform. The recruits stood in 95 degree temperatures expecting to take a five-minute rest, then jump back into a double-time march in unison. An hour lapsed, then they rested for five minutes. The marching pace persisted for another two hours. The chief was merciless and uncompromising. One or two of the guys fell to the ground, completely unconscious from heat exhaustion.

Any of the sailors who could still breathe and think clearly speculated the chief hated them so much he punished them for being black. He pushed, tested, and demanded, determined to break down his beleaguered subjects. In succession, marching shifted to exercises, sit-ups, pushups, knee bends, in sets of 20, then 30, then 40, then 50. The men crawled, climbed rope, jumped over obstacles, and broke for lunch. An hour later they were back to marching for one hour in the afternoon.

Subsequent to the most brutal training experienced by any of them in their lives, they cleaned up for an hour-long movie that kept playing beyond their capacity to stay focused. Depleted and disinterested, they struggled to learn essential tips for survival in an uninspiring, black-

and-white military-issue newsreel on the finer points of tying Navy knots, rolling clothing for packing sea bags, and packing hammocks for sea duty. Other required instructions included using a gas mask while walking through a gas-filled room. They also learned to salute officers, recognize insignia, and respect the hierarchy of authority in the U.S. Navy.

During the second week, John's true birthday came along on July 5. He hated that he could not receive a birthday cake and special privileges like other sailors, but what could he say? That he was told to lie about his age? Nobody would believe that anymore than they would the notion that his grandmother could cure anything with a drop of kerosene in sugar. He fumed over the matter, knowing full well he could do nothing to change it.

After the second round of shots, John's arm was so sore he could barely lift it to scratch his chin. Distracted by soreness, he walked right past an officer without saluting. A subordinate never walked past an officer without saluting him. John was immediately put on report. As a result, the chief ordered him to salute the wall 200 times, letting the pain do the teaching.

Both black sailors and white sailors ate three meals a day. White officers and sailors ate first. A rumor circulated that German prisoners of war dined with the white sailors. Black sailors had separate chow lines and their own eating area. Sometimes there wasn't enough food or the food they got was cold and hard. For example, the morning oatmeal was frequently cold and lumpy. They were tired and hungry like any other sailor driven to the point of near-collapse. Factor in having to wait until everyone else ate – including German POWs – being fed the remains, and not getting enough to eat due to a miscalculation or an act of cruelty by the staff, and one could set a timer as to how quickly patience ran thin. Youth, hunger, and angry emotions instigated several heated disputes among the crew, most times focused on the mess hall staff or snickering white sailors.

Regardless of how long subjugation of their personal rights persisted, most black sailors could never grow accustomed to the same treatment they experienced in civilian life. In the service, black sailors could not sidestep acts of malice as if they occurred on city streets due to sheer proximity and being severely outnumbered. Most everyone traveled in packs. Black sailors had no choice but to use reason and restraint in every social interaction where their rivals obviously did not. Thus, the pervading attitude became "us versus them." Rarely did a black man fight another black man because they were out of control. They fought each other because they couldn't withhold retaliation against their oppressors one more second.

While segregation in civilian life divided and diminished blacks individually, in boot camp, it bonded them. Of course, many black sailors would invite the chance to return the intentional cruelty of the white gangs forever flaunting their numbers, power, and standing in society. None of the white sailors, officers, or staffers knew or cared how much discipline black sailors needed. Ultimately, rigorous drilling galvanized the small circle into a tight one. They were not just preparing for military warfare. Without knowing what challenges they faced at any given moment, they trained for each other.

All recruits were required to attend a formal meeting being held in a segregated auditorium. The commanding officer wanted to speak to everyone new to boot camp. The black group sat in the top rows at the rear of the auditorium. When "The Star-Spangled Banner" played, all the white sailors stood up. Nearly all of the blacks had never heard their national anthem and did not know why the white officers were standing.

John looked around the auditorium and saw the black sailors still in their seats. They didn't know any better. The white sailors had been trained to respect the national anthem and saluted their nation's flag. Few blacks recalled who to salute based on their rank. The plain truth was they had to salute everyone because no one else was ranked below them. But the chief had said nothing about what to do when the national anthem sounded. Maybe he assumed everyone knew what to do and never expected otherwise. Maybe he preferred the black recruits to experience everything the hard way.

The difference between innocence and ignorance was a judgment call the chief had to make. Innocence meant training; ignorance elicited another interpretation – defiance. In this man's military, an act of defiance required immediate punishment. Dishonorable behavior would not be tolerated. Any time the chief became embarrassed by his black apprentices, he took it personally and dealt with it harshly. He ordered the volunteers to march around the barracks with their sea bags full of gear on their shoulders for one hour before bedtime.

Boot camp did not provide a great deal of recreation, but everyone needed somewhere to release pent-up frustrations. The Navy built a makeshift recreational section outdoors away from white sailors, allowing blacks to hang out, relax, clown around, and box. Four barrels and rope immediately converted an empty space into a boxing ring. Spread the barrels into a good-sized square, wrap the rope around the barrels, and either get in or wait your turn. Navy personnel called it "the smoker" and gave black sailors the opportunity to get in the ring, put on gloves, and let off some steam. No one provided instructions, so they made it up as they went along.

Occasionally a small purse went to the winner, motivating sailors to get in. Thinking about the money, almost everybody wanted his turn in the ring but not everybody made a thrilling fight. Once two guys chose a ring man and jumped in, the ring man refereed and encouraged them to mix it up. Someone on the sidelines threw a nickel in the ring to make the clash more interesting. One or two others tossed nickels in while someone else passed a sailor's hat around. The longer the fight, the more the winnings, winner take all.

The first time in the smoker, John knocked the other guy down a couple of times. His defeated foe had had enough, got up, and quickly climbed out of the ring, conceding the fight. Even thought the hat got passed around, John got some change out of it but wasn't satisfied. The second time in, John faced a tougher opponent and did not fare as well. He knew the game, thinking he needed to stick around if he wanted to make some money, but ended up with a busted lip and got beat up a little bit. The hat got passed around, but needless to say the other guy took the winnings.

Side wagers got as much attention as the fight itself. Hustlers always had more money than anyone else and made bigger bets. They thrived on gambling, coaxing the bigger guys to get in the ring and square off, like any good fight promoter. A hustler interested in waging a bet looked around for the most fascinating matchups and instigated a match, yelling, "Anybody want to get in the ring and take on so and so? I'll bet this amount he whoops anybody's butt!" With or without odds, the fight had to be compelling to be worthy. Once two fighters agreed to take each other on, they jumped into the boxing area and then the bets began to fly, raising both the ante and the volume with every solid blow. Sometimes the fight got contentious, with boxers going toe-to-toe until someone got knocked down a couple of times, called it quits, or finished running away from a beating. No one cared how long matches lasted so long as the entertainment value exceeded the boredom.

Most times the intrinsic benefit of getting in the ring had nothing to do with the money. Camaraderie counted for something. Everybody grew stronger, more confident. Getting in the ring seemed to be more of a test to see how far each man had come than anything. Even a busted lip was good for a few laughs, plenty of jawing, and bragging rights afterward.

One morning John found himself losing a fight, though not at the hands of someone else. Shortly after breakfast he fell ill from food poisoning and became extremely weak. He did his best to ignore his condition and fell into ranks for morning drills. John tried to keep up and the nausea got worse. He told the chief he was getting sick and the chief responded, "So am I."

Marching in the fierce sun, John could barely hold on, losing his grip on consciousness. He sweated profusely and could not help but get progressively dizzier, eventually falling to his knees. The chief walked over to him and said, "Stick out your tongue!" Barely able to do that, when John stuck out his tongue it was pasty white. Immediately the chief sent John to sick bay.

For three days John lay in bed. Sometimes he felt guilty sitting around while the other guys endured at the hands of their punisher. By the end of the third day, the chief paid him a visit and told him if he didn't rejoin his group soon, John would have to start boot camp all over again. An hour later John convinced himself he'd rather get back to the grind and drop dead than see this man through another boot camp.

Five weeks in, John took his turn on night watch at the front security gate. His group filled a duty rotation, and his number had come up. Six white sailors coming from town casually strolled through the gate without acknowledging him. Military protocol required that they show the security guard their passes to enter the base. Instead they waltzed past John as if protocol excluded black security guards. John yelled, "Halt!" His arrogant counterparts kept walking. For all the compliance requirements the military demanded of subordinates, this situation surpassed civil rights according to Navy regulations and John went by the book. Pulling out his .45 caliber sidearm, he fired a round in the air. That got their attention.

Startled, the insubordinate sailors stopped walking. John told them to show their badges. They still refused to answer his demand. To them, this was a social issue, and they would not answer to a black man. As citizens, they would not hesitate to do what they did. As military personnel, they were willing to take the risk that they were right. By their logic, John should be put on report for "inappropriately" firing his weapon. John did not appreciate their disrespect and stood his ground.

The smirking sailors located the chief, John's superior, and appealed to him as though the sanctity of their race was at stake. Through all the commotion they caused, the noncompliant malcontents succeeded in getting John put on report for firing his weapon, but they were required to march right back to the guard station and show John their badges or they too would be put on report for violating security protocols.

While John pondered whether segregation applied to military security, the chief stormed toward the security gate, annoyed by such nonsense during his down time. Would the chief take disciplinary action against him for not permitting the white sailors to walk through the gate without showing their passes to a black security guard? Details caught up by circumstance forced the hand of authority.

How would the chief decide to handle the proper action of a black sailor who performed his security duties to the letter, exposing a clear violation committed by white sailors in a white man's Navy?

Without hesitation, the chief jumped in John's face and asked him, "Sailor, what right did you have to fire your weapon?" John knew the Navy manual because the chief threatened them all if they didn't. John even tutored some of his colleagues who struggled to read. In response to the chief's demand, he recited a summarized version of a clear directive against a specific violation, "Correct action was if anyone passing through the gate did not identify themselves, I should fire in the air. If they don't stop, shoot them. I was doing my job, sir."

John knew he wouldn't have shot them, but they didn't know that. He wasn't surprised when the chief simply turned and walked away without saying another word. Striding back to his favorite chair, the chief masked his satisfaction that one of his recruits performed well under pressure. John wasn't positive he was off the hook, not knowing procedure for a "racial policy" question. In time he received his answer.

He never heard a thing about the matter again and got no extra duty. It was, however, part of his permanent record that he fired his weapon. John began to figure out the nuances of regulation enforcement between the lines in the Navy. He said to his friends, "If you do it by the book and white sailors are involved, they'll write you up, then let it go. So make damned sure you do it by the book."

It became routine that the chief hammered his black recruits every day for six weeks. John wondered whether the chief hated them or was more worried about being embarrassed by them. John and his colleagues debated this and many other topics involving their teacher. They felt betrayed by him for lying to them when he originally said he would tell them "when to move and each and every move they must make." They believed him and trusted that he would keep that promise. He didn't. In turn, they blamed him for not telling them what to do with many things: boxing in the smoker, standing up for the national anthem, making sure they had enough food. They assumed the chief made boot camp an uphill battle because he hated them. True or not, they believed his extra duty made them better.

Some of them saw the benefit in what he did. They got up an hour before reveille to march around the barracks with their sea bags. They scrubbed the decks in their barracks with toothbrushes. They took everything he dished out and did not complain. The members of this now tightly-knit group had pride. They hated his attitude, but they had become sailors in spite of everything, or maybe because of it.

Word came down that before graduation from boot camp they had the opportunity to perform before the base commander. They got to compete against their white adversaries for top honors as the best recruiting class. All forty black recruits attended a meeting before the event. They decided no one could take their dignity from them after six weeks in hell. Add up all the disrespect, the lack of food, brutal drills just for them, especially the torment from their white rivals, everything prepared them for this moment. By the meeting's end, they agreed excellence would be their best weapon, and they would have their revenge.

Demonstration drills proved to be competitive as the battle of the best raged on. White sailors glared with the entitlement that the honor was theirs from the beginning. The black sailors' rebuttal was to excel in everything: double-time marching, drills, endurance, cadence, timing, and precision, every phase. John and the others knew they had to do everything possible to prove they were the superior sailors to their counterparts, and nothing would stand in the way of them making their point clear.

They made their point. The awkward second-class citizens who entered Basic Training on June 28 emerged as the top recruiting group in their head-to-head competition

August 8. When it was all said and done, they could graduate with the last word.

The chief derived great pleasure from the event. He tipped his hat to his fellow drill instructor, then stood at attention and saluted the base commander. When the demonstration ended, he congratulated his recruits for an outstanding performance, the first kind words he spoke to them during their entire six-week stay. The base commander followed that with his own complimentary remarks to support a perfect score. In his final words to his men, the chief made no apologies for his methods, assuring them that their commitment and hard work changed his opinion of their kind.

Those few heartfelt words challenged the men to draw a new conclusion about their drill instructor. He was a decent man. And they did the impossible. They earned his respect.

John left boot camp on Wednesday, August 11, 1943, with orders to go up the coast to St. Simons Island.

CHAPTER 8

ST. SIMONS ISLAND

"We are all faced with a series of great opportunities brilliantly disguised as impossible situations."
— Charles Swindoll

St. Simons Island lay off the Georgia coast of the Atlantic Ocean approximately sixty miles equidistant between Jacksonville, Florida, and Savannah, Georgia. During the late 1700s, four plantations set the tone for the plantation system: Hampton, Cannon's Point, Hamilton, and Retreat. The foundation of labor that made every plantation work came from slaves. Slave laborers outnumbered white owners 20-to-one, but the owners ran their labor-heavy businesses very efficiently and profitably.[8]

Slavery and several related industries, including tobacco, rice, cotton and flowers, flourished on St. Simons from 1749 until the Emancipation Proclamation in 1863.[9]

On a portion of the beautiful coastal landscape once inhabited by bustling plantation activities was built over 70 years later, in 1935, The King and Prince Club, opened as a seaside dance club. While little was known to authenticate the dance club's history over the subsequent half-dozen years, by July 2, 1941, the main facility reopened as the King and Prince Hotel. Sources described it as "immediately praised for its modern features and magnificent ocean views."

Not long after America's entrance into World War II on December 7, 1941, the Navy took over the hotel, using it as a lookout for enemy vessels. After midnight on April 8, 1942, both land and sea security was compromised, allowing an undetected German U-boat to lie in wait off the St. Simons Island coast. Submarine U-123 pursued and sunk two tankers, the "S.S. Oklahoma" and the "Esso Baton Rouge," killing 22 of their crew.[10]

At any time in its history, St. Simons Island possessed enduring splendor and beauty like few places in America. John and several others boarded the train from Jacksonville to a junction where they caught a bus to the King and Prince Hotel. When John arrived, he temporarily forgot the reason he was there. He was still in his home state, but he had never seen anything like this.

The sunny coastal breeze offered a dramatic contrast to the swamp-like conditions in Jacksonville. As far as John could tell, the officers lived a luxurious life at St. Simons. After settling in, he and the others briefly toured a portion of the facility under supervision, if for no other reason than to learn the limits of their station in the U.S. Navy. He was still very much in the South.

John didn't know about the Virginia and Maryland facilities or St. Simons Island, Georgia, for that matter. He had been focused on North Chicago, Illinois, since before boot camp. He was only aware of the construction battalion because his buddy George told him. That's why he wanted to be a Seabee.

Now trained Navy personnel, the group of black sailors was told to get to know the new officer graduates and get acquainted with the work ethics of some of the officers who they might encounter in the near future on whatever ship they would be assigned. To John, his responsibilities seemed unspecific.

Once the newest influx of black sailors settled in, they assembled to meet their immediate boss, a black chief petty officer dressed just like Jackson. He handed out their apprenticeship assignments. John received his orders to report to one of the officers. When he reported to the officer's quarters, the officer told him what his duties would be. The list included shining his shoes, making his bed, ironing his uniforms, and delivering fresh water every day, everything a servant would do. John looked around the room, looked at the officer, and found himself speechless.

In that moment, John had the presence of mind to know that whatever he said next could and likely would get him thrown into the brig. Fresh out of boot camp, he knew the drill. If he stuck to the book, and it involved a white sailor or in this case an officer, he should do what he was supposed to do and he would be left alone. Without speaking, he left the officer's quarters.

Walking away from the officer's room, John feverishly organized what he knew. Southerners, servants, white officers, black sailors… wait a minute. Bracing himself for an epiphany, he stopped walking and collected himself, thinking, "Am I recruited to be a servant for the U.S. government? Was that what I signed up for? Oh no, no, no!"

Seizing up like someone had kicked him in the gut, John agonized over the possible ramifications of his discovery. He heard himself saying, "I can't believe this." Memories of the day he signed with Graham Jackson flooded into his heart with heavy regret. Now he really knew how it felt to be captured and sold into slavery, modern-day slavery. He revisited the promise he made to himself, swearing he would do something with his life if he had a chance. Had he fallen into the same pit? Fired up about the servant conspiracy he uncovered, John frantically needed to share his findings with his colleagues.

Looking into the eyes of three or four recent boot camp graduates who had all gone through hell to get here, he asked them, "Were we deliberately recruited to be servants?" They stared back at him. This was not what he had in mind when he visualized a bright future. All he saw was the-same-old-sweat-box-nowhere-job back home like some busboy bussing tables at the local restaurant as if he cannot do anything else. In pure frustration he blurted out, "Are you kidding me?"[11]

When the Navy took over the King and Prince Hotel after WWII began, they used the facility as a watch station for enemy vessels as well as an Officer's Training School. Due to increased demand for officers, and with the Virginia and Maryland installations providing "steward's training," the Navy deemed this location ideal for preparing more officers and stewards to get them both acquainted with the demands of sea duty.

To be honest, John didn't know "general service" from a "steward's branch." Now that he was going to be trained in a steward's school, what did that mean? John knew not everyone from the South went into the steward's branch because his friend became a Seabee, but did everyone in the steward's branch come from the South? In other words, did the Navy presume that southern black men most readily accepted subservient roles to whites, making them the logical choice to fill the role of personal servants? Most of the black recruits accepted their fate, preferring a meal ticket over the scraps of the lowly economy; a few never would.

Reality sunk in. It all came together as if he woke up from a nightmare, one in which he felt the shackles around his ankles like before a slave auction. The steward's branch of the Navy consisted of all black sailors serving white officers. If any other race of people performed the same duties for the so called steward's branch, he didn't see any. Then again, how exactly could the Navy publicly articulate the specifics of his steward school apprenticeship when black civilians used unflattering terms to describe it?

He learned his new professional title was "Steward's Mate," a recent differentiation from the previously-exclusive title "Mess Attendant," changed earlier in 1943. As far as he was concerned, there was no training. The full extent of his job description stipulated that he obey white officers, starting with a laundry list of domestic chores.

Having a meltdown for a minute, John made one final observation about his experience to date. The military thought it took a drill instructor to teach him how to defend America. Then, rather than handing him a gun, the military handed him cleaning rags and an iron. Forget it. With all the bad press the Navy was taking over the racial issue, John was not only up in arms, he was not alone. He just didn't know it.

Equally outspoken and pessimistic about the government's "opportunity" for blacks to serve their country was the powerful black press. *The Pittsburgh Courier* and *The Chicago Defender*, among other newspapers, along with the National Urban League and the National Association for the Advancement of Colored People pressured the Navy publicly, using their circulations or leverage as much as they could to influence policy decisions and cultural change. Black officials in higher-ranking civilian posts encountering pressure to do something could do nothing for fear that their positions and safety were in jeopardy. Their best defense was telling everyone to be patient. But the reality of most civilian black businessmen showed they had limited influence outside their communities and would not force the hand of the American government.

Thus, sailors resorted to guerilla warfare, seeking a voice in the press to tell the truth behind the veil of patriotism. The story of the "Philadelphia Fifteen"[12] made the black press and national news, advising black volunteers to choose another branch of service over the Navy.

John's discord with Navy racial policy positioned him against a network of black chiefs who had already achieved the highest rank possible in the Navy for a black officer, telling other black sailors whose room to clean.

There was nowhere else to go. "In response to the question of why Negro sailors were restricted to the position of mess attendants, the [N]avy said that Negro seamen who were elevated in rank superior to that of white men could not maintain discipline. Therefore it was in the interest of efficiency that the policy of restricting Negroes to the mess attendant's position be maintained."[13]

Angered and determined, John went back and told the black chief that he did not join the Navy to be a flunky for white officers and he didn't go to boot camp to shine anyone's shoes. Wearing the hat of both chief and head steward, his immediate superior answered, "You will do as you are told or you will be sent to the brig for five days of bread and water." John dug in and refused. The chief, having not yet incurred such adamant insubordination, said to John, "For today, you will be assigned to working in the scullery washing dishes." Sensing a moral victory, John agreed to the compromise, knowing he had done that before.

After dinner the chief said to John, "I'll talk to you about this later. You could have an easy job. You come to my quarters at 2000 hours tonight. I'll put someone else over there to take care of it." Relieved, he agreed, hoping there was another option in the Navy besides being a servant.

John knocked on the door to the chief's room at eight p.m. sharp. When the chief opened the door, he let John in and went into the bathroom. He came out of the bathroom undressed down to his underwear. John was puzzled and didn't know what to do. The chief walked up behind him and grabbed his privates. The first thing the chief said was, "Oh I like your privates! I want it!" He told John to pull his pants down. His touch alone made John cringe. John turned around, pushed the chief away, and turned toward the door. Reaching for the door handle, twisting, and pulling the door open in one motion, John lunged out the open doorway. Before he headed down the hallway, he looked back into his superior's quarters and spat out, "You queer bastard!"

John returned to his bunk so aggravated that he had only one thought in his mind, "How do I get out of this damn Navy?" Later that night the chief arrived at the stewards' quarters and singled John out. As soon as the chief walked in the room, John saw him and braced himself for some kind of assault. The chief walked up to John and said, "Seagraves, I'm putting you on scullery duty tomorrow morning. Report there at 0650 hours." John anticipated worse punishment for rejecting him and felt relieved the assignment wasn't more sinister. After the chief left, the other guys in the room looked at John and asked him what just happened.

The next morning John reported to the dish and pot washing area. The chief was waiting for him, came over, and said, "I am going to put you in the breakfast area." From that point forward he had nothing else to say to John. However, the chief was bound and determined to make John's life miserable. He planned to escalate scorn into torture and he would have his vengeance by giving John more and more work to do.

Every day it was something new on top of the old. One day John decided he had enough and exploded. He said to the chief, "I'm tired of your work detail. Does the mess officer know your little secret? Maybe it's time he found out!"

At the next sunrise, John approached the mess officer and asked if he could have a word with him. John began to tell him about the chief's overtures and punishment because he rejected him. The mess officer tuned John out. At once he looked at John and said, "The chief says you're a trouble maker and he wants you off this base. So, I'll tell you what I am going to do. I am going to send you so far away that it would take six months for you to get home!" Then he just walked away.

Of course, John wanted exactly that. However, his wish was not immediately forthcoming. Instead of an early release, the torment of an indefinite stay took its place. John remained in the steward's school for the next 14 weeks.

By late November 1943, he finally got his orders. On Friday November 26, 1943, the day after Thanksgiving, John shipped out to Shoemaker, California.

CHAPTER 9

ON THE MOVE

"To accomplish great things, we must not only act, but also dream; not only plan, but also believe."
                                                            Anatole France

With orders in hand, John was thrilled to ship out to Shoemaker, California. He had never been out of the state before going to Jacksonville, and California never entered his mind until signing up for the Navy. But he would have gone anywhere they sent him as long as he could leave boot camp and steward's training behind. He felt strongly the government should have called steward's training "butler's school." Segregation was a curse. John battled it by refusing to give in. Two other steward apprentices and he left the facility together. They bought train tickets according to instructions to ride from Brunswick, Georgia, to New Orleans, then change trains for Los Angeles. From there they were to ride a train to San Francisco and make their way to Shoemaker.

So far John's Navy experience had produced mixed results but he chose to remain positive. Surviving boot camp, getting his butt beat up, chewed out, poked, stuck, burned out, grabbed, and pushed past his limits, he emerged better for it. No doubt the Depression created a responsible young person who entered a harsh military factory and came out an especially well-trained teenager. He and his friends held themselves to a higher standard, a new code, one that U.S. Navy sailors lived by. Now he headed to California to see the world and fight for a cause, courtesy of the U.S. government.

John Seagraves in uniform

Like anyone who had never been to war, he and his fellow recruits had not experienced the horrors yet. They were gung ho. As crazy as it sounds, they were fearless, if only because they were U.S. Navy sailors, something bigger than they ever imagined. Being black meant they had to deal with segregation and racism; being a sailor meant they could overcome that, hold their heads high, and fight for their country if the chance ever came. They managed to bond and stick together through a trying ordeal. Each one had a story to tell of how he wanted to quit or kill the drill instructor, and each walked with a proud posture that lesser men of any color who never had to survive boot camp would not understand.

They may have been required to travel in uniform, but they were proud of what the uniform represented. They looked like respectable members of an elite group, handsome and prototypical. That said, the Navy manual stated regulations for mandatory action including wearing uniforms at all times. To be seen in civilian clothes brought charges of desertion. Their basic sailors' uniforms were dress blues, dress whites, and dungarees for casual situations. Dress black shoes and white hats were standard for all of their uniforms.

Passing through Biloxi, Mississippi, on the train, the three sailors sat in the dining car. A black curtain separated them from other passengers. Their dinners had just been served when the train stopped. They were so hungry none of them paid any attention to the outside world.

Suddenly a brick came flying through the window where they were sitting. Glass shattered everywhere, including all over their food. Shocked and dismayed, then furious that their hot meals were covered with shards of glass, they jumped up, cursing while surveying the damage. The conductor broke through their privacy curtain as they examined the extent of the mess and their meal. He told them to leave the dining car and not come back. No other food options could be found the rest of the way to New Orleans.

The three-man crew arrived in New Orleans with barely enough time to grab some food and change trains for California. The trip from New Orleans to California took three days, twenty-four hours just to get through Texas alone. The long ride and almost unbearable heat drained the military men in full uniform. After three days without a shower, they smelled so bad they avoided speaking to anyone until they got cleaned up. Black military personnel were not assured accommodations, so they bunked with whoever would have them. Ultimately, they heard the YMCA in Los Angeles would take them in, and they spent the night there.

It so happened that while they were in L.A. the local United Service Organization chapter organized a celebrity mixer with a few Hollywood stars such as George Raft, Lena Horne, and others in attendance. Showered, fed, pressed, and dressed, John and his friends looked forward to a little excitement. A USO bus picked them up and shuttled them to the Canteen for entertainment and refreshments.[14]

Once at the USO, they socialized freely in an ethnically-diverse crowd, found something to drink, and picked up a program outlining the festivities. The L.A. center was a far cry from Jacksonville in look and feel, though on par with St. Simons Island for military fashion. Yet an entourage of celebrity guests automatically elevated their experience to sensational. For John, the event turned utterly magical at the sight of his favorite movie star actress and world-class singer, Lena Horne.[15]

John made his way to the middle of the floor to get a closer look at her. Seeing Lena Horne in the flesh struck him as a subtle reward for getting through boot camp, surviving steward's training, and getting all the way to Los Angeles without any major incidents. She was the pinup girl of the century in his mind, and he could not believe he was looking at her with his own eyes.[16]

Autographed photo of Lena Horne in 1943

The talented star sauntered around the room mingling and socializing with everyone. Then she caught John's tall, handsome countenance admiring her. He could not hide his captivation, wearing an obvious grin. Lena Horne loved performing for USO boys because they were so sweet and honest. She'd seen this look dozens of times during her career doing USO events, and it always reminded her of why she did it. There was no mistaking John's infatuation, a sign that she would make this sailor's day simply paying him a visit.

Before he knew it, she headed his way. Matching smiles with his, she asked "What's your name, sailor?" "Seagraves, Steward's Mate Third Class," he answered quickly. Everyone present including his buddies gawked at the luckiest man in the room. Some music played, and she asked him if he cared to dance with her. He froze, confessing to her that he didn't know how to dance. She laughed graciously and put him at ease. They chatted for a short time and he told her he wanted a picture of her. It impressed him even more that she personally took his forwarding information. Before circulating some more, she gave him a kiss on the cheek.

A star-struck teen labored to remember where he was. His pals whistled and teased him about his delirious glow. They reminisced over how stunning and friendly she was. In John's mind, at least for a moment, all was forgiven between him and the Navy. He knew this was the start of a life-changing experience because he had already changed. The boys decided to walk back, taking in the city lights and talking about the evening. Still stricken, John declared he had the time of his life.

The next morning, on Tuesday, December 7, 1943, John and his friends headed toward the train for the long trip north to the Camp Parks Shoemaker Training and Distribution Center in Shoemaker, California. On the second anniversary of the infamous attack on Pearl Harbor, John and his buddies had joined the fight ready to avenge the unprovoked assault. Boarding the train, they talked about Lena Horne, the whole event the night before, things they heard they could do in San Francisco. The train ride to San Francisco took several hours with only one transfer, a bus to Shoemaker. Despite the challenges of three young sailors not knowing anything about their journey and less about their destination, they finally arrived.

Three worn-out travelers checked in at the receiving barracks in Shoemaker. The installation had tens of thousands of men, like a small city. They were told where the segregated section was, to hang their hats after a long trip, and what to do. Standard military-issue sleeping quarters consisted of large, wooden, two-story boxes with flat tops and wood corner posts, five or six boxes wide and many more rows of them deep. Directions pointed the young men toward the back of the complex to drop their things, settle in, and get a good night's rest.[17]

The next day they woke up, got cleaned up, and grabbed some chow. Typical of John to not sit still for long, he went to find some work to do and got put to work in the kitchen. With a mountain of potatoes to peel, he and another black sailor named Wyatt went to work stuffing potatoes into the peeling machine. Every day they shared duties and quickly became friends.

John grew to be Wyatt's closest friend, if one could call it that. It didn't take much to see the loner and born hustler in Wyatt. His cagey, quiet presence projected a suspicious, even dangerous disposition, the inevitable expression of a man who didn't trust anybody and who wanted to be very hard to read. All that mattered was that he trusted John. Rumor had it that he was kicked out of steward's training early because he refused to do anything he was told. Rather than throw him into the brig, his base commander gave him an early release to make him someone else's problem.

One day Wyatt had the bright idea to take in a movie. Wyatt asked John if he felt like hanging out in San Francisco with him for the day. John had not seen a movie in so long that he thought it was a great idea. Going to the movies had been one of his favorite hobbies on a day off in Atlanta, so he thought, "Why not?" But John was broke. Wyatt assured him not to worry about money. The gift of a hustler was that he always had plenty of pocket money, and he told John he would loan him a few bucks until his pay arrived in Shoemaker.

They made the trip to San Francisco, found a movie theater, and stood in a short line to buy tickets. Being in uniform, they attracted plenty of attention. John mused that the uniforms made them handsome and mysterious. As they walked into the lobby, Wyatt kept making eyes at a girl. He kept talking about her, staring at her. Frankly, John was more interested in the movie. He knew they needed to get back to the receiving station, and there wasn't any time for messing around.

As soon as they got situated with seats inside the theater, Wyatt scanned the theater in search of the girl. The next thing John knew, Wyatt spotted her and abruptly jumped into the aisle to go speak with her. The movie had not yet started, giving Wyatt a chance to make a move. He said he would be right back. As John sat there waiting and checking out the crowd, the lights turned off and the movie began without Wyatt's return. The way John looked at it, Wyatt was wasting his money, and he wanted to get his money's worth. He stayed put and sank down in his seat ready to enjoy the movie, figuring Wyatt would be back any time.

The movie finally ended. John considered staying for the credits but instead got up to leave, pleased with his decision to enjoy the show and not worry about his unpredictable friend. He hoped to find Wyatt in the lobby talking to the girl. When he entered the lobby area, Wyatt was nowhere to be found. John hadn't been worried about it before, but now he was. Wyatt never gave John the money he promised so John could get back to Shoemaker. Wyatt just left him behind in the theater, went off with a woman, and never came back. What was John supposed to do now?

John literally had to panhandle and finagle his way back to Shoemaker. He begged some guy to take pity on him and contribute some spare change so he could take a bus from San Francisco to Oakland. In Oakland he had to ask people for money for the rest of the way and, because he was in uniform, people helped him. Many knew how far he had to go. Dropped off at the last turn before a long stretch of road took him back, John began the walk back several miles to the receiving station. He walked for miles before a military bus spotted him and picked him up. John was so angry with Wyatt that all he thought about was punching his buddy in the kisser.

Mad as a hornet, John finally turned up at the receiving station where 30,000 servicemen were coming and going. Many waited to board troop ships and head overseas. It was a mob everywhere. John looked for Wyatt but knew he had wasted enough time already stewing over the matter. Who knew what happened to Wyatt? All John knew was that he got stranded in San Francisco with no money, and he could not risk getting lost or sidetracked while he waited for his orders. John caught up with some of his other buddies and killed time waiting for word that he was shipping out.

The following morning Wyatt, of all people, finally showed up. John stared at Wyatt, ready to explode, and the streetwise gangster from Texas knew it. John walked toward Wyatt with a deep desire to deck him for being dumped over a girl, and he probably would have if Wyatt allowed it. Wyatt exchanged a rare burst of humor in place of subjugation. Describing the particulars of his impromptu soiree, he eased some of the tension as the others gathered around him. John stayed back, but the story reluctantly drew him in. With a belly full of laughter, John eventually let Wyatt off the hook, waving his finger at him and calling him by his new nickname – "slick."

The good thing about getting to Shoemaker was that the Navy finally had a pay voucher waiting for John. The Navy paid him $60 a month. He asked the Navy to send half of his money to his mother. The Navy matched his $30 with another $30, like an early pension. John never intended to stop providing for his family after enlisting in the service, especially given that his mother and siblings counted on him, with or without King's help.

The financial arrangement amounted to John's mother receiving $60 a month between him and the Navy every month while he kept $30 for himself. The deal made sense, given that his mother received almost the equivalent of an entire month's salary from the Peachtree Theater. Meanwhile, the Navy paid John's salary plus travel and meals. He covered his own expenses, but what could he spend his money on anyway? As soon as he got his cut, he went crazy. He ended up splurging on cartons of cigarettes for a dollar each, candy bars, snacks, whatever he wanted. John assumed he would be at sea any time, only to end up blowing his money while waiting endlessly at the receiving station. An entire week passed in common military fashion – waiting at the ready. Suddenly thousands of men shipped out.

Nearly two weeks after leaving St. Simons Island, John was finally on the move, getting on a bus to Treasure Island where he would board a ship for his final destination. At Treasure Island he boarded the *USS GENERAL JOHN POPE (AP-110)*, a troop ship that served as a transporter for the U.S. Navy during World War II. The brand-new ship had already had a busy schedule, beginning in Newport News, Virginia, and making stops in Scotland, Australia, and New Guinea before arriving in California.[18]

On Friday, December 10, 1943, she began her voyage into the South Pacific with several thousand troops on board. Only about ten percent of her passengers were black sailors. Using limited armaments for defense, troop ships carried soldiers both during peacetime and wartime.

Once John and his friends were at sea, they learned that the ship was headed due south, relatively close to western shores of the United States and Mexico, before finding deep water along the Central and South American coasts. Rather than sail directly toward the islands on a southwestern course where the Japanese were looking, the Navy determined they could minimize exposure taking the unexpected path along the southern route to yield better results. Then they would turn due west and push straight across, essentially crossing the International Date Line much farther south, to avoid contact with any Japanese submarines.

Pacific waters were very dangerous. Liberty ships, mainly carrying supplies, and troop ships were primary targets for submarines. Japanese logic was sound. If the Japanese could cut off supply lines and kill American forces before they could get positioned to fight, the Imperial Japanese Navy could more easily advance their plans to control the Pacific and eventually take over half the globe. In response, the U.S. military kept sending more troops and finding more effective ways of getting them across the Pacific.

As expected, the black sailors were assigned to a segregated compartment with bunks stacked five high and double sided with a small locker to store their sea gear. Each bunk was numbered.

John considered himself lucky he got a bottom bunk. Having to climb in and out of a bunk at sea proved to be an acrobatic exercise. No one knew the floor plan of the troop ship to be certain, but the sleeping quarters for blacks must have been near a boiler room because it was so hot it was literally a steam room. Black sailors had no choice but to explore the ship and get some cool, fresh air.

Both black and white sailors pushed their way toward the galley serving area for lunch. The chow line meandered in all directions, seemingly forever. When they got within sight of the steam tables, they picked up tin compartment trays, and servers dumped spoons or ladles of food into each compartment. As much as they were famished, many sailors and marines got seasick the first day, including John.

Whether chow times or between meals, the entire ship could agree to that one single priority. After lunch everyone rushed to their favorite spots on the ship. Sitting around shooting the bull or playing cards filled the short list of activities. John and his buddies walked, talked, congregated, contemplated, whatever they could do to pass the time. Bodies hovered everywhere. Sometimes they found places to sit, most times not. After seeing everything on the ship once, curiosity quickly turned to boredom. By the second day, boredom morphed into restlessness.

On December 12, the first Sunday at sea, the chaplain held a church service on the main deck to reach the broadest possible audience. At the conclusion of the service, the chaplain announced, "We hope that you will join us next Sunday for service." John thought to himself, "That's seven days from now." He had hoped the journey would be over sooner and wagered the chaplain knew more about this trip than he was letting on.

Any peace derived from Sunday's chapel service drifted off by Monday, the fourth day. Day five at sea, restlessness spiraled downward toward tension. Sailors and marines were trained very differently. They stuck together, both in tightly-knit groups, creating nicknames for each other passed on from boot camp instructors and others loyal to their branch. Fights broke out on various parts of the ship for no reason except the aforementioned descending emotions, starting with boredom.

Like a lot of guys, John felt more content staying busy; unlike a lot of guys, he went looking for work. Essentially, having something to do meant finding something to do. During transport, nobody handed out busy work. He tried to volunteer for several duties without luck. It wasn't enough for him to be at sea for an uncertain timeframe with nothing to do.

Fear played a central role in putting everyone on edge. Passengers and crew alike worried about Japanese subs and dying in the vast Pacific Ocean. They were on their own until dry land came into view, wondering every time they looked overboard whether the sea would become their grave. Ironically, the reference to John's last name, "Seagraves," never came up. Enough people believed in superstition to leave it alone.

Some funny moments kept the men preoccupied. Sometimes a group of guys got together and provided entertainment, completely unplanned stuff. Any sign of entertainment drew a crowd, even if the entertainers had no talent. Even noise provided temporary relief. Anything to break up the monotony was worth investigating. Occasionally, a few musicians got together and played some real music. Black and white performers didn't play together. Not because they couldn't, only because they didn't.

As the ship proceeded across the Pacific, the days grew longer and hotter. The closer they came to the International Date Line, the hotter it got.[19]

As the troop ship crossed the IDL, the crew decided to entertain their passengers. Lord knows, they needed it. Apparently the crew cooked up some passenger initiation as they pretended to beat servicemen with hoses. Crew members dressed up as pirates and ran around on the deck, shooting in the air and putting on a show. Everyone got a certificate for crossing the IDL for the first time. Invariably, John and his buddies looked at their certificates, weighing the possibility they may never cross it again.

CHAPTER 10

THE SOUTH PACIFIC

"The average person puts only 25% of his energy into his work. The world takes off its hat to those who put in more than 50% of their capacity, and stands on its head for those few and far between souls who devote 100%."

Andrew Carnegie

The *USS GENERAL JOHN POPE* arrived at the Naval Receiving Station in Nouméa[20], New Caledonia[21], on December 23. Nouméa sat approximately 915 miles northeast of Australia. The French-owned island served as a significant military hub in the South Pacific.

The southern part of New Caledonia boasted heavy occupancy, mostly by servicemen, and this particular receiving station dispatched Marines and sailors assigned to submarines, battleships, cruisers, and destroyers. In many ways New Caledonia earned its reputation as a big playground for Navy personnel. Graham Jackson told the truth about one thing: John would travel to exotic islands in the Pacific.

Troops being transported finally found dry land 14 days after their departure from Shoemaker, California. Every man aboard cheered upon setting foot on land. Freedom from claustrophobia, Japanese attack subs, hot-tempered servicemen, and even hotter boiler room temperatures gave everyone something to be happy about.

Colonizing New Caledonia represented an important strategy, called island hopping, for U.S. Armed Forces."US forces moved from island to island, using each as a base for capturing the next."[22] "Building on their success at Guadalcanal, Allied leaders began advancing from island to island as they sought to close in on Japan. This strategy of 'island hopping' allowed them to bypass Japanese strong points while securing bases across the Pacific. Moving from the Gilberts and Marshalls to the Marianas (left), US forces acquired airbases from which they could bomb Japan."[23]

"With its central Pacific location, New Caledonia provided a strategic air base as well as personnel and logistics support for the war."[24] Nouméa's small city population naturally gravitated to different aspects of the island outpost. More often than not, men chose where to spend their time based on ethnicity, branch of service, division, rank, or activity. When so many personnel landed in one spot, it was nearly impossible to predict what priorities mattered most. Like an internal compass, people ended up where they felt most comfortable. The same rang true at the beach.

The many beaches throughout New Caledonia made the stop a favorite among all military personnel. Officers, subordinates, sailors, and Marines took advantage of the island's peace and tranquility. Newcomers savored the locale most because they had never seen anything like it anywhere stateside unless they came from south Florida or southern California. Contrast the lingering signs of depression stateside against a massive youthful island installation in the South Pacific and it became plain to see why military personnel loved passing through there.

John's first exotic port of call provided heavy doses of tropical heaven on earth. He and his buddies had arrived in paradise. Everyone had smiles on their faces. So many things about New Caledonia put a surreal stamp on John's new life.

With economic challenges at home and vacation paradise abroad, one central theme appeared ostensibly wedged between them: war. World conflict complicated the exclusive lifestyles of the troops, resources, and assets committed to the islands they currently inhabited. The Navy and Marines knew they must defeat a powerful enemy in the Japanese, while the Army and Allies took on the Nazis in the European and North African Theaters. Taking into consideration what was really going on, many men could only enjoy themselves temporarily. Beneath the playful exterior of many sailors and soldiers lurked unsettling fear and anxiety. Swiftly the glow of paradise takes a dark turn toward its true purpose: to spell the fatigued and prepare fresh personnel for battle.

Some of the men who had not been dispatched struggled to make sense of their environment. Among the restless, John could not quite get the hang of doing nothing for any length of time. Beyond beach activities, his options included movies twice a week, softball, and checkers. John showed little interest in games before he enlisted in the service. Like he had on the troop ship, he looked for things to do, and food prep gave him plenty to do.

As he awaited reassignment, he requested kitchen duty, with a virtual guarantee he would find plenty of work to do. In fact, the mess officer was only too happy to accommodate him. Needless to say he got his wish. John's temporary duties again involved peeling potatoes and vegetables for 15,000 to 20,000 sailors and Marines, a military city not quite as large as Shoemaker in personnel yet equally voracious in appetite. As much as he wanted to be assigned, he enjoyed working rather than sitting around.

John wanted a fast track to the front lines. No one really understood why he was in such a hurry to enter the war. On the one hand, he never had so much free time while being paid. On the other, he had no prior experience with paradise, so who could blame him for saying paradise bored him? His buddies wrote him off as a workaholic while they refined the art of doing nothing.

Some of the guys wanted to check out Australia. New Caledonia was in close proximity if they could figure out how to get there. Seeing the world caught John's attention, and he was interested if they could sort it out. As a few black sailors stood around debating their general interest outside the transport office, a few white sailors came out making preparations of their own. One of John's buddies asked them what the process was to go visit Australia. One of them retorted, "Well, I don't know. You coloreds can't go over there because the Australians think you are all like monkeys without tails." The group broke out in laughter as they walked away. John was not one to give up on anything easily, but after that comment, the four of them looked at each other, thinking any comparison to monkeys completely turned them off. In an instant none of them had any further desire to go to Australia.

The troop ship provided clear leading indicators of life at war in the South Pacific. The heat and humidity started to wear the men down. Predictably, tolerance ran thin. The military police threw servicemen in the brig left and right for five- and sometimes ten-day stretches. Any time the guys thought about starting a fight somewhere, the sight of MPs reminded them that the reward for stupidity included bread, water, and the brig. That straightened out any nagging itch for mischief. When the MPs got tired of picking up the same jarheads over and over again, they sent the persistent troublemakers to the rock pile. One MP told another, "Thirty days on the pile, a sledge hammer, and sun… does the trick every time."

While hot, humid weather conditions in the South Pacific caused most of the bad behavior throughout the receiving station, regional weather proved equally volatile. On New Year's Day, howling winds woke everyone out of a deep sleep. Before noon, a full-blown typhoon[25] began to tear up the place. Incredibly high winds wrecked their light construction facility like it was a house of cards attached with string. The lethal winds destroyed nearly all the living quarters, called Quonset huts, pulling the tin roofs from their framing and easily folding the mesh screen siding. Made of the same materials, sick bay had to be tied down by dozens of sailors and Marines to protect the wounded.

Quonset huts stood about fifty yards from the toilet facilities, which were nothing more than glorified backhouses. Halfway around the world, John just shook his head in amusement. The military version also had no running water, though built large enough to seat ten and designed without interior walls. For the sake of efficiency, the government-issue design did not require privacy. The construction battalion built these quick-assembly latrines on the logic of military engineers, who rationalized their design by concluding that all men do their business the same way. Men willing to die for each other had nothing to hide. More to the point, privacy costs extra.

High winds blew the tops and sides off the latrines, knocking men down into the sewage pit below the ten-man bench seat. As makeshift materials landed on servicemen, some got pinned down, became trapped and submerged in the sewage. Waste acted like quicksand drowning them. Other men were blown off their feet and lifted into the air with nothing close enough to anchor them. John found a tree and literally hung on to save his own life. Approximately 50 lives were lost because they could not tie themselves down fast enough. John had been in New Caledonia for only ten days. With all the mayhem he had already seen, he was ready to leave.

After the typhoon, a lot of men were transferred to other islands. John's group received assignments at Espiritu Santo, which was part of the New Hebrides Islands. Once again their quarters were Quonset huts with open sides. This time the familiar hut design had no screens. They were instructed very clearly from the beginning to tuck the netting under their mattresses to keep the island wildlife out of their beds. John assumed that what he couldn't see could not hurt him. He also presumed that Espiritu Santo could not possibly be any worse than New Caledonia. So he ignored the suggestion.

One night at the tail end of a long, busy day, John was sleeping peacefully when he felt something odd around his legs. Still groggy, he woke up and reached for the chain light hanging over his bed. With eyes barely adjusted to the light, he threw the blanket and sheet back. Before John could focus, he distinguished a foot-long green lizard. He nearly jumped three feet straight in the air and out from underneath the tin roof in one continuous motion.

He had never seen anything that big and green in his life! The creature startled him so badly his eyes were still wide open. He actually forgot to breathe. Not knowing whether to swing at it or freeze until it ran away, he hesitated before shooing it off his bed. Now wide awake, he turned in search of netting. More willing to cooperate, he hoped to avoid more reptiles, malaria-carrying mosquitoes, and any other undesirables.

The effects of island living began to crawl under John's skin. The fate of his mental health hinged on keeping his mind focused and his head uncluttered in this completely foreign environment. Always preferring to use his hands to keep his mind occupied, he found work down at the docks. His work duties on the island included unloading Liberty ships full of cargo such as food and other supplies. Underneath all the busy activity, John had to wait for everything. Thus he discovered a critical secret.

The hardest thing to do in the military was stay busy. His new mission, even on a short term basis, was to keep from losing his mind through boredom and repetition. That's where the fighting, the restlessness, and all the anxiety came from. He figured that out and then no longer cared to hear all the whining and complaining of others. He made up his mind to tend to his own business and he would get through this. His formula proved most successful.

Espiritu Santo had become just another island at this point. The exotic pleasures of island living had gone by the wayside and now the mission was to stay busy to block out the noise. His colleagues would rather sit around and complain. Admittedly, everybody managed depression that stemmed from a myriad of sources. Homesickness, uncertainty, and talk of war all dissolved courage and took a piece of each and every brave sailor or soldier who remained idle too long. It all added up to fear, and fear poisoned the mind. However, even the best psych ward doctor could not tell whether unknown fears did more damage than known ones.

Some guys were petrified after warnings that the Japanese were holed up in the hills above the outpost. Everyone heard the warnings: "Do not stray beyond secured areas." Recovered remains suggested the enemy had cannibalistic tendencies.

At first John didn't believe it, until he thought back to the lizard incident. He was so far out of his element that anything was possible. Every now and then he and others were informed of victims who had been attacked, killed, and dismembered. He clearly did not know how to categorize this type of danger. He only wanted off the island, and new evidence convinced him to leave immediately. In utter disbelief he spoke a thought, "What kind of people eat other people?"

The admission brought the atrocities of war closer to all the men in the South Pacific. John refused to fathom what else to expect. Four months passed on Espiritu Santo by the time his new orders came in. Without hesitation he boarded a destroyer, destination unknown. He honestly did not care where it went as long as he left this island.

Looking back, the search for a permanent assignment had begun with New Caledonia and Espiritu Santo. The obvious modus operandi of military personnel management suggested that many sailors were shipped into the Pacific Theater with no specific assignment, making their unofficial assignment to wait. John's work ethic kept him sane. Maybe the Navy had spread the cliché about "people waiting for their ship to come in" because everyone in the Pacific waited for their orders, fortunes to be determined. Only now did he begin to understand the possibility that his search for an assignment was a metaphor for life. And if that were true, then as best he could tell a great many people around him were lost.

Even when some had ship assignments, they either waited for their ship to arrive or they were sent on a wild goose chase searching for their assigned ship. John wondered whether the Navy moved sailors around sometimes just to keep them busy. In other words, would the Navy dole out assignments to move a sailor from one installation to another rather than onto a ship? He never knew, but if so, did this procedure have a name or did it represent a breakdown? With so many sailors to keep track of, missed assignments and miscommunication led to all kinds of problems.

The true story of one sailor went that he received his assignment, chased down his ship, and narrowly missed her as she pulled away heading out to sea without him. Before anyone on board had a chance to report that he was not on board, the ship got fired upon by an enemy vessel and sunk. The Navy got notification of the ship's sinking, and the correspondence pool sent out letters in the form of telegrams. On behalf of the U.S. Navy, his family received the "death notice" telegram delivered by a junior officer. In the meantime, the sailor naturally became upset that he missed his assignment and he sought reassignment, regretting that he missed his chance to join the war and fight for his country. In all the confusion, his name went back into the pool. It might have even gotten lost among all the other names. The bottom line was that his family thought the sailor perished at sea.

Once John got to the undisclosed checkpoint, the officer on the destroyer told him he was being assigned to a submarine. Subsequently he boarded a bus to the submarine base. Reporting for duty, he climbed on board the sub and down the ladder. As he approached a landing area inside the sub, he moved toward the captain. The captain looked up at him and said, "How tall are you, sailor?" John responded, "I'm not sure sir," so the captain said, "Stand over here." A mark on the wall indicated that John exceeded the maximum height limit for duty on a submarine. The captain informed John, "I'm sorry, sailor. We will have to reassign you. You are four inches too tall."

After looking around the confined interior of the sub, John privately breathed a sigh of relief. The waiting was killing him, but living in an underwater coffin scared him to death. Walking away from the sub, he confronted the mental picture of getting claustrophobia while sneaking around the Pacific, dodging depth charges, and chasing down enemy ships. By his calculations, when a submarine got sunk no one lived. With no chance of survival, a sub was the last place he wanted to be. John thanked God for letting him be tall.

Before he knew it, John received new orders. The officer's voice conveyed urgency. This time there was no mystery to where he was going. He was shipping out immediately to meet up with Battleship *USS NORTH CAROLINA*. A battleship finally! He didn't know much about it, but he felt he was ready for anything.

For the first time, he and six other black sailors really entered the war. The time came to be a sailor. He and the others boarded a PB4Y Privateer amphibious seaplane. John did not know all his colleagues yet, but that soon changed as they flew to Pearl Harbor, Honolulu, Hawaii, to board the ship together.

CHAPTER 11

THE SHOWBOAT

"Consult not your fears but your hopes and your dreams. Think not about your frustrations, but about your unfulfilled potential. Concern yourself not with what you tried and failed in, but with what it is still possible for you to do."
Pope John XXIII

Hawaii had to be as beautiful as anywhere on Earth. On the island of Oahu, Honolulu[26] maintained a bustling city life full of civilians with the military playing an important role in the local economy. Honolulu's uniqueness resulted from its transformation into an American city in the middle of the Pacific. With its interwoven plethora of ships, personnel, citizens, commerce, urban activities, and lifestyle, this critical center functioned as the U.S. military's Pacific Theater Operations Headquarters. Pearl Harbor prominently stood out as Honolulu's primary port of entry, essentially a large parking lot for U.S. military vessels, hardware, and activity.

John and his fellow sailors arrived in Pearl Harbor and reported to the dispatch office. All seven of them walked into the plainly-furnished, busy little building responsible for so many lives. John asked the Dispatch Officer how to get to the *USS NORTH CAROLINA*. The officer reviewed John's papers and suddenly looked perplexed. Then he said their group must have just missed the ship. After looking at a clipboard and asking a few questions, he came back and said, "You boys better catch a ride to Majuro Atoll. The *NORTH CAROLINA* was restocking there and you'd better get going or you'll miss the war."

He told them where to catch a ride, who to catch a ride with, and to hustle. The officer described their taxi as an aircraft carrier named the *USS BELLEAU WOOD*, a "small" carrier they couldn't miss. John looked at his buddies and shrugged, knowing he wouldn't know large from small, having never been on a carrier before. When they arrived at the dock number provided, they saw a carrier that looked plenty big enough to them, the *BELLEAU WOOD*, Hull Number CVL-24, a light aircraft carrier converted from a light cruiser hull.

They showed up at the carrier and asked for a lift to the *USS NORTH CAROLINA*. Given permission to come aboard, they entered the aircraft carrier, showed their papers, and received instructions to go down to the hangar deck where they would receive further instructions. Once down below, one of the carrier's officers advised them to make themselves comfortable in a secured area near the airplanes.

The smell of metal, fuel, and seawater flooded the air. Just the sight of the planes spelled "war" to John. Hammocks had been hung between some planes as temporary sleeping accommodations for just such occasions. No one knew how long the trip from Pearl Harbor to Majuro Atoll would take, or where Majuro Atoll was, for that matter. But they were no strangers to waiting, so they settled in as best they could.

After debating who got which hammock, the small band learned something the Navy didn't want them to know. While snooping around, John's buddy "Slick" Wyatt stumbled over a trade secret: pilots commonly stored their .45 caliber pistols in their cockpits. He reached in one of the planes and helped himself to one like he was plucking an apple from a tree. Proud of his easy catch, Wyatt flashed a familiar grin and asked John if he wanted one. John told him, "No, I'm not stealing a gun." The others remained indifferent to Wyatt's criminal tendencies. Each found himself more concerned about going to war, and every moment brought them closer.

As the carrier entered the mouth of the bay of Majuro Atoll, from the open hangar doors the sailors could see a land mass to one side leading to several wooden docks full of crates, trucks, personnel, and activity. The carrier slowed down a great deal, signifying an end to a long journey for all of them. Moored and quiet, the carrier opened its doors and extended its ramps, and busy men commenced with fulfilling their duties.

The wide-eyed sailors walked off the carrier in search of the *NORTH CAROLINA* and this time they did not have to wait. Someone spotted her right across the bay. A couple of them scanned the roadway surrounding the bay for a direct path to the ship. Others let their eyes adjust to the menacing man-of-war. John's first impression of the *USS NORTH CAROLINA* was… awe.

The Battleship at sea with Measure 32 paint scheme in 1943 –Courtesy of Battleship NORTH CAROLINA

He heard what the others were saying, but he was not paying attention. He wrestled with meeting his destiny. This was what he had been waiting for. Here he was, a 17-year-old seeing the world for the first time. After what he'd been through already, he needed a moment to gather his strength. Compared to what he expected, one look at that ship told him he needed a bigger vision. He had never seen 16" guns before. To him, they were legitimate cannons. He audibly mumbled to himself, "What the heck do you shoot with that?" John could not help but notice while carrying his sea bag and all his belongings that anxiety and anticipation had set his heart pounding.

As the seven young men circumnavigated the dock to the ship, he could not take his eyes off the battle fortress. For a split second he remembered when he was 13 or 14 years old what that fortune teller told him at the "81 Theater." He could hear her voice like it was yesterday: "You have two dimes in your pocket, you'll experience many things, and will live a long life." Reflecting on then and now, he had two dimes in his pocket that day, he had already experienced many things, but would he live a long life?

Against the tropical island background, this battleship was all business. The ship's deck had been painted camouflage blue to blend in with the ocean and mitigate becoming obvious targets to the Japanese fleet. The sheer logic of this detail escaped him because he could not imagine how anybody would miss anything this big.

John no longer had to prove he was a U.S. Navy sailor. His chance arrived when he boarded his permanent assignment, the *USS NORTH CAROLINA*, on May 4, 1944. It took five months to the day between when he signed up for the Navy and when he left St. Simons Island. Add another five months and a few days on the long road from St. Simons Island to his assignment on the *NORTH CAROLINA*, and John could say objectively that a lot had happened over roughly 300 days.

Boarding the ship for the first time, John knew everything would be brand new to him. He had been assigned to a living legend nicknamed the "Showboat," the proud fighting symbol of the "new" U.S. Navy. When the ship first pulled into Pearl Harbor late that afternoon of July 11, 1942, seven months after the Japanese sneak attack on Sunday, December 7, 1941, the terms "sight for sore eyes" and "Godsend" described both the awe and the hope the ship represented to a battered Navy and a bruised nation. The first of a new breed of warrior, the *USS*

NORTH CAROLINA, Hull Number BB-55, fast battleship class, had muscle, was built for speed, and possessed the kind of power that could swing the balance in the war against Japan. It proved then and now the United States of America had the will and the resolve to change the course of history.

America had proved to be totally unprepared for the surprise attack at Pearl Harbor and definitely got its proverbial butt kicked, but Americans apparently needed a galvanizing moment to assert themselves and change their future. The American colony at Pearl Harbor lost in battle, first through political and communication misdirection by the Japanese, followed by a maneuver no U.S. military leader expected: the Pearl Harbor attack. The bold move caused significant damage to most of the Navy's battleships, conveniently lined up for the Japanese to destroy with the ease of shooting fish in a barrel. Luckily, the aircraft carriers were at sea at the time, thus the Pacific Fleet was not left completely wiped out. When the *NORTH CAROLINA* entered the harbor the first time, any advance warning about the extent of the damage from the attack could not prepare the Showboat's crew for what they saw that day. The impact must have been so unsettling, so disturbing, that every sailor immediately knew what needed to be done.

Seven steward's mates reported for duty to the Officer of the Day, who subsequently notified the Mess Officer Lieutenant, Polark Slaborda. When Lt. Slaborda came to meet them, the Officer of the Day called, "Atten-tion!" The new crew members came to attention and saluted him. The lieutenant greeted them, then immediately clarified their roles and responsibilities. He said, "You men are here to work in the Officer's Mess. Your duties will be assigned by your chief." After a brief tour of the ship, the lieutenant proceeded to show them to their sleeping quarters below Main Deck.

Carrying their gear, the men enjoyed a brief tour of the ship on their way down to their quarters, located on the third deck. The ship gave a deceptively large impression as they walked around it, suggesting perhaps they would not see the light of day very often. Nearing their destination, they walked past some junior officers' quarters, noting officers had their own shower. As the sailors entered their berthing area at the end of a hall, John saw beds hanging from the ceiling using chain links, stacked three bunks high to the left and right with lockers in the middle and corners. He knew this was going to be home for a while and looked around for an ideal bunk.

The room was about 400 square feet with lockers approximately 28" by 32" to store all their worldly belongings. A telltale sign of the times placed 66 black sailors packed and stacked like towels in a steaming closet. John brushed off his disappointment. This was not the Hotel USS North Carolina.

Some of the resident black crew members happened to be hanging around in their bunks or in the room. Different points of view occupied the sleeping quarters. To a man with experience on a battleship, one or two of their new roommates appeared too young to be Navy men. A few strongly felt that misery loved company because they hated the ship. Still others welcomed the newcomers to their new home, accepting their lot in the Navy. A small cast had lost their minds and acted in compromising ways. Some more remained neutral, did their jobs to the letter, and loved the opportunity they were given. Combined, they represented the cross-section of personalities responsible for running the most successful seaworthy force the Navy possessed.

The only thing they all agreed on was the *NORTH CAROLINA* ran like a Swiss watch. The executive officers knew their business. Do what they say and everyone lived. The new guys heard various versions of how lucky they were to be assigned to this ship. One of the black sailors told the improbable story of the ship surviving a torpedo hit with a hole big enough to drive an automobile through. One fellow said the ship had nine lives. No matter what happened to it, the ship did much more damage to Japanese positions and vessels while protecting fleet carriers, other battleships, destroyers, and planes.

To John, any crew that managed to withstand a direct torpedo hit already earned his confidence. Regardless of his new job description, everything he heard satisfied his curiosity. Looking back at his journey from boot camp to Majuro Atoll, John had no interest in any more bad news.

The Battleship *USS NORTH CAROLINA* was nearly 729 feet long, almost 109 feet wide, and carried a feast of fire power. "The first commissioned of the Navy's fast, heavily-armed battleships with 16" (410 mm) guns, *NORTH CAROLINA* received so much attention during her fitting-out and trials that she won the enduring nickname 'Showboat'... As the first newly designed American battleship constructed in 20 years, *NORTH CAROLINA* [was] built using the latest in shipbuilding technology."[27]

Despite the challenges awaiting him, John increasingly became excited to be on the ship. The Navy showed him the world in exchange for his time, effort, maybe even his life. If he had to go to war, at least the Navy put him on the ship most likely to survive. The vessel, overpowering armaments, a diverse crew, and its efficient chain of command had somehow developed a successful system. But how?

Social norms that separated black and white men in civilian life did the same, magnified 100-fold on a ship. White officers expected black sailors to do what they were told, and it was never that simple. Entitlements that passed from civilian into military life complicated the situation when an order resembled a social-class demand. Southern officers in particular shared a taste for entitlement, which struck a very personal chord with black sailors. But it was not just white-on-black control issues that sparked passionate differences. Black sailors resisted the dual role of black chief petty officers with equal fervor.

Black or white, officers expected sailors to do what they were told. Black chief petty officers directly supervised black stewards, who worked for the officers individually in most cases, and messmen, who served in the dining areas. No matter how smart or how well educated they were, black chiefs could only command black stewards and black mess attendants and could not give a command to a white sailor even if the white sailor was below them in rank. Herein defined the "glass ceiling" for every black chief petty officer, and they each must have felt squeezed by black sailors below them who despised them and white officers above them who only tolerated them. A black chief had no choice but to show respect for men who had no respect for him. If he had special requests or disciplinary problems, his orders were to report to the executive officer. Overall, black chief petty officers in the Navy were powerless, so naturally they took their anger out on the few below them. Bad blood may have rolled down hill, but not without a surprising amount of backlash.

John's biggest complaint was directed at any black chief who traded in his dignity for acceptance. The common trend involved a black chief talking to a white officer like a plantation slave with his subordinates standing by, then turning to his subordinates and expecting them to march to his orders. Few followed a man who had no dignity. The black sailors all knew their chief had his job to do. They just hated how so many chiefs acted one way around officers and another way entirely around them.

The thorn in John's side specifically involved domestic work. He would rather peel a thousand potatoes a day than shine one shoe. Everyone had to eat, yet there was so much more he could do. He expressed his willingness to do anything asked of him as long as it was something worth doing. In this controversial regard, he expected more from the Navy.

His intentions to see more of the ship suffered a redirection. Right after the sailors became acquainted with each other, Mess Officer Slaborda walked in the room and introduced their chief petty officer. The chief restated his name and started calling out names from the ship's manifest to see who was present. The new guys had been added to a typically accurate list. As soon as the mess officer left the room, the chief showed his butt. He said, "Y'all are here to serve these officers!" As he handed out assignments, he looked at John and said, "You, Seagraves!

You're assigned to Officer Curley's room." John thought to himself, "Here we go again!"

Twenty-five-year-old Officer George Curley made John's acquaintance. For the first time, John would benefit from a northern officer as his assignment. Curley spoke differently from southern officers; he brought professionalism to the job. The racial hierarchy bit wasn't personal with him. John could have been Filipino, Chinese, or from any other ethnic group. Officer Curley respected people and the work at hand.

John learned after their first meeting that Curley's father was a powerful man. James Michael Curley (1874-1958), a well-known politician in Boston, Massachusetts, orchestrated an exceptional career. By mid-1944, he had served as the Mayor of Boston three times and Governor of Massachusetts once, and he was in his second term in the United States House of Representatives. Officer Curley's grandfather Michael Curley (1850 - 1884) was a first-generation Irish immigrant who worked as an unskilled laborer, settling in Roxbury, Massachusetts, in 1864.

When John reported to Officer Curley's quarters, he expected to be told what his duties would be. He had also rehearsed his lines, knowing exactly what to say for a reassignment to the galley. Rather than go through the whole situation one more time like at St. Simons, John simply told the officer he was not comfortable doing that work, he had experience in the kitchen, and he preferred that work. Officer Curley accepted that and said he would notify the mess officer. Curley simply said, "John, if you have a better way to serve the Navy, I suggest you get on with it then!" It was so quick and to the point, John was caught off guard. He thanked Officer Curley for his understanding and left his cabin.

There came a point when he wondered how many times he would have to deal with the same situation. Of course, his particular objection to steward's duties would never be documented somewhere. That afternoon the chief showed them how to set the table and serve dinner for the officers. John knew his time doing this would be short. Every time the road to food prep was different. As a temporary resolution until his commanding officer could determine what to do with him, John was told, "You go to the dishwashing area!" That evening he ended up washing pots. He was disappointed again.

The next night the chief said to John, "Tonight you have officer's watch!" The job required John to hang around the pantry all night, essentially waiting for the phone to ring. If an officer wanted coffee or tea, he delivered it. At least he would not be shining shoes.

That night he took coffee to an officer's room. The officer asked John to put down the tray. He said he liked John and he could make things easier for him. Intolerant with the familiar ploy, John ignored him, replied "Good night, Sir," and left the room. When the officer called the watch room a second time, another sailor named Jesse helped John maintain officer's watch. Tiring of this in general, he asked Jesse to take the call. Jesse left to deliver the coffee and came right back. When Jesse returned to the pantry, John asked him what happened. Jesse just said, "Nothing." John tried not to shake his head, but the sexual thing grew exasperating. Still, he kept his thoughts to himself.

The next morning Mess Officer Slaborda ordered John to report to the dining room as a server. After reporting for duty, John noticed as the mess officer kept a watchful eye on him. John knew he would get thrown in the brig on rations of bread and water if he disobeyed this order. The chief walked into the dining area, saw John, and asked him what he was doing. John told him Lieutenant Slaborda gave him an order and if anyone had a problem, they should see him about it. The chief responded, "If you speak to him, then you have a problem with me!"

Whenever the sailors spoke candidly, the chief threatened to put them on report. Maybe that was normal chain of command protocol, but it also validated why sailors despised him. John was well aware that he had a history of rejecting domestic work. He had ruffled a few feathers with his obstinate behavior at every stop in his short military career, but his senior officers worked with it because they needed help everywhere else regardless.

Very few of his fellow sailors really knew what he was doing when he went to work in the kitchen. It was almost as hot in their sleeping quarters as the kitchen, so the heat was not an obstacle from John's point of view. The reason he preferred it was he had more independence. People gave him a task and left him alone. He knew what he was doing. What he didn't know, he would learn. Besides, he always ate well and he made friends. On the ship, food was like currency. If he needed anything from anybody, he had something to trade. If someone went around harassing people, he was not one of the guys they messed with. He took care of the guys who did something about it and they watched his back. At sea, sometimes people needed friends when other people got a little crazy.

The next morning while John was finishing up his breakfast, Mess Officer Slaborda walked through the dining area and asked, "How are all the new men doing?" John said, "Sir, I have a lot of experience cooking and I would love to be a breakfast cook. I know they need help in breakfast prep and cooking." The lieutenant said that he would tell the chief to transfer John to kitchen duty and to assign someone else to take his current duties.

During his down time, John got a visit from the chief. He indignantly accused John of going over his head again. So he had to get up at 0500 hours every morning for one month. His regular wake up time was 0600. He was to be in the kitchen at 0650 hours to start breakfast.

The following morning when he arrived to cook breakfast, the chief was there. The chief informed John, "You will be washing pots in the galley." John didn't argue

Cooks in officer's galley – Courtesy of Battleship NORTH CAROLINA

with him and went to the galley to wash pots and pans. When John finished, he decided to ask the first cook if he needed help. Getting overdue, unexpected support, the cook reacted, "Sure, kid!" After three or four days passed, the mess officer came to the kitchen and said to John, "Tomorrow you report to the breakfast kitchen." The mess officer said to the chief, "I like the way this kid works." From then on the chief left John alone.

Finally! And once again he landed on his feet doing what he enjoyed doing most. John became friendly with the officers who wanted their food cooked a certain way. In fact, that was how he got to know Commander Joe W. Stryker. Stryker rarely ate meat. Usually he just wanted a soft-boiled egg and toast for breakfast.

Commander Stryker was the Executive Officer, the XO responsible for the crew and, in John's opinion, the most respected officer on the ship. Stryker didn't see color. He saw Navy personnel and he led with an even keel. As the liaison between captain and crew, he was straight with everybody. Typically, captains were assigned to a ship for four to six months, then reassigned. Stryker continued to hold his post throughout every new captain's tenure. He knew the temperament of the men and how to handle situations when men came apart under pressure. Stryker's recommendations got done, no questions asked.

As simple as Stryker's meal preferences were onboard, other officers took full advantage of the menu. The ship's officers dined separately from the crew, paying extra money each month so they could enjoy a more customized menu from that of the crew. Officers paid for their food with a mess bill that might average one dollar a day. They were served the best of everything - fresh cream, fresh

Commander Stryker: BB-55's Secret Weapon – Courtesy of Battleship NORTH CAROLINA

eggs (not the powdered eggs the rest of the crew ate), and the best cuts of fresh meat. The wardroom breakfast menu included eggs cooked to order, bacon, ham, grits, hash browns, coffee, and canned fruit juice.

Preparing breakfast was definitely no problem for John. At first he began by just cooking eggs any style the officers wanted and hash-brown potatoes. After a few days on the ship, he was preparing entire breakfasts, which was what he wanted to eat, too. He cooked his own meals and no one cared. The officers' cook prepared the food in the officers' galley, one deck below the wardroom. Then it was sent up the dumbwaiter to the officers' pantry directly above for final preparations. The navigator was served breakfast on the bridge by a wardroom steward's mate. The captain had his breakfast served by his personal steward's mate who brought it to the bridge on a tray.

When breakfast was over, there was a break for one hour before general quarters sounded. At that time, John would report to his battle station assignment. Most stewards and messmen had battle stations like every other crewmember. His assignment required working in the 16" turret gun powder room, which was also segregated, probably due to a confined work area. Sometimes "powder room" crew members did drills at their battle stations for hours.

In late morning John proceeded back to the kitchen for lunch prep, mainly sandwiches. As a general rule, the officers selected a lighter meal at lunch, usually served at noon in the wardroom. Typical selections on the menu included soup, sandwiches, cold cuts, potato salad, fresh fruit salad, and assorted cheeses, with pudding or cobbler for desert. Iced tea and coffee were always available.

After lunch they had an afternoon break before various training sessions to prepare them for anticipated clashes with the Japanese and their battleship's part in each campaign strategy. For dinner, they usually prepared an extremely light menu for the officers, salad and bread. After dinner they had time to relax, unless general quarters sounded.

CHAPTER 12

LIFE ONBOARD

"Life means to have something definite to do—a mission to be fulfilled—and in the measure in which we avoid setting our life to something, we make it empty. Human life, by its very nature, has to be dedicated to something."
                                                      Jose Ortega y Gasset

For the first 10 days on the *USS NORTH CAROLINA*, the newest crew members got a taste of waiting, not for an assignment but rather for the opportunity to enter the war. The ship and its crew remained in Majuro Atoll while dock crews attempted to repair damage to the vessel's rudders. Apparently the rudders were so badly corroded the port rudder had large holes in it. When that effort proved ineffective, Battleship *NORTH CAROLINA* headed to Pearl Harbor for repairs. After hearing that the executive officers had dodged one torpedo, got hit by another and survived, John agreed with whatever they decided to do.

Five days later the battleship maneuvered into Pearl Harbor channel. The next day the ship entered dry dock for permanent repairs. Out of curiosity, John asked one of his shipmates where the ship had been, fishing for the truth concerning its most recent whereabouts. The *USS NORTH CAROLINA* had not been to Pearl Harbor for quite some time, implying the seven sailors did not miss it after all. He learned the dispatch officer misled him and his colleagues. John guessed the dispatch officer got a laugh at their expense.

For all the waiting necessary to receive an assignment and find the ship, John and his associates had plenty of duties to keep them busy now that they were onboard. The lowest-ranking crew members were confined to the ship at Pearl Harbor. The only exciting news John heard involved a collection of rumors pertaining to sailors who frequented cathouses on the Hawaiian Islands. Pearl Harbor suffered from epidemic levels of socially-transmitted diseases among servicemen. The rampant spread of venereal disease, syphilis, and gonorrhea forced the U.S. military to intervene and unofficially "manage" the cathouses to insure the entire military was not infected.

Out of the blue John received a piece of mail from an address he did not recognize. When he opened the envelope, he remembered. Inside, he found a short letter and photograph of Lena Horne from when he and his buddies passed through Los Angeles. The USO Hollywood Canteen forwarded the picture provided by Lena Horne, and the mail finally caught up with him. Sure, it took months from early December 1943 to late May 1944, but John did not care; frankly, he had forgotten about it.

All the guys hooted and hollered, reminding him of those unforgettable moments talking to her and getting a kiss on the cheek. His cohorts teased him once again over the matter and agreed that Lena Horne was the most beautiful woman they'd ever seen. That he had a signed photograph of every black sailor's favorite pinup girl in his locker nearly made him a celebrity.

At this point John grew bored again. Life aboard a battleship still had not reached its potential. Given that time-consuming repairs were necessary for optimum performance, he and others utilized their advanced skills in waiting to see any action.

General quarters, a big part of the obligation to the Navy, meant practice time for both officers and crew. They spent a lot of time practicing what to do during wartime to prevent any confusion over responsibilities and to ingrain automatic responses under fire. That was why every man called himself a Navy man. In a war, there were many moments of reckoning. Incessant drilling insured this crew would be prepared for every single one.[28]

When general quarters sounded, John went down into "the hole," the powder room of the main battery, a 16"-diameter, 3-cannon turret. The ship was armed with three turrets, two mounted in the front and one in the back. John's duty was to put bags of gunpowder on a powder hoist, an electric elevator which transported canvas bags of gunpowder up four levels to the gun deck. His gun crew toiled in the lowest level of the turret. At least the tight environment benefited from air-conditioning down there, though sometimes it was too cold. Gunpowder residue seeped into a seaman's lungs like coal dust to a coal miner.

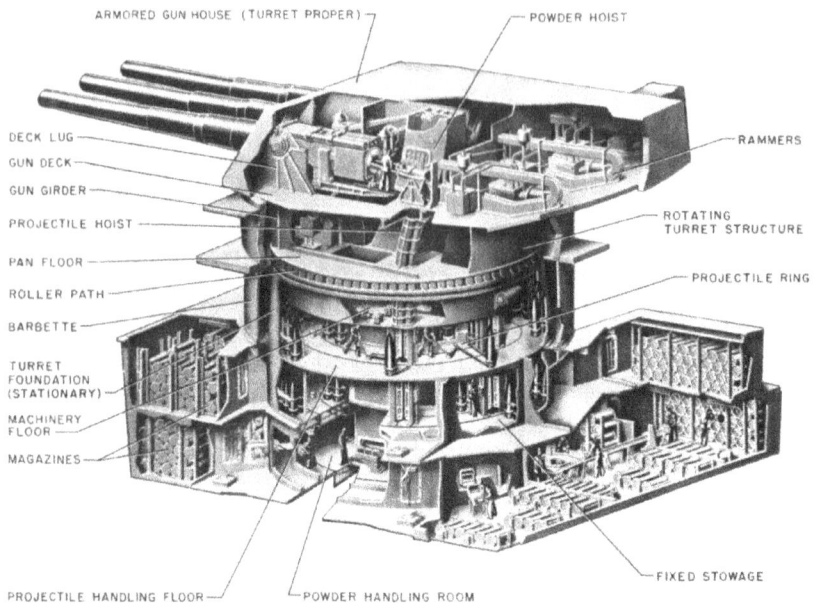

Cutaway of the 3-16" cannon turret, gunpowder room at the bottom level – Courtesy of Battleship NORTH CAROLINA

Normally, 90 pounds of gunpowder in three separate 30-pound bags could launch a single round from one of the 16" guns to maximum range. Young sailors like John used their youth, agility, and strength to sling the 30-pound bags. The armor-piercing, 2,700-pound, 16" shells, which standing upright were as tall as some men on the ship, were moved to the gun deck through a separate hoist. Once on the gun deck, the projectiles and powder were loaded into the breech of the gun for firing.[29]

The fundamental rule of a battleship during racial integration was that no one had to like each other, but they had to work together if they were going to win the war. Lest anyone need a reminder, the enemy was not each other, but Japan, and America needed to stop the enemy from taking over the Pacific. That was the common goal, even when staying focused on the goal resembled a moving target. The distractions behind the scenes took a toll on the performance of every ship, save potentially one.

Commander Stryker's talent for personnel management ensured the ship's mission would remain locked. Stryker understood people better than anyone else on the *USS NORTH CAROLINA*. For this reason, he was thought of more highly than any other executive officer during his time in service onboard. The XO's position on the ship gave him a high vantage point to view his men's actions, affording him the capacity to identify with each group. He was a man of few words, and those were to the point. His wisdom placed him heads above other officers as the voice of reason in a room full of bias. In many ways, he was the secret weapon other ships did not have, knowing when to allow and when to intervene, when to reprimand and when to turn the other cheek.

Commander Stryker executed his duties as if to say, "Running a ship was not brain surgery if the right people were doing what they did best." That was how he filled positions on the ship as well as address challenges. Put the right people in the right places, drill them until they could perform in their sleep, keep them busy so they did not succumb to the agitations of domestic and international conflict, and mix discipline with anticipation for a positive outcome.

But what made Stryker special was he never attempted to manage the debacle of race relations. His secret? He never took sides. He applied his knowledge of the crew and his "feel" for the influences of war impartially and efficiently. His advice to black sailors only made sense if it applied to white sailors as well. He recognized the key to long-term success for black sailors rested in both their safety and preparation for fighting a war, just like white sailors. Outnumbered black servicemen would not be accepted in white circles privately. He knew that. Their only choice was to stand tall in the face of adversity with their white shipmates and live long enough to work it out. His whole philosophy was simple: "Do your job, use your instincts, give your best."

All seamen adjusted to the predicament of free time. If they were not on duty working or drilling, they had plenty of idle moments with limited options. During their personal time, black sailors felt the impact of segregation the most. Despite relatively free movement throughout the floating village, they found no escape from segregation except their own quarters. But this came as no surprise; it was merely a continuation from private life. Docked at an island, maybe they could go ashore, loosen up some, and find things to do.

Little wonder that John and nearly every black sailor questioned how well the Navy thought integration through. Living on a battleship, one could obviously see why the Navy resisted integration and why a recruiter said whatever necessary to recruit black citizens into the service. The circumstances were what they were. The situation was not great, but the ship was no different than life outside the Navy. Finding out blacks were not wanted by white sailors in close or popular areas was part of life onboard. Sometimes white sailors would bump a black sailor along tight corridors deliberately to instigate a fight.

Friction continued between black and white sailors in segregated areas, leaving common areas to be utilized in shifts. "Unofficially," there were many segregated places.

One of those areas was the mess deck at the stern of the ship, because that was where the ice cream stand, the commissary, and the post office were, all right beside each other. The ice cream stand was also referred to as the "gedunk" by white sailors. The commissary sold tobacco, stationary, toothbrushes, and so on. The post office offered "V-mail," a little form to send a quick message home.

The more the black sailors looked for things to do, the more they encountered boundaries. On one extremely hot day when a few black sailors attempted to buy ice cream, white sailors prevented them from entering. Later, the guy running the ice cream stand told them that black sailors could not come down whenever they wanted to. That did not bother John much because he had access to ice cream in the officers' mess, which made John very popular. However, they also learned that only one black sailor could visit the post office at a time. For dental work, the special day chosen for black seamen to come in was on Mondays. After falling down the stairs, John was taken to sick bay and they put him on a bunk against the back wall in case a white sailor came in needing medical assistance.

Of course, when black seamen grew tired of looking for something to do, they sat around the bunks telling stories. Shooting the bull one afternoon in their quarters, a black sailor shared a story he overheard and wanted to warn others in the room. Some stood, others sat huddled around him. The story went that one of the black sailors got into a fight with a white sailor and the white sailor told him, "I hope we do not catch you niggers on deck at night. You are going to be drinking a lot of seawater!" The sailor told his associates to watch their backs on deck at night.

No black sailor ever got thrown overboard, but the threat lingered in John's mind.

Like the powder room, John liked to call their quarters "the hole," too, except it was hot like the kitchen rather than air conditioned. The heat intensified everything. For the most part he was used to the heat, spending so much time in the kitchen. No doubt he was human, too. Constant exposure wore down his ability to think, and a couple of his bunkmates got on his nerves. Occasionally he argued with one of them, but for the most part he minded his own business and others stayed away from him. John was not looking for a fight, but he would not back down from one either.

One day, one of the guys in the galley got extra duty polishing silver for doing something wrong. While on duty in the kitchen, John had no problem staying busy and ignored him. For some reason, though, this guy kept running his mouth. John lost his patience and said a few things to him, and they traded verbal jabs. Before they could control their tempers, the confrontation escalated and they stood nose to nose. The guy pushed John, who pushed back. Powerless, voiceless, and out of his mind, the irrational sailor took his pain out on John by throwing silver polish at him. The polish container fell to the floor, its contents splattering about. The two wrestled for control slipping on the polish. They messed up the place pretty good.

Getting into a fight was strike one, making a mess strike two. The fight broke out in the wardroom where the officers dined. That was a big problem. Strike three.

Commander Stryker walked into the wardroom and looked at them. That was all it took. Stryker assessed the situation. The two guilty parties, covered in gray-colored silver polish, stood at attention without hesitation, saluted Stryker, and waited for him to throw them both in the brig. For behavior unbecoming of a sailor, they expected the worst, but Stryker understood the stress of the job and their situation. He told them to clean up the floor, return to their quarters, wash up, and cool off. That's that.

The ship distributed one set of clothes to every sailor when they first came onboard. Considering the boilers, the engine, the ovens, the steaming tropical air and the density of personnel throughout the ship, everyone should have a change of clothing daily, but few did because they had to buy their own replacements. Additional uniforms were not very expensive, maybe a couple of dollars. Unfortunately, some of the guys did not care much for personal hygiene or spending their money on a change of uniform. Disbursements provided sailors laundry bags and their names got stenciled on their clothes, blankets and towels. Without personal identification, sailors would not get their personal effects back.

After some time, sailors really needed grooming. Because the ship's barbershop was for white sailors only, black sailors used the head (toilet area) as their barbershop. White sailors paid 15 cents for the standard "buzz cut." John started cutting black sailors' hair for one or two of the guys to stay busy. Eventually the word got out that he cut hair, and a few more guys asked John to cut theirs, leading to an occasional barter of sorts, though generally free of charge. He offered one style, a basic cut similar to a buzz cut to whoever asked him. Sometimes he got a dime as a tip.

One day Wyatt wanted his hair conked (straightened) since that was fashionable in the States. White and black sailors did not want much to do with each other, but a black sailor could have hair like a white sailor. John remembered how to conk hair from back home and gathered supplies for the job. He grabbed some lye (a strong solution of sodium hydroxide or potassium hydroxide in water that was used for soap), added some bacon fat or grease, mixed it and applied it. John put the mixture in Wyatt's hair and let it sit for a while to straighten his nappy curls. Having never seen this process before, a few of the guys watched with a mixture of curiosity and humor.

Loosely estimating the correct amount of time to leave his concoction in Wyatt's hair, John decided arbitrarily when the time came to rinse out the lye. He ran Wyatt's head under the faucet. As the water flowed through his hair and across Wyatt's scalp, the water seemed to be pulling clumps of hair along with it into the sink. The onlookers watching in disbelief tried not to laugh, but frankly it looked bad. Wyatt wanted to know what the snickering was about and demanded to look in a mirror. One glance at what was left of his crop and Wyatt started cussing in all directions.

The other guys scattered, fearful that Wyatt would grab his gun. John took a step back, thinking Wyatt was going to beat the hell out of him. He didn't, but that was the last time John touched Wyatt's hair.

The ship was full of characters. "Slick" Wyatt was John's favorite. To everyone else, Wyatt was the guy to be afraid of, the crazy guy. Since they had been buddies going back to Shoemaker, California, Wyatt did not rough John up over the hair thing. In fact, he never even considered it to be revenge for leaving John stranded in San Francisco over the girl at the movie theater either, but maybe he should have. They had history together and laughed it off later, something no one else could have done. Fortunately, very few were brave enough or dumb enough to provoke John, because Wyatt watched out for his young, teenaged friend. As for the other cooks, Wyatt sort of liked them, too, because they had something he wanted.

John preferred to spend most of his free time on deck despite the warnings to watch his back, if only to avoid situations that caused him trouble. He had a few friends that he chummed around with that constituted his pack. John's best buddies included Lindsey, Ramus, Woodward, Simpson, and, of course, Wyatt. He loved to share Wyatt's antics because the legend of Wyatt never stopped. Lindsey, who was a chief petty officer in charge of several stewards and mess attendants, was from Atlanta as well. John and Lindsey talked about Georgia all the time and planned to meet up back home when they got out of the service. Ramus was a Portuguese guy he buddied around with. Woodward worked in the stateroom. Simpson's station was in the kitchen scullery washing pots and helping with food prep.

As for Wyatt, the dangerous Texan was the oldest, probably in his mid-twenties. He usually called John "little kid," not because he was small in size but because he was young. Sometimes he showed John his hustles, knowing John would never tell anyone. Wyatt had all the qualities of grifter, and he plainly did not just pick up his bad habits after joining the service. John had watched Wyatt's gambling activities at the receiving station in Shoemaker, on the *USS GENERAL JOHN POPE*, in Noumea, New Caledonia, Espiritu Santo, Majuro Atoll, Pearl Harbor, and anywhere the ship went. He carried a knife at all times. Wyatt was so reckless and notorious that he threatened to cut the chief's throat if he ever messed with him. He was definitely a character.

Maybe the real mystery was how the Navy had kept these two together since they left the States. The nonstop stories about him confirmed Wyatt was no angel. If his name was hypothetically linked to even the most outrageous speculation, John more likely believed it than not. Most of the wild stories John repeated about Wyatt John either saw firsthand or Wyatt told John personally, and Wyatt wasn't the type to tell lies. He didn't need to.

Two facts about Wyatt were that he rarely showed up for any battle station drills and he was a loan shark. If John ever needed money between paydays, Wyatt loaned it to him without interest. Anybody else paid extra. Of course, he had the cash mostly because he cheated at cards.

One day John walked into the head to pee and found Wyatt sitting in a stall doing something to his cards with a knife. He asked John, "You play cards?" John, still 17 years old, answered, "No." Wyatt asked him next, "You know what I'm doing?" John looked blankly at Wyatt, knowing he did not know a thing about cards, and said, "Nope." "I'm marking cards," Wyatt confided. That's how he knew what everyone else had. Needless to say, no one ever accused him of cheating. People just quit playing with him, so he was always looking for new victims.

During a smoker on the *NORTH CAROLINA*, Wyatt and John were sitting on a turret watching the festivities. Wyatt rolled up some tobacco and started puffing on it. Turning to John, he asked if John wanted any. He said no, assuming it was a cigarette. Truthfully, John had never smelled anything that bad with such a pungent aroma before. John squinched his nose, looked at what Wyatt was holding, and asked him, "What is that?" Wyatt laughed and said, "You don't know what weed smells like?" With the two of them sitting on a turret by themselves, going unnoticed was quite fortuitous. Luckily, no one else could smell it. They sat up there while Wyatt smoked marijuana on a U.S. Naval military vessel in broad daylight.

Back when they were on Espiritu Santo, Wyatt was there working the docks with John when seven of them received the same assignment to catch up with the *NORTH CAROLINA*. They were loading cases of food onto ships when Wyatt noticed sheets of plywood stacked on wooden sawhorses, with canvas over the top of them, sitting next to a warehouse near the loading area. Curious about what the Navy was hiding, Wyatt decided to look under the cover. What he discovered were cases of liquor. He helped himself to the secret stash, stealing the booze and selling every bottle with the exception of two bottles of Scotch. They became part of his private collection.

Everyone kept their mouths shut about that, just like they did when Wyatt stole the .45 caliber pistol out of one of the planes back on the *USS BELLEAU WOOD* aircraft carrier hangar deck on their way to Majuro Atoll. After they had left the carrier, they never heard anything about that gun from anyone. They assumed the pilot who lost the gun would get in trouble if he mentioned it. No one ever said anything to them about it. Wyatt carried that gun with him almost everywhere.

John recalled that once when general quarters sounded in the middle of the night, everybody jumped out of their bunks and raced to their stations. They drilled for several hours and then headed back to their sleeping quarters to grab some shut eye. On the way back, they saw Wyatt being taken away in handcuffs by MPs and wondered what was going on. Apparently he was thrown in the brig for a couple of hours and released. Later, John learned that Wyatt went to the brig for sleeping through general quarters, but no one knew how or why Wyatt was able to get out so quickly.

The real kicker happened when the alarm sounded one quiet night at sea. Someone yelled, "Man overboard!" The rumor accused Wyatt of throwing a Filipino steward overboard. No one ever knew for sure. John knew Wyatt could have done it. Without witnesses, no one knew what really happened. Wyatt never told John and John didn't ask.

The life of Wyatt was more colorful by far than any movie, although the occasional movie offered some relief from the black-and-white necessities of drilling and routine. At sea, a sailor could get court-martialed for lighting a cigarette at night and potentially giving away their position. Movies were shown on deck when the ship anchored near a port or safe zone. When a movie was showing on the main deck, it was not segregated. Down below, movies were off-limits in some areas. The officers had their own movie showings in the wardroom, the white sailors were in the mess hall, and the black sailors could watch movies in the galley. Destroyers pulled alongside the battleship to refuel and exchange movies, and the *NORTH CAROLINA* supplied them with ice cream.

The fun never lasted very long. The ship's personnel were reminded that their breaks served as relaxation and they still had a war to fight. Every day general quarters sounded. John admitted to his buddies he'd grown sick and tired of being in the gun powder handling room day in and day out, smelling and inhaling gunpowder all the time. The rollers had great big steel canisters that were packed with ether. Sailors got high as a kite on the airborne toxins. To make matters worse, one sailor had become such a loose cannon that he threatened to get them all killed.

The term "loose" implied a danger to the well-being of the ship and its crew. The guy was a real country boy, always threatening to light a cigarette in the gun powder room. Obviously he thought he was being funny, but no one was amused. John told him not to play games down there. The guy looked at John as if he was insulted, and suddenly the country boy charged at John like a bull. The nutcase tried to choke John because John did not want him to detonate the powder room and blow them all up. The others pulled him away from John. Later, everybody joked that one day the country boy would get his way and blow everybody up, but nobody had the guts to speak up about him. Right then and there John knew something had to be done.

The rogue sailor became a liability to the entire ship the moment he blurted out he didn't care what happened. A cancerous crew member created the kind of volatility usually resulting in severe consequences if not handled promptly. John explained the circumstances to Commander Stryker and one of the gunnery officers. Being on the ship for any length of time could affect a reasonable man's state of mind, and Stryker knew that. He and a side-armed marine escorted the country boy away with swift and surgical precision. The temporarily insane crewmate was sequestered behind bars for a few days and permanently banned from the gun powder room.

John did not know what happened to the country boy because he had not returned to their sleeping quarters for a while, but it was not uncommon for Stryker to use hard labor as a motivator. Even if Stryker sent a man to the brig, he made the sailor do things to keep him alert. That always brought a man to his senses. In addition, a ship at sea needed a lot of cleaning so the salt would not damage the ship. Seamen made effective deck scrubbers. Besides, cleaning the decks served as actual duty the same as extra duty. In other words, whether duty or punishment, the work had to be done.

The silver polish incident, handling the country boy, and many other situations verified how Stryker, the venerable XO, ran a tight ship. The *NORTH CAROLINA* was already legendary because it did what needed to be done and did everything extremely well. Stryker believed he had the most gifted crew in the Navy, allowing the ship to do things faster and better than any other. He was probably right. With personnel and character decisions in his hands, Stryker undoubtedly made sure he got the best men for the job and kept them ready for anything.

CHAPTER 13

TASTE OF WAR

"Above all be of single aim; have a legitimate and useful purpose, and devote yourself unreservedly to it."

James Allen

From August 7, 1942, to May 4, 1944, when John first boarded the *USS NORTH CAROLINA*, the ship and its crew had seen nine battles. According to Stryker, their original intent as a fast battleship was to "slug it out" with enemy battleships from 20 miles away, shooting at each other like a deadly game of dodge ball. The Showboat was designed to use its speed to outmaneuver enemy fire while using their 16" guns to shoot at and sink enemy battleships. From that distance, it appeared that fast battleships had a significant advantage. Maybe the Japanese learned this, leading to a different kind of war.[30]

In a changing war, the *USS NORTH CAROLINA* took a leading role in a number of tactical and strategic offensives. Operations focused on relentlessly shelling island targets, such as coastal defense guns, anti-aircraft batteries, and airfields, or on land assaults. Additional responsibilities ranged from protecting their aircraft carriers against Japanese air attacks to playing big brother to dozens of destroyers and cruisers only a fraction of their size, weight, and capacity while supplying them with fuel and supplies. Along the way, the ship survived a torpedo attack, sustained rudder damage, and frequented Pearl Harbor's repair docks. All the while the ship's command wanted nothing more than to return to the fight and get revenge against the Imperial Japanese Navy.

Following repairs at Pearl Harbor, the *NORTH CAROLINA* returned to Majuro Atoll to rejoin its Task Force and head out to sea for its next assignment, the Mariana Islands south of Japan, north of New Guinea, east of the Philippine Sea.[31]

It seemed everything at sea took days. Once John started helping the chef, he got pretty comfortable around the kitchen, learning where things were and what had to be done. The chef complimented John on his smarts and felt John would excel in the breakfast area. So he paired John up with another cook and gave him more to do.

In a very short time John mastered the breakfast menu. Before long he helped out with the lunch menu, too. Limited menu or not, the kid showed confidence and speed. John worked on cold sandwiches, salads, and whatever else the menu called for. Hot food came up to the pantry by dumb waiter. The same routine included the dinner menu. There were times when John helped the head cook. Before he knew it, John was doing a lot of cooking in the kitchen, and he understood how the system worked.

Food came in from supply ships or wherever they docked – Pearl Harbor, Majuro Atoll, Ulithi Atoll, and so forth. The chain of command from top to bottom started with the Mess Officer, Petty Officer-Chief Steward, Petty Officer-Chief Cook, and the Petty Officer-Store Keeper. The store keeper checked in and dispersed the food. The chief cook or the chief steward filled out requisition forms to get food from the store keeper. They sent runners to pick up the requisitions from the store keeper. As a chef's helper, John did what the chef needed done. He loved all the work and was a quick study who enjoyed kitchen duty, unlike 99 percent of his colleagues.

If John wasn't cooking in the kitchen, he was slinging gunpowder in the hole. The kitchen was hot; the powder room was cool. His activities showed him gaining confidence.

General quarters, the highest condition of battle readiness for all hands, sounded frequently between meals. Since the officers had to be fed, too, John was constantly on the go. Sailors were expected to perform multiple tasks under all conditions, and John accepted the challenge with enthusiasm. Stryker believed in cross-training for non-specialized servicemen, getting men ready in as many tasks as possible. Finding men like John, who brought genuine interest to work, made fighting a war many times easier. He was happy to be busy but even happier to learn, making him a sponge for knowledge.

The ship's assignment called for protecting the aircraft carriers while carrier planes attacked from the air, initially on Guam, Saipan, and Tinian. John did not know the details of specific operations, but the fact that the ship was there meant he was getting his first taste of war. The

NORTH CAROLINA crew stood at battle stations waiting to jump in if needed. John guessed their turn was coming at some point. Eventually they moved into position along with other ships and got in on the act.

John did not know where they were exactly or who they were shooting at. Kitchen or hole, his work kept him below deck. No one could be on deck when the big guns were blazing without ear plugs anyway.

In one instance, John worked security duty on deck during targeting exercises when he noticed turret two's 16" guns moving over his head. Because he had not been ordered to get himself below deck, John did not abandon his post and stayed put. Suddenly one of those 45-caliber cannons went off, almost breaking his eardrums. His ears were ringing for three or four days. John got a set of plugs and never went on deck security duty without them after that.

In the world down below, John did not know whether the sun was up or down, what time of day, or sometimes what the day of the week it was. To him, it didn't matter anyway. Time only mattered when planning officers' meals, because they lived by the clock, or general quarters, which had nothing at all to do with a clock except for how quickly the crew could man their stations. Ordinarily, general quarters could sound anytime day or night. That assured their XO would remain predictably unpredictable to keep his crew sharp.

When John was in the powder room, both he and the entire crew lost all track of time. The ship shuddered from the 16" turret recoils. Three turrets firing to one side tended to push the ship sideways a little at a time. All John knew was, in his first day of live fire, his turret alone fired off over 100 rounds. Three hundred bags went up the lift. Working in rhythm, these youngsters proved the powder room was definitely a young man's job. Furthermore, everybody put everything they had into doing one thing. Hours and hours of general quarters engrained that value into their brains. No other priority could be permitted or everyone would die. Sometimes being angry or frightened could make sailors stronger and faster in controlled situations. Stryker knew how to get the most from his crew. Shelling lasted for brief, intense stretches, then the ship and big guns retargeted for another barrage.

The only kind of time that mattered was as long as it took. "Whatever it took" was a measurement of effectiveness. The unwritten mantra around the ship was to maintain its record for the highest success rate with the lowest number of casualties in the Pacific Fleet. It never felt like the crew's actions were the result of desperation or danger. Instead, the feeling was more like quiet urgency, professionalism, excellence.

The entire crew just kept up their pace and never thought about anything but their jobs. The talk swirling around Navy circles began to trickle in through various channels. Carriers wanted them, destroyers and cruisers followed their lead, fellow battleships had confidence in them. The rumor was the *NORTH CAROLINA* was the best in the business.

Meanwhile, in Saipan, a whole other rumor circulated. John had heard the completely insane talk and propaganda being passed around. They all had. Japanese people were told by their own propaganda machine that Americans would capture, imprison, rape, pillage, and eat them. Even more absurd rumors, spread by the same fear mongers, targeted their own women and children, accusing the Navy of being brutal murderers and encouraging them to kill their own. John was not close enough to see the suicides with his own eyes, but American sailors from other ships witnessed mass murder and suicides committed by Japanese women and children or Japanese soldiers throwing their own people over cliffs. The thought of this made John angry and put a sour taste in his mouth.

Like most young Americans, John knew nothing about the Japanese or their culture before being on a battleship that would ultimately bombard them. Naturally, he was not prepared to understand what made a person lie to his own people to sacrifice them in the name of war. Was it more honorable to not let women and children fall into the hands of the enemy? Did they think so little of life that they would rather kill their own than lose a battle of leverage? Spreading rumors and fear in psychological warfare among opposing forces seemed a common practice. Suicide and cannibalism were unfathomable. In the end, John did not know whether to respect the Japanese for their discipline or consider them completely insane.

In truth, John now knew what he needed to know about the Japanese. They were dangerous because they were willing to trade the lives of their own people without hesitation, a complete contradiction to America's policy to protect and preserve the lives of its own. Dying for one's country topped the list of heroic sacrifice. A nation willing to kill its own to win a war offered absolutely no logical explanation. The Japanese crossed the Pacific to attack

America at Pearl Harbor. That kind of ambition had to be stopped.

Suddenly John understood why so many Americans volunteered. He appreciated why he signed up. In hindsight, he didn't sign up just to see the world. He respected the uniform, the opportunity to defend his country. He had never equated another culture with genocide before. For one second John contemplated what life would be like if the Japanese won. The best he could surmise was that it would be far worse than American racism. Imperial Japanese logic would eradicate American freedom completely.

Personal differences between black and white Americans paled in comparison to what the Japanese were prepared to inflict upon America and its allies. Any motive as absolute as that most certainly trumped slavery legislation and divisive social norms. The Japanese aimed to kill Americans, and all Americans could agree that must not happen. John understood the need for war much better. The need to shell islands and back up the Marines trained to hit the beaches was a critical step toward the outcome of the Pacific War. Japan would be difficult to defeat. If John had any doubts about why he joined the fight, he did not anymore. To take a lesson from the Japanese, it was win or die.

With all the expectations of a grueling war ahead, it would be nice to get some easy victories. After the Saipan invasion, the U.S. Navy moved on to the Philippine Sea. Again the *NORTH CAROLINA* supported the aircraft carriers which, John assumed, would take the fight to Japanese land and sea targets. He walked up on deck for a brief look. What John noticed was something interesting. It seemed the ship was part of a big circle.

From previous operations, John knew the ships traveled in clusters to shell Saipan. He assumed the ship was changing positions in the pack by moving back and forth, but it was hard to tell. When the big guns fired, he was down below in the powder room. The only indicator he had to determine the boat's position in the formation was which side the ship would lurch toward when firing. The big guns switched sides, and the impact of the 16" guns sent the ship sideways from starboard to port to starboard to port. That's how he could tell where the ship was within any given formation.

At first it was always calm, as if the ship's leadership was waiting. There was not a lot of activity at all. But John got the impression the fleet was watching for something, because their circle consisted of battleships, destroyers, and cruisers. He wondered how many circles were out there like this one. Then he went below.

Sailors were not granted a peek at the big picture. No one would tell them why something must be done, just that it must be done. Defending the Philippine Islands when the ship had Filipino Steward's Mates onboard made sense. If the Navy was defending their island, the Japanese must have taken it and the Navy was taking it back for them. But by being here, the question was how far from mainland Japan was the fleet? As for the Mariana Islands, how close were they to Japan? Now John realized the fleet was setting up to attack positions in Japan's backyard. It took guts to defeat them on their own soil.

The Pearl Harbor attack made Americans as bold and committed to destroying the Japanese as the Japanese were willing to risk so much to defeat the United States. But an attack on Pearl Harbor was not the same as an attack on California, Oregon, or Washington along the western coast of the United States. The United States was much larger than a cluster of islands in the Pacific. What possibly could have been Japan's rationale in attacking a single port? In other words, the Japanese did not attack the heart of the American spirit, only the core of the American Navy. Attacking Japan the same way they attacked Pearl Harbor meant bringing the fight to them, away from American soil or an American colony. To destroy the enemy, to crush Japan's spirit, defeat had to take place on Japanese soil.

All John's information came from discussions circulating among the officers around the wardroom. Of course, they were not speaking to any sailor, black or white. They were speaking as if the mess help was not there. Bits and pieces of information meant nothing unless someone paid sufficient attention to the details to assemble a picture of the world unfolding above.

With crews at battle stations, anticipation was heightened, but everyone was still playing the waiting game. Time seemed to stop. Nothing mattered now except doing what each man was trained to do. Right now, that meant waiting. Being down below had its advantages. It was not John's job to make decisions that saved or lost lives. The mission and history of the ship suggested the crew was the best in the Navy. That was a comforting thought amid uncomfortable circumstances. Life and death crossed their minds a great deal when they sat idle waiting for orders. That was why John loved to stay busy. Ironically, loading one of the biggest guns on the ship served as evidence that he was still alive. Unfortunately for the moment, he had to load gunpowder.

Vibrations of gunfire off in the distance indicated gun crews were firing on deck. They must be under attack, but they were not firing 45-caliber shells. Instead they were firing the smaller rounds, anti-aircraft rounds, lots of them. The powder room crew remained at battle stations while the battle raged on forever above them. Minutes seemed like hours, and they heard much less than what was really happening. Even in the cool environment of the hole, their clothing stuck to their skin, saturated with sweat.³²

Though John was not keeping track of time, the U.S. Navy waged war against the Japanese for almost three days. Then the *NORTH CAROLINA* and a few others withdrew to open water away from the action. John did not know what the outcome was, but judging from the general mood of the officers, the campaign went well. In fact, maybe they got that easy victory John had hoped for. John heard discrepancies among how many the fleet lost against how many "Japanese Betties" they shot down, but the Navy won big so the specifics did not matter. Some other ships, including the *SOUTH DAKOTA*, took hits but none of America's sea vessels were sunk. Talk indicated the *NORTH CAROLINA* was escorting them back for repairs while looking for American pilots downed at sea. One officer whispered that the extent of U.S. offensive casualties came from a few planes running out of fuel. Translated, their pilots rarely got shot down.

Reporting for kitchen duty broke up the monotony for John and gave him updates. He listened in on the objective to head back to Saipan to support the effort there during the occupation. Sifting through what he was hearing, John repeated to himself, "Occupation? The Marines must be taking the beaches there." Once the ship arrived in Saipan, they continued supporting the carriers for several days. John and the powder room crew were on battle stations but not firing very much. So there was quite a bit of high intensity waiting, waiting for orders, word, anything.

Time flew by so fast John almost missed his 18th birthday. The day after Independence Day in 1944 the *USS NORTH CAROLINA* conducted strikes on Guam, 1,500 miles south of Tokyo, and Rota, 900 miles from Eniwetok and about halfway between Tinian and Guam.[33] The Navy, of course, did not acknowledge John's birthday, but he and his buddies did in passing. He wasn't concerned. These were busy times.

The next thing John heard was that they were headed back to Pearl Harbor, something about repairs without knowing what they were talking about. Then he picked up Bremerton, Washington, as the destination for upgrades and repairs. It was hard to believe that the second week of July 1944 had already come and John had experienced war. He first came aboard the ship in early May and personally witnessed her in action. Now he knew how the Showboat earned its reputation. He could now appreciate serving on a battleship that operated like a well-oiled machine no matter what, putting all differences aside for a single cause.

After performing at such a high level, everyone felt relieved the United States won the battle. Glowing remarks by Navy brass branded the *NORTH CAROLINA* and her crew the best of the best. The mood throughout the ship felt upbeat. Now everyone needed a breather from general quarters, long drills, repetition, being at sea, and, above all, waiting.

CHAPTER 14

SHORE LEAVE

*"Look at what you've got and make the best of it.
It is better to light a candle than to curse the darkness."*
Proverb

Coming off a victory in the Mariana Islands, the *NORTH CAROLINA* headed stateside to Bremerton, Washington, for the ship to be dry docked and overhauled. This was necessary periodically for all naval vessels due to the toll the sea took on them. In this case, maintenance and a Combat Information Center (CIC) upgrade were planned. The crew had been out at sea in war conditions long enough that everyone was ready for a break. Once they arrived in Bremerton, the crew was given 25 days to get away from sea duty and do whatever they wanted.

Upon docking, most of the ship's personnel were given liberty ashore. Some officers and sailors stayed behind to handle their duties on the ship. Of the 66 black sailors, six of them took the ferry from Bremerton into Seattle and made a plan for what they wanted to do for a few hours. It was time to get reacquainted with civilization, relax, and let their hair down. Right off the ferry in Seattle, they asked around for a good nightspot that hosted military personnel, and they learned there was a USO nearby. The cheerful group stopped by the Cantina, but they were too early. The USO opened at 2000 hours and it was only 1600 hours. No problem. The guys were all starving anyway.

Seeking recommendations, they got directions to check out a diner a couple of blocks away. So they walked to the diner, went inside, and sat down. The young men found a booth and waited for service. They were so content to be off the ship, each visualized ideas of finding a place to have some fun, maybe see some girls. About ten minutes passed and the waitress still had not greeted them. Getting irritated, John began to watch her and realized she was ignoring them. He had enough of waiting and called to her, "Are you going to wait on us?" At least she addressed the question, "We do not serve colored people here." Being up to his eyeballs with this segregation crap, first in the South, then on the ship, and now Washington, John lost his cool and said to her, "We are United States Navy sailors. We are not colored people."

The cook who owned the place came out of the kitchen and told them to leave. The insulted seamen looked at each other and got up to leave, but not before giving the diner staff a few choice words. They finally went outside. This was not the South, and John did not see any signs out front about segregated services. In fact, he had envisioned that Washington would be as open-minded as California. He thought Californians respected the uniform and the men that wore them. This outrage was the last thing he expected. They loitered outside the diner, still angry about not getting served, not to mention starved.

Debating their next move, three of them wanted to retaliate; the other three just wanted a hot meal. One of the guys standing next to John looked around for something to throw and noticed a row of brick trimming the flower garden in front of the restaurant. He bent over to pick one up, joined by John and another buddy. All at once they threw the bricks through the diner's two large front windows. John's friend shouted, "We've been out there fighting the Japs for our country and we come home to be treated like dogs? To hell with you!"

John's heart raced out of control, as he'd never been blatantly destructive before. All six sailors just stood there as surprised as the restaurant owner, waitresses, and patrons, looking through the window at each other. The main offenders gloated while the other unwilling participants argued about the next course of action. Caught up in the error of their ways, they ignored how much time passed or the possibility of police nearby. They began to run away, but did not get very far before the Navy's Shore Patrol cut them off and arrested them. The SP did more than just put them in handcuffs; all six of them were shackled together in irons like chain gang convicts and transported back to the ship. On the ferry from Seattle to Bremerton, people looked at them as if they were common criminals. The injustice gnawed at John the entire way.

The minute they boarded the ship, Marine escorts walked them straight to the brig. Thinking of a legitimate excuse to avoid lock up, John told ship security he had to report to the wardroom to prepare the officers' meals. In reality, if John were still on shore he wouldn't be thinking twice about officers' meals since he had expected to visit the USO, but the chief told a Marine guard to let him out because he had to cook.

Deep down, the chief understood very well how John felt. The chief didn't have John released because he owed him anything, or even because he liked him for that matter. He did it because black servicemen had the right to a hot meal after risking their lives to defend their country. The people who refused the young men table service were to blame. Society was to blame. He could not say it, but he respected what they did. These sailors were really just kids, with nothing to lose. The chief had too much to lose to do something like that. Duty in the officers' mess was John's "get out of jail" pass. Rather than a home-cooked meal, the other guys received rations of bread and water.

When the time came to face their disorderly conduct and destruction to private property charges, they all stood in front of the Captain's Mast side by side to determine whether their commanding officer would impose non-judicial punishment. Each of them was given an opportunity to justify their actions. One by one on down the line the guys would not say anything to defend themselves or incriminate one another. John was the last one. When his turn came, he told the captain how difficult it was being at sea so long and all they wanted was a home-cooked meal. After fighting for their country, they were angry because the restaurant refused to serve them. They shouldn't have been treated that way. They knew what they did was wrong, but what those people did was not right either.

Commander Stryker attended the hearing. After listening to their side of the story, he whispered something in the captain's ear. The captain, a Michigan man, said he was changing his sentence. Instead of sending them to the brig, he put them on probation, gave them 25 hours of extra duty, and told them they would have to pay for the damages.

To anyone's knowledge, none of them ever received a bill or noticed a reduction in pay. In fact they never heard about it again.

After their run-in with the law, John decided to take advantage of shore leave and go see his family. He was tired of being an outsider. The thought of getting some home-cooking and special treatment appealed to him. John knew it was going to be a long trip, but the crew was granted 25 days leave for maintenance and upgrades so he decided to go. He packed for a few days, jumped back on the ferry to Seattle and headed to the train station.

Many service personnel arrived, departed, or passed through Seattle on trains. About 10,000 service people frequented this station every month. That day was no exception. Union Station at South Jackson Street and 4th Avenue South was crowded with a mix of tired and exuberant servicemen in desperate need of a break from war. John heard others planning to go home and see their honeys. Many intended to get married. He quietly bought his ticket from Union Station-Seattle to Union Station-Chicago on Great Northern Railway, the main train line carrying freight, passengers, and mail between the Pacific Ocean and the Great Lakes. While John pondered the similar names of train stations, he minded his own business, still agitated over the disrespect and detainment he and his buddies suffered during their last visit.

After boarding the train and finding a seat, John was surprised at how many people were on the train to Chicago. He wondered how many were going as far as he was right before he dozed off. The train route passed through Montana, Idaho, North Dakota, Minnesota, and Wisconsin, then went south into Chicago. In and out of slumber along the lengthy journey, John found himself thinking about many of his experiences since enlisting in the service. He had no interest in talking much, so he just kept to himself the whole way.

The outside world was a sobering experience. John wondered how it would be different if Americans abided by the Navy manual. The official bible of the United States Navy, best known by Navy men as "The Bluejackets' Manual," was first printed for the United States Naval Institute, Annapolis, M.D., in 1902. A little Navy knowhow might straighten out a few things in civilian life. Everyone got a copy following completion of Basic Training. A multi-generation Naval Academy Class of 1935 graduate named Frank B. Herold once told his family "there were three ways of doing anything: the right way, the wrong way and 'the Navy way.'" More precisely, "... Honor, integrity, reputation, chivalry and acceptance of responsibility that calls for leadership — this was the old Navy way."[34] Despite integration issues, the Navy still lived by a code, a higher standard than civilian populations.

The Bluejackets' manual documented procedures for everything a sailor needed to know on a broad range of topics. A rebellion by several black sailors in Seattle could be ascribed to violations of civil rights they did not yet have, but the manual gave them guidelines for being proud American leaders, led by men like Stryker who believed in what that manual stood for, people who fought for principles. To Commander Stryker, principles were above differences between blacks and whites. Principles were in black and white – clear as a bell – whether they fit the outside world or not.

True, every branch of military service had its own code of honor, and equally true, Navy men cared little about any other branch. One unspoken Navy tenet suggested it was almost all right to cheat, steal, and lie to anyone on shore, but it was not permitted with another sailor. A Biblical quote once shared about naval comrades in arms stated, "Greater love hath no man than this, that a man lay down his life for his friends." - John 15:13 (King James Version).

The brick thrown through the window in Bremerton resulted from the evolution of a few young men. They stuck together, even though all six of them did not agree to throw bricks. Specific names of the actual culprits didn't matter. No finger pointing took place. Mutually they remained silent until John spoke up to challenge the dark side of American morality. He was a kid when he left home, but he had a sense of responsibility most kids didn't have. His mother Rhunette and grandmother Lizzy had a lot to do with his values going into the service. Now he saw the world from a whole new perspective.

John's thoughts drifted to their Navy uniforms. It did not matter where a sailor went. Everybody recognized what he was and perhaps who he was. On ship they wore their "blues," a form of cotton pant, and white sailor cap on deck. During the summer months, or when it was warm, they wore all white jeans or blues and jumper, with hashmarks on their sleeve. Because John was wearing all white, people noticed him even when he did not want to be noticed. If it had been winter, he would be dressed in blue. They had dress blues as formal clothes that they rarely wore, particularly on the battleship.

Navy pride came from wearing the uniform. It must have been something to see as the *USS NORTH CAROLINA* pulled into a shell-shocked and nearly defeated Navy base in Pearl Harbor, its crew lined up on the side of the ship as it pulled into port. Such a momentous occasion that must have been.

Most times, people respected the uniform. But as much as John was surprised and angered by what happened in Seattle, he had no delusions about the South. The uniform said everything anyone needed to know about the man. Sailors were willing to give their lives for their country. Like him, many of the black sailors saw the Navy as an adventure, despite the obvious fact that there were no jobs, no opportunities, no money, and no food. The adventure quickly turned serious business when John first saw the *NORTH CAROLINA*. With so many guns, a battleship was the emblem of a nation's might, the symbol of a nation's power. As best John could tell, America was flexing its muscles for the entire world to see the moment his fast battleship arrived in Hawaii and in every operation since.

When he got to Chicago, John needed to switch stations without knowing what time the connecting train left and he needed to get there in a hurry in case he could make the next train. Not knowing how far he had to go, he walked out of Union Station in search of another station at Dearborn and Polk Streets. As John walked out of the station into the busy city, he looked around to see who could give him directions.

Seeing a policeman on the sidewalk, John approached him and asked him for his advice. The officer was a good person. John could tell the officer respected the uniform and did not seem to care what color a serviceman was. The cop told him how to get there, but realizing John might get lost, he walked out into the middle of the street with one hand up, stopped traffic, and waved a cab over. John jumped in and the officer instructed the cabby, "Take this sailor to Dearborn Station and make darn sure he gets there safely. He has a train to catch."

The trip from Seattle to Chicago was harmless and peaceful. Once John changed trains heading south from Chicago to Atlanta, however, he knew the environment would become more hostile. At that time The Nashville, Chattanooga and St. Louis Railway (NC&SL) was a popular southern U.S. railroad providing a route from Memphis through Nashville to Chattanooga and then Atlanta. From Atlanta heading on to Florida, it was called "the Dixie Line." During the 1930s and 1940s, the Dixie Line was the carrier of choice for the Chicago to Florida-bound Dixie trains.

Once John got to Dearborn Station he bought a ticket, stuck it in his wallet, found out where the train line ran, and checked the departure time and correct track on which to catch the train. Now he was free to relax a bit. With money in his pocket and several hours to kill, John stashed his duffle in a train station locker and decided to take a look around Chicago. From the way the policeman treated him, it did not seem segregated like other parts of the country, and he wondered what he missed when the Navy sent him to Jacksonville instead of North Chicago.

John walked to an area called Rush Street and looked around. A sidewalk barker grabbed his attention outside a speakeasy and asked him if he wanted to come in for a drink. The perceptive solicitor gave him some impromptu line about special prices for sailors. Combining a robust thirst with little drinking experience, John took him up on his offer and walked in. A pretty girl caught his eye, and John flirted with her. The place was crowded but he felt comfortable. The girl was nice to talk to and she held his attention.

He bought her a drink and enjoyed the small talk. As the crowd thickened, someone passed by John and nudged him. John looked at him as he walked through the crowd but chose to ignore him and resumed his flirtation with the girl. After some time John checked his watch so he did not miss the train. He assumed he had time for one more drink and he reached for his wallet, normally sticking out of his back pocket. It was gone. All his money, his ticket, his Naval ID, everything gone! His heart sunk in his chest as he realized he had been robbed.

He turned to the girl and briefly interrogated her. She claimed to know nothing about the theft and denied that she had anything to do with it. Frantic, John asked the barkeeper if he recognized the man that bumped him, wondering whether the guy might have robbed him. The barkeeper said the guy just walked out the door.

John ran out into the street after the man, who was nowhere to be found. Maybe he never left. Not sure who to trust or what to do, he struggled to recall exactly what happened. Did the stranger work alone or was the girl his accomplice? The longer he examined his recollection of the events in search of clues, the more he came up empty. John was penniless, ticketless, and embarrassed, but he still intended to get home to Georgia.

Suddenly it dawned on him. If he could find a USO, he could get help. Without a USO in the area, he located a Red Cross center nearby and took off to find it. Fortunately for him, the location was just a few blocks away. He went inside and explained his situation.

A Red Cross administrator who was very sympathetic and understanding came up with a solution to get him home. He gave John money for another ticket and enough extra for food. All John had was his U.S. Navy identification information, so he shared that with the administrator and signed an "IOU" so the money could be deducted from his pay. Shaking his head in disgust on the way back to the train station, John considered himself very lucky he could find help in time to make the train. He got his duffle out of the locker and hopped on the originally scheduled train to Atlanta.

Continuing south from Chicago on the segregated train, John was grateful for the kindness shown him by strangers in Chicago and was completely annoyed with himself for not protecting his wallet from a thief. He agonized over his own guilt, realizing he got hustled by some rogue city hustler. Struggling to accept the loss, he wrote it off as over and done with. The train's passage, originating in Chicago and connecting from Evansville to Nashville, proceeded quietly through the night. John's angry mood following the theft debacle made the time pass quickly.

When he reached Atlanta, John grabbed his duffle bag and asked for directions to get to Smyrna. The ticket agent told him to get on a particular streetcar headed northwest. The streetcar took him and a few other passengers across the Chattahoochee River and through thick wooded areas.

When John left to join the Navy, his family was living on Hunt Street in Atlanta right in the middle of the city. John could not understand why anyone would want to live in rural Georgia. Hearing the motorman holler, "Next stop, Log Cabin," he lifted his duffle and readied himself to jump off. He was a little shocked to see the area where his mother lived as he walked a long distance on a dirt country road. She had moved into an area that was totally undeveloped. Semi-visible in the setting sun, John recognized silhouettes of little shacks in the woods along the road.

As John approached the apex of a hill, he thought he saw his grandmother off in the distance, hobbling on her cane. The closer he got, the more certain he became that it was her. They recognized each other, and she threw her cane in the air. She carried on so much that her performance in the street gave him a hearty chuckle. Since John didn't tell anybody he was coming home, the rest of the family got in on the excitement. All of a sudden his mother and others rushed to greet him from one of the houses. As it turned out, his mother lived right next door to his grandmother.

Everyone was thrilled to have him home again. John was dressed in uniform and made quite an impression. Everyone was so proud. A neighbor offered to roast a fresh pig to celebrate his homecoming. It was a happy time, and it was great to see everyone again. But John still could not understand why, after living in Atlanta, his family moved out here in this remote place with no basic human necessities or comforts.

He was pretty hungry after all the travel, and there was not much food in the house to speak of, so John offered to go buy something to eat. His mother told him she shopped at a little country store down the street. John walked there and looked around to see what they had. Frankly, he was not impressed with the store at all. The place was rundown, and as he walked around trying to find something decent to eat, John could hear the white storekeeper haggling with a young black kid over some candy or something. He was talking to the kid like he did not care whether the kid bought the candy or not.

Apparently this was how the storekeeper dealt with everybody. He did not just take their money, he berated his customers, sputtering and complaining like a senile old fool. When John heard what he charged one woman for some groceries – rice, flour, salt, basic stuff – he thought the guy was a crook. He remembered what it used to cost down at old Bronner's General Store years ago when he was a kid. John figured prices had gone up a little, but not the ridiculous prices this man was charging.

Three people stood in line ahead of him. John listened to the man tell a woman how much she owed him. All she had was a small check from her job. He took her entire check as partial payment toward her balance. These people had no choice. The next closest store had to be miles from here. He bought a few items with the money he had left from the Red Cross and carried it back to cook. He was going to cook the family a world-class, naval-officer-style breakfast.

The neighborhood was full of small wooden houses in various stages of decay on the other side of some freight train railroad tracks. John doubted passenger trains came through here, and if they did, they did not stop. When the trains rounded the bend, some of the coal fell off the coal car to the ground. Mothers sent their young kids to the tracks to scoop up what they could find and carry it back to their houses to burn for heat. He saw himself in those children some ten or twelve years ago. The thought ruffled him.

He knew there was not much he could do. There was no hope for improvement because nobody here could afford anything. They had no running water. They relied on a spring for water, much like the well his family used back in Armour. Without electricity, they had to use oil lamps. The fireplace became the sole source for heat when the winter got really cold. With no bathrooms, people resorted to backhouses. These were good-hearted, hard-working people. They may not have known any better, but his mother and grandmother did. That's why John did not understand their motives.

All along John had been sending half of his $60 Navy pay to his mother to help her out, and the Navy matched his $30 with an additional $30. His mother got $60 every month, which was considered quite a lot of money. Put that together with what Mr. King earned, and John thought his family should have been living better than this. It was very disheartening to see the living conditions his family chose.

Of course, his stepfather was not around much again since he was still a heavy drinker and gambler. King never did take care of the family properly, in John's opinion.

With John giving his mother money before he went into the service, then sending her money once he got into the service, King had stopped taking care of the family years ago. John would bet a year's pay King continued to get revenge after John's mother called her 11-year-old son the man of the house. John found out over breakfast that King was working at the Bell Aircraft plant in Marietta. His sister Virginia worked as a waitress at Aunt Fannie's Cabin, a little restaurant in Smyrna. Having jobs in the area might explain why they lived in Cobb County, but it did not explain their living conditions.

The whole situation depressed him. John wanted a change of scenery and began to feel an urge to go somewhere. He had left all this behind for a reason and nothing had changed. If anything, it had gotten worse. After a week or so, John grew restless and bored. He went into Atlanta and wandered around, exploring his old stomping grounds. Aunt Fannie and Uncle James had been in Boston for some time now. Consequently he paid a visit to other relatives or went to the movies. Everything was different, yet things remained the same.

To keep his mind occupied, John traveled back and forth between Atlanta and Smyrna by streetcar, sometimes very late at night. John's gut told him, "Do not go back to your mother's house," but he had not made up his mind to return to the ship either.

John's grip on his patience for civilian life began to slip. When he went to see The Inkspots and Mills Brothers at The Boisfeuillet Jones *Atlanta Civic Center* downtown, he knew black and white people mutually agreed that popular musical acts were worth the price of admission, but, of course, whites sat on the floor level and blacks in the balcony seats. After working with black and white men in the Navy, coming here resembled taking a step back.

When he left the show, it was late and pitch black outside. John walked down to Five Points and hopped on the streetcar headed to Marietta. He found a quiet place to stand toward the back, minding his own business. Then two drunken white patrons climbed aboard as the trolley left the station.

They held onto the hanging strap, swaying back and forth as the trolley car made its way northwest. The two southern boys snickered, with bloodshot eyes looking for trouble. One of them still had a bottle of beer in his hand. Per Navy regulations and by choice, John proudly wore his Navy uniform, giving them something to talk about. One of them looked at his buddy, then he looked at John, and said, slurring his words, "Boy, what you doin' with that uniform on? You ain't no sailor. What you in, the nigger navy?" They both started laughing.

John ignored them at first, but the talker holding the bottle walked toward him and shoved him in his chest. The force pushed John back a little. He managed to hold onto the strap with his right hand. Being left-handed, he balled his left hand into a fist, used his right hand to hold himself upright, and, without hesitation, punched the talker in the mouth with his left. John hit the intoxicated bigot with a clean shot. The drunk immediately dropped the bottle off the streetcar, which broke on the ground against the railcar ties, and grabbed his face. His buddy, seeing what had happened, lunged toward John face-first, making him an easy target. John clocked him right in the nose.

Lying on the floor of the streetcar, both of them tried to stand while bumping around the moving carrier holding their faces. The talker was bleeding from his mouth. They started cursing at John while flopping around on the floor. The motorman looked back and must have only seen John standing over the two white guys squirming on the floor. He pulled the hand brake, stopping the streetcar between stations, and told him, "Nigger, get off!" The talker was lying on the floor of the streetcar holding his mouth in so much pain that John thought he must have knocked one of his front teeth out.

He got off the streetcar and started walking along the tracks, watching as the streetcar passed him. John knew he had a few miles' walk ahead of him to get back to his mother's house, an awful long hike in the dark. He stewed all the way home about how much he hated the way things were here, almost everywhere. "To hell with Jim Crow, whoever he was, whatever he was. I'm not going to live this way anymore. The family could have it." Right then he made up his mind.

After a little over a week and a half, John was ready to head back to the ship. This was no longer his home, the South was not, Atlanta was not, his mother's house was not. John said his goodbyes to family and neighbors and headed toward the train station in Atlanta. Once on the streetcar, he began to look around, thinking it could be the last time. He wouldn't be returning to this place to live after the war.

Traveling through the United States in the 1940s was a challenge. Most of the country was still divided and prejudiced. Segregation was everywhere, even in northern cities like Seattle, although John did not feel that way about Chicago. The war was dangerous, but living in America felt worse. If anything, John was safer in the military. At least they had rules for right and wrong that were enforced by the U.S. government. But John would not, no, he could not swallow the very fact that a black serviceman going home dressed in full uniform with battle ribbons on his chest still had not earned respect. Some were hanged by white lynch mobs because they were black men. How could this be? How could men willing to give up their lives for their country be hated so much and treated so badly? Is this what his father experienced and why he was so angry? These thoughts deeply disturbed him all the way back to the ship.

When John returned to the battleship, he was satisfied to be back. The *USS NORTH CAROLINA* was his home now. The ship was segregated like most civilian places, but in the Navy they could earn their respect as black sailors. They could all be killed during their next operation. The Navy, or at least some people in the service, respected them for their contributions. John always felt he could handle most anything life threw at him most times, but this past visit really opened his eyes. As far as he was concerned, the things he did not like about the ship were easier to deal with than the South… including the Japanese.

It was the end of August 1944 by the time he set foot on the battleship again. The ship was still in dry dock, though engineering had almost completed the installation of the new Combat Information Center. What really caught his attention was the fresh coat of paint. The U.S. Navy offered approximately 25[35] conventions for painting a ship in camouflage to reverse the inevitably corrosive effects of the sea. Once again, the executive officers chose the original "Measure 32" camouflage scheme John remembered in Majuro Atoll.

Asked to report for duty early, John gladly agreed. With his heart steadfast he emerged from shore leave more committed than he thought possible. He was a sailor on the most accomplished battleship in the U.S. Navy. When the *NORTH CAROLINA* became ready to return to the war effort, so was he.

Uncommon Hero

CHAPTER 15

GUNNER SHOT

*"Enthusiasm is the mother of effort, and without it
nothing great was ever achieved."*
                                        Ralph Waldo Emerson

John was onboard for about a month before the executive officers began weapons trials to test their new CIC equipment. As sailors returned from their respective shore leave adventures, everybody had stories to tell. Several sailors saw their families and sweethearts, some got married, others told a variety of tales. John could not stop thinking about the life he wanted after the service, somewhere other than the South.

America's racial imbalance stood in the way of him living a good life. His shore leave stories had few happy moments to speak of compared to the others'. After hearing stories of those who got married, he wondered when that day would come for him. In the meantime he remained preoccupied with the persistent resistance of a nation not quite ready for a person like him. To live life by his terms would take everything he had, and he was up for the challenge. Meanwhile he would serve the Navy as a sailor until his time was up.

By the second week in October 1944, the ship loaded up with enough fresh ammo and supplies to serve a small city, then set out for San Clemente Island for gun firing practice. New leadership came as Captain Frank George Fahrion USN relieved Captain Frank Pugh Thomas USN of duty as commanding officer. The new CO enjoyed a ceremonial introduction to his new crew with some fanfare, but John assumed the new captain's presence had little to do with the crew directly. As XO, Stryker maintained control of personnel, making the transition for any new CO seamless.

The return to the war took weeks. True to form, general quarters sounded early and often to get the men focused and battle-ready again, particularly a freshly-rested crew, new targeting equipment, a new commanding officer, and several newly-married servicemen. Down in the hole, they knew their jobs inside and out. There was nothing new about what they did. Most of the time they sat around while things happened beyond their rank and pay grade. When it came time for them to jump into action, the 16" guns got tested for accuracy like every other weapon onboard. No question the powder room had become boring.

One day John mentioned to the chief that he would like to get out of the hole. John said to him, "With all the guns up on deck, how can I get on a gun? Can you get some of us on one of the 20-millimeter guns?" The chief tolerated

John but was not likely to stick his neck out for the kid, and John knew that. He also knew his request fell on deaf ears but he had to try him first. Almost immediately he considered his options to go above the chief.

A few days later, when the gunnery officer complimented John on a well-done omelet, John saw his opportunity and replied, "Thank you, sir. By the way, I would like to do more to serve the ship. Is there a chance that some of us could get on a 20-millimeter gun?" The gunnery officer responded, "I have no objections. But I would have to look into the possibility."

The answer seemed positive, neither a yes nor a no. But John was no more confident of the outcome with the gunnery officer than with the chief. So he decided to continue working his way up the chain of command. Hoping for better results, he singled out Commander Stryker and requested gun duty.

All the black sailors knew about Dorie Miller, who John believed to be responsible for changing the perception among white officers that black sailors could not fire anti-aircraft guns successfully.[36]

Who knew where these crazy ideas came from in the first place? Did Navy generals sit around smoking cigars, sipping brandy, and concocting wild stories to tell the press, or did the thought of black men with guns make them uncomfortable?

Rumors swirled, but none of the black sailors knew for sure. Speculation pointed to decision makers not letting blacks fire weapons on a ship because they feared that blacks with knowledge of weapons in a segregated war might lead to an untimely rebellion. Fear of insurrection complicated matters. It was much easier to put a lid on the discussion by declaring black sailors incapable of firing weapons accurately.

Stryker must have spoken to the gunnery officer to get them on the 20-millimeter guns. Somewhere along the line, the gunnery officer passed on to the mess officer that he had a spot for eight black sailors on two 20-millimeter guns forward starboard. The mess officer complied and set out to assemble a short list of interested messmen and stewards to take part in armament exercises. With CIC testing underway, the crew incurred a myriad of drills when they left Bremerton heading to Pearl Harbor, with more prospects for practice from Pearl Harbor to Eniwetok Atoll and Eniwetok Atoll to the Admiralty Islands over the next three weeks.

Given the gunner shot he strongly desired, John learned another important lesson about the Navy and life: Nothing he wanted would come easily. Had he not spoken up for kitchen duty and now the gun opportunity, he'd be shining shoes and doing someone's laundry. John harbored no ill will against other black sailors for doing what they were told. It was just the thought of doing domestic work genuinely made him angry, and he looked forward to cooking. Putting up with the aggravation of positioning himself for what he wanted was, to him, impossible to avoid and definitely worth the effort. Feeding the officers held a level of dignity that made his experience of the Navy palatable, maybe even sustainable after the war.

He and his buddies got in some gunnery practice after Pearl Harbor. He watched and listened very intently. Three-pound shells, short range, rate of fire, etc. Their group captain was in charge of their gunnery officer and eight men, two teams of four. They fired Oerlikon single-barreled 20mm anti-aircraft cannons. The group captain communicated first with the gunnery officer for orders, then he relayed those orders to his gun groups consisting of the gunner, loader, trunnion operator, and spotter.[37]

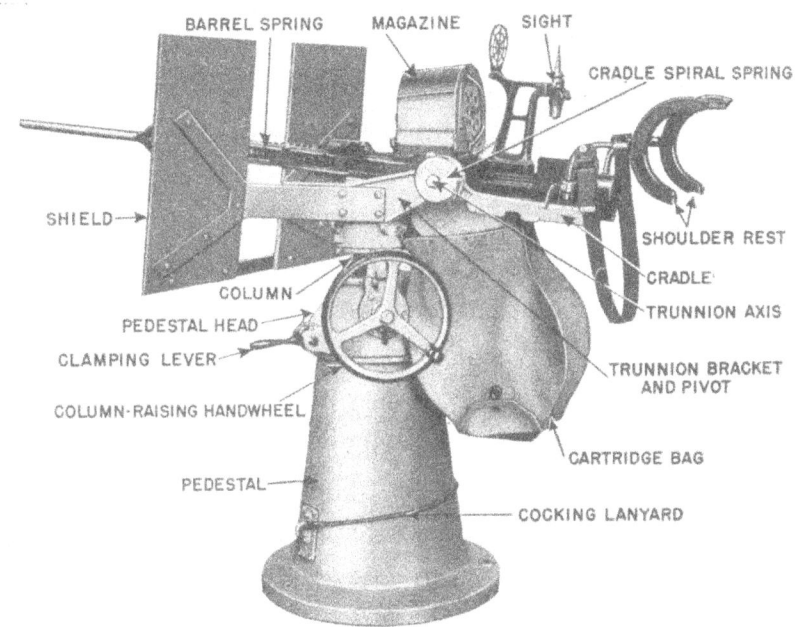

Oerlikon single-barreled 20 mm antiaircraft cannon - Courtesy of Battleship NORTH CAROLINA

U.S. Marine Corps Private First Class Harry W. Clark served as their Group Captain. Stryker's habit of cross-training trickled down to periodically alternating and substituting the gunner with the loader in the event the gunner became disabled. Both four-man gun crews manned guns next to the 16" cannon turret II. Their training involved shooting at drones, moving targets pulled by neighboring destroyers. The drones sailed in the air like massive kites while ship gunners honed their skills firing at them.

John let his excitement get the best of him at first. It took a couple of turns for him to settle down and get used to what his gun group mates were doing before he got all the moving parts figured out. He learned to organize his mates while integrating anticipation and communication into a system, allowing him to track his tracers for accuracy while locating and striking targets. After a few solid rounds, John and a few others on deck realized he had a knack for coordinating his team.

So good was he, in fact, that his accuracy in leading targets proved consistently superior to both the loader and the other group's gunners. As the only lefty in both groups, John entertained the idea that he had an advantage somehow with the trigger in the right-hand grip. He felt comfortable controlling the direction of the gun, maneuvering, balancing, and rebalancing in the pursuit of multiple moving objects. He couldn't prove his theory so he didn't take the idea seriously. To an observer, though, he was flat out better than the rest.

John didn't know his loader beforehand, having seen him around without having a conversation with him. Because the loader and gunner needed to communicate initially about round status, they used sign language to speed up their performance. Ultimately they got to know each other more by deeds than by name. Matthew J. Marchand, Steward's Mate, acted as his spotter, and his buddy Hansel L. Simpson, Jr., Steward's Mate, became so fascinated with how the pedestal worked he assumed the trunnion operator's duties by default.

Spotter Marchand was the shortest guy on their crew. John and Simpson laughed and teased him about being too damn short to spot anything. Simpson loved war planes the way a car buff back home could automatically recognize any car by year, make, model, and specifications. He knew U.S., Japanese, German, and British fighter planes, paint schemes, performance specs. Anything anyone wanted to know, he repeated verbatim with enthusiasm. Coordinating with Simpson made being the gunner as easy as two kids at play in a sandbox. After a while, the recoil did not bother John anymore.

Everybody had a job to do and something to learn. His loader learned a valuable lesson the hard way – quickly replacing full cartridge bags with empty bags to catch the red-hot shell casings. A full bag caused the shell casings to bounce out, hitting him. If he reached out with his hands at the wrong time, the shell casings burned his hands as if they were stung by wasps.

As John reached a cognitive comfort zone, the team grew efficient, excelling in drills.

No one expected them to do well. Judging from some of the grumblings John and the others heard, they were all pretty sure a few onboard, both black and white, did not want them to succeed. Sticking together made their team better under pressure. To some, perhaps, they were just drilling. However, make no mistake about it, they were under pressure.

They were not being shot at by the Japanese, but they were being tested by Navy brass. As far as John was concerned, every eye on that ship was on them. The bad things politicians and the higher-ups said about black sailors either were true or they were false. John took it personally to prove them wrong. He and his team never spoke of it on deck. However, an unmistakable opportunity had presented itself for them to join forces and silence their critics.

In the final analysis, the young sailors impressed. The word was that, for first-timers, they scored high enough marks during drone practice to create a buzz on the ship. Working together, they took their results to higher limits, supplanting doubt with evidence that they would soon be an asset under fire. John and his crew were so pumped up they could hardly wait for another chance. They had just left the Admiralty Islands and were heading toward Ulithi, Caroline Islands when they heard, "All hands, man your battle stations." Japanese planes were in the area. The eight men returned to their stations below.

Moments like these didn't go unnoticed. Sixty-six black sailors served on the *NORTH CAROLINA* out of roughly 2,600 men. John's request led to the first black sailors to ever fire any kind of armament in the ship's history. His actions broke the color line and convinced key *USS NORTH CAROLINA* decision makers to abandon popular fabrications and propaganda distributed about black sailors.

John contained his exuberance, satisfied he'd won a critical victory toward demonstrating his worth. Indeed, he craved the taste of live action. But neither that nor changing the record books meant a thing to him. What compelled him daily was the chance to dispel the infuriating untruths about black people.

Deep inside, the search for validation had become his private war. This drove him, motivated him, and consumed him. He saw how far the Navy would allow him to go.

Killing the enemy represented the greatest honor a black sailor could achieve. In gunner duty he sought to prove himself worthy – to his country, to the Navy, and to himself. Proving he could do what others told him he could not meant everything, absolutely everything. His obsession with doing more set him apart from the others, as if he alone stood willing to shoulder the burden of a race on the ship and in society entirely by himself.

John began to detest indifference, and he fought anyone who defended the status quo with the vengeance of opposing his oppressor. Once the chief learned of the achievement, he said to John, "You can't keep your mouth shut!" John responded, "Chief, I asked you and you did nothing about it. Why are you so afraid to speak up for us? You have been in the Navy for ten years and you treat us like we are your slaves. I am sick of the way you treat us. You can't hurt me because I do not care how you feel about me. I am not your slave. I'm not anybody's slave!"

They broke new ground on a United States Navy vessel that day in 1944 and returned to their battle stations knowing they would be brought up for wartime experience. No one knew exactly when, but Stryker told them they would get their chance during battle. A long, difficult confrontation with the Japanese ensured that. The Navy's plans progressed steadily against Japanese strongholds. Unfortunately, a nonpartisan enemy aided the Japanese resistance in disrupting America's naval advances.

CHAPTER 16

TIPPING POINT

"Courage is almost a contradiction in terms: it means a strong desire to live taking the form of readiness to die."
G. K. Chesterton

After being anchored in Ulithi Lagoon briefly in early November 1944, the *NORTH CAROLINA* left port with several ships. Following a Task Force switch, the *USS NORTH CAROLINA* caught up with a different group with orders, called the Leyte Operation, to attack Japanese positions on the Philippines island of Luzon. En route, the Task Force encountered near-impossible weather conditions at sea.

John did not know where they were headed nor did it matter. When John signed up for the Navy, he had no prior understanding of life at sea. After a couple of days off and running with a large group of ships, the *NORTH CAROLINA* ran into heavy winds and high seas. Waves crashed over the main deck, flooding a vent which knocked out two turbo-generators and the switchboard. They had to reduce speed because the raging sea effortlessly tossed the ship around like a toy boat.

Typhoon winds stirred up the ocean into a vicious assault of white caps and deep swells. John and the vast majority of the crew held on, unprepared for the severe conditions. He knew the damage a typhoon could do on land, throwing people around and destroying buildings. It was different being in the middle of the Pacific. Any minute they could be swallowed up with no chance of survival.

The next day they heard that the gun shield on turret one had blown off, partially flooding the inside of the turret. Other complications piled up, slowing them down even more. John volunteered to take coffee up from the officers' pantry to the officers on the signal bridge three decks up. It was not the seasickness that got him like other guys; it was drowning at sea. He could swim, but not in this. Much worse, he feared the ship breaking in two.

The 36,000-ton battleship shuddered unlike anything previously seen. The way it was thrown up in the air and slammed back down on the water did not inspire confidence. Regardless, everyone had duties to perform, and they did their best to carry them out with one glaring observation: no one could sleep.

This enemy never slept. If necessary, neither would the men aboard the ship. As the weather subsided, they pressed on to support strikes at Luzon. The moment the weather changed for the worse again, logic dictated that they return to Ulithi and rest before resuming attacks on Luzon. The crew was grateful for their CO's decision to dock, even if the call likely came from above to back off during bad weather.

Ulithi Atoll had become a full-service American base a couple of months before. The Seabees had built a primary support facility for the Navy. Because Ulithi was 900 nautical miles from Iwo Jima, 1,200 NM from Okinawa, 360 NM from Guam, and 1,300 NM from Tokyo, its location gave the Allied forces the hub necessary for continuous strategic warfare.

The now-infamous "Marianas Turkey Shoot" and significant losses by Japanese air defenses led to far more unpredictable aerial attacks by Japanese kamikaze pilots.[38]

The Japanese displayed enormous capacity to adapt to conditions. When they learned of the new capabilities of America's fast battleship replacements, they considered fighting off their aggressors from the air. However, the lack of experience of Japanese pilots compromised their plans, causing strategic and tactical changes in their battle plan yet again. Japan embraced a "death before capture" philosophy, desperately seeking any effective countermeasure to the advancing U.S. military. In light of deficiencies in aerial skill, deployed kamikaze pilots traded one life for many lives in hopes of breaking American resolve.

America fought for runways, bases, and adjacent land masses to gain stations for repairs and to replenish their forces by destroying enemy air and land defenses scattered throughout the region. Tactically, battleships shelled those defensive positions while planes flushed out hidden targets and attacked airborne Japanese planes. Strategically, the Japanese were losing control of their own airspace, forcing them to deploy their kamikaze tactic as a full-blown strategy. To the besieged Japanese military, using their planes to knock out U.S. battleships and carriers was far more important than losing pilots and airplanes in one-on-one dog fights they knew their inexperienced pilots could not win. Because their pilots lacked maneuvering ability, they could at least fly straight into American assets. However, the Japanese may not have had enough planes to stop American vessels without the help of their own warships, too far away to bolster resistance.

Aggressive, frenzied use of kamikazes was the only direct counter-strategy they had left to defend their islands. Though this was not the first time the U.S. Navy had seen kamikaze pilots, the increased frequency of kamikaze attacks against Navy ships indicated the Imperial Japanese Navy was desperate and the U.S. military was winning. As much as that was good news, the Japanese became a more dangerous adversary.

Intense kamikaze attacks damaged the *ESSEX* aircraft carrier, and other carriers were largely defenseless against the attacks. Battleships like the *NORTH CAROLINA* did their best to protect the carriers, which had limited weaponry as they kept planes in the air to attack Japanese targets. The darkened skies had been dotted with anti-aircraft shells, aircraft explosions, and flack. Courageous pilots withstood perilous conditions, knowing their chances were almost as bad as their less-experienced Japanese counterparts. American flyboys made them all proud.

By the beginning of December, several ships were sent back to Ulithi Atoll. Their officers and gun crews were overworked and exhausted. Some of the officers complained of nightmares. All of them below deck did whatever they were asked to do, knowing their lives were held in the hands of the officers and sailors above them. Conditioning, endurance, and training prepared them to react when they were too tired to think. Moments like these reminded John why they trained so much. It was so they didn't have to think. All those long stretches of boredom actually built stamina. Welcome to Stryker's Navy.

They stayed in Ulithi for a week. As always, when resting, time passed quickly. By the end of it John ensured his readiness to get back to sea and return to work by showing up early. He was surprised to find that a lot of other men were ready, too. Many moaned and groaned, of course. Duty called, and not everybody acquiesced as willing participants. Someone asked only half-jokingly whether they were still winning. Even the complainers were ready. John began to see that as patriotism – Americans defending their way of life in spite of their differences.

When they headed back to the Philippine Sea, they were part of a large group of ships, maybe 20 or 25. For the next week they were part of a major attack to secure Luzon. Weather conditions were growing worse again. Little did most of the crew know that they were part of Task Force 38 with Halsey in charge.

Admiral William F. "Bull" Halsey USN was the General Patton of the Pacific, an old-school bulldog who loved the Navy and loved a good fight even more. The Navy respected him, some said even feared him. The admiral definitely believed in pushing the envelope.

Weather conditions had become as bad as ever. The ship was tossing around so badly that John became nervous. It must be another typhoon, only this one was much worse. Wind velocity had progressively climbed to over 100 knots. Wave swells were so high it felt like the ship would be summarily devoured. John balanced himself in the galley when an officer called for more coffee. It was probably best to not catch a clear view outside. The ship would rise up in the air, straining, shaking, almost suspended in mid-air, when all of a sudden WHAM! The ship just pancaked down on the ocean's surface. Anything not nailed down was thrown around. Dishes flew and broke everywhere. What did Halsey get them into?

Every minute felt like eternity. New Caledonia was a mild coastal breeze compared to this. On Nouméa, John was on solid ground, lucky to find a tree to hang onto. On a battleship surrounded by 36,000 tons of steel, a sailor had plenty to hang onto, but the ocean pounded the ship violently. The ship hit the water so hard John never understood how the hull didn't crack. Few things scared him. So much water offered no escape, though, and that scared him. He was not the only one. Every man aboard wondered whether they would survive. December 18, 1944, was probably the worst day of his life in the Navy.

The next day the gusty winds died down significantly, but the work was just beginning, with one big mess to clean up. The *NORTH CAROLINA*'s crew was eternally grateful that they sustained very little damage. However, they lost a Kingfisher aircraft to the sea. The Chance-Vought OS2U Kingfisher was an American catapult-launched observation floatplane, a compact mid-wing monoplane, with a big central float and small stabilizing floats.[39]

The good news was that the *NORTH CAROLINA* had not lost any sailors from her crew, despite teetering on the brink of a treacherous tipping point. The bad news was that three destroyers had been lost to the lethal storm, the *HULL*, the *MONAGHAN*, and the *SPENCE*... 800 men. Several other ships were badly damaged. The *NORTH CAROLINA* circled back to help anyone it could.

The battleship and its crew returned to Ulithi by Christmas Eve, and they stayed in port for almost a week. By now Ulithi had become their permanent base of operation. Ship gossip suggested that after the loss of the three destroyers and getting a new Task Force commander the Navy blamed Halsey. Maybe it made sense, since he was the Task Force commander held responsible. But how could anyone say with certainty the catastrophe was his fault? Would he knowingly risk so many lives? The higher probability suggested his information underestimated the severity of the storm.

Halsey's reputation as a renegade did not justify accusing him of committing a blunder. However, the Navy needed a fall guy to atone for the loss of so many men and ships. The weather continued to interfere with deployment deadlines for weeks, from the beginning of 1945 on. Strikes against targets in Formosa, Okinawa, Luzon, Saigon, Cam Ranh Bay, Hainan Island, and Hong Kong were all cut short.

Their next trip to Formosa was business as usual for them, but it became a nightmare for the *TICONDEROGA* aircraft carrier, which took two kamikaze hits. Light carrier *LANGLEY* got hit with a bomb. Incredibly, that did not stop them because the *LANGLEY* stood shoulder to shoulder with the *NORTH CAROLINA* the next day for strikes on Okinawa. Even the *TICONDEROGA* refused to leave the offensive, choosing to return to the fight only one day after being hit, before hobbling back to Ulithi. The memory of Pearl Harbor must have been the reason these devoted ship captains and crews were so unyielding.

In the last week of January they returned to Ulithi a couple of times. The first time, John and his buddies really wanted to enjoy their time away from the ship. The guys horsed around, jumping off a dock in a lagoon, enjoying the warmth of the shallow ocean water. In the middle of the Pacific, the temperatures were warm already. Paradise had regained its allure.

John decided to dive below the dock, messing around with his buddies, when he noticed what looked like seaweed floating all around him about ten to twenty feet below the surface. He did not concern himself with the mysterious substance, assuming it was harmless whatever it was. When John came up for air, one of his friends yelled, "Watch out for the snakes!" Not entirely aware of what was said, John responded, "Snakes, where?" His friend responded, "All around you!"

He swam toward the dock, reached out, grabbed hold, and looked below the surface. Realizing the "seaweed floating all around him" was actually venomous sea snakes swimming about, he climbed out of the water so fast they seemed unfazed by his presence and did not react. Unknowingly, John's calm demeanor until the last minute likely saved his life.

The next time back to Ulithi the ship received a new commanding officer. Captain Oswald S. Colclough USN relieved Rear Admiral Frank G. Fahrion USN. They stayed in port a while to let the new CO learn his way around. There was no doubt in John's mind that Admiral Fahrion's three-plus months at the helm of the *NORTH CAROLINA* chronicled some of the toughest conflicts of his entire life. On his watch, the captain and his crew saw two typhoons and enough bad weather for a lifetime, multiple kamikaze attacks on the Task Force, other Task Force ships struck, sailors from other damaged ships lost, and risky refueling efforts. He kept those under his charge out of harm's way during some difficult times.

For the next two weeks they headed north as a part of Task Force 58. This was going to be a major offensive on a Japanese island. They were headed to Iwo Jima.

The gunnery officer put John and his gun crew back on the guns. Their time had come to see live action. The Iwo Jima Operation was bold and dangerous. Their pilots were proof of American fortitude, flying into the teeth of their enemy's home territory. The *NORTH CAROLINA* took part in air strikes in Tokyo, Chi Chi Jima, and Iwo Jima, along with rescue missions. The main and secondary batteries saw all of the ship's action, taking turns with other ships firing salvos on Iwo Jima, east, central, southeast, west.

Once the big gun crews stopped shelling, they had fired over 800 16" and 2,700 5" salvos into the island. They refueled a couple of times on their way to Tokyo, delayed an attack due to bad weather, launched a brief attack, and withdrew with more bad weather coming. By then they had gassed up again and headed back to Ulithi.

After a brief regrouping in Ulithi, the ship was part of a massive undertaking to land on Iwo Jima along with sweeps of Tokyo in the beginning of March 1945. After repeated attempts to land Marines on the beaches, the high cost of so many fatalities most certainly challenged the Operation's command.

Like most battleships, the *NORTH CAROLINA* transported a Marine detachment to provide security and other specified duties onboard. Often Navy men referred to the Marines as "seagoing bellhops," the same unflattering term used with the same condescending intentions as black newspapers to describe black steward's mates. Ironically, they both served executive officers.

The Marines going ashore must have been a proud, gung-ho bunch to do their jobs. Probably the toughest of all their difficult assignments was to take a beachhead. Observers with binoculars or within close proximity could see landing barges unloading hundreds of Marines as they ran onto the beaches. Most never had a chance against large-caliber machine guns, land mines, and rocket launchers.

The ship would do its part and head back to Ulithi for more ammunition. Incredibly, a kamikaze plane struck the *RANDOLPH* in the Ulithi Lagoon! The question everyone wanted to know was how did it get there without getting shot down? It was not likely a Japanese carrier was sitting off shore launching planes because Ulithi Atoll could port over 600 American ships. So it had to be one lone plane using all its fuel for a one-way mission. That was all they heard.

The attack must have shaken up the brass, because a new Task Force was formed which included carriers, battleships, cruisers, and destroyers. This formulation appeared to be an angry reaction cut short as cooler heads prevailed. Before that Task Force organized and set out to sea, it was dissolved and the *NORTH CAROLINA* rejoined another Task Force.

CHAPTER 17

DEFINING MOMENT

"Occasionally in life there are those moments of unutterable fulfillment which cannot be completely explained by those symbols called words. Their meanings can only be articulated by the inaudible language of the heart."
Martin Luther King Jr.

The Okinawa Operation started March 17, 1945, and promised to be more brutal than Iwo Jima. U.S. Navy and Marine personnel attempted the same kind of landing on the Okinawa beaches. Frankly, John couldn't imagine setting foot anywhere near that beach. Marines going ashore could not overcome Japanese coastal defenses hiding in caves and bunkers, as they continued to cut through American flesh until another plan could be devised. A lot of good men were slaughtered trying to climb above the Iwo Jima beach head.

The ship pulled back and later returned for Marines who got shot up. John and his gun crew stood alert from sunup to sundown and on long rainy days, knowing they might spot a bogey. Within five seconds, the canvass covers could hit the deck and the 20mm guns be cocked and ready to fire upon the slightest provocation. On a couple of occasions they had false alarms due to boats being out of range or planes not attacking.

Life on the edge all the time permitted little or no sleep. John's job included getting up to work in the pantry to serve breakfast at 0700 hours. His routine woke him up at 0500 hours without an alarm. Whether he got any sleep or not did not matter. If the officers needed meals and he just got off battle stations, he got no sleep. A less enthusiastic person would have wilted from exhaustion, but he thrived under the pressure.

The Japanese battle culture required self-sacrifice in a way with which Americans could not agree. American pilots and shore Marines faced the threat of instant death, but no American was asked to arm himself and commit suicide. The Japanese proved they would send one kamikaze plane to surprise the Americans against all odds or a squadron to attack them regardless of the odds.

The *NORTH CAROLINA* provided cover for the planes taking off from the *USS FRANKLIN* aircraft carrier to launch strikes on airfields on Kyushu. In addition, they were covering launches on strikes and sweeps of Kobe, Kure, and the Inland Sea. Prime directives called for bombing and destroying both air and shipping targets and facilities. The *USS NORTH CAROLINA* anti-aircraft effort had some success shooting down enemy planes, but the chaotic barrage of kamikaze attacks could not be stopped. The kamikazes damaged several large aircraft carriers in their area. Now the *FRANKLIN*'s early-strike air corps "friendlies" were returning to the carrier and their gun crews were under strict orders to hold their fire, leaving them open to attack.

In lousy weather, both crews watched closely as pilots made their final approaches. Limited visibility, a low cloud ceiling, and a short runway at sea demanded solid aviation skills and undivided attention. Cease-fire orders effectively handcuffed any defensive initiative from gun groups. Kamikazes rarely achieved total surprise unless they encountered visibility and communication breakdowns simultaneously, explaining the key reason for their relative lack of success. However, the Japanese could exploit an American weakness. Japanese attackers deliberately traded lives whereas Americans did not, nor were Americans willing to risk injury to comrades in arms to stop an offensive.

Japanese kamikazes did their jobs by dying and taking the enemy with them. Willingness to die was a prerequisite for the apparently limited Japanese pilots. An opportunistic suicide pilot looking for holes in opposition protocols and war ethics would find vulnerability within specific and narrow crosshairs if he positioned himself at the right place at the right time. Consequently, the *FRANKLIN* took a massive hit only a few thousand feet from the *NORTH CAROLINA*.[40]

John's gunner group was quite familiar with increasingly elusive kamikaze methods. The ability to consistently limit that type of strike depended on the flight angle of the attacking plane and enough advanced recognition to react in time. If a kamikaze dropped straight down from the sky, it was unstoppable. With this method, one kamikaze succeeded in carrying out the worst attack either vessel had seen in the Pacific War.

The *NORTH CAROLINA* crew tried to save as many men as they could, throwing anything overboard that would float. While the ship maneuvered away from injured men blown into the water, they did whatever they could to help. The red hue saturating the ocean surface told the story. Men screamed everywhere. The sounds of agony were horrific.

The *FRANKLIN* was listing badly toward starboard, like it would tip over and sink any minute. But her captain and skeleton crew managed to limp all the way back to Ulithi. Very busy *USS NORTH CAROLINA* 20mm and 40mm gun crews shot over 400 rounds each. The 5" gun crews shot almost one-third of that. Perhaps they all could have done more to prevent the disaster, but that is highly unlikely.

While the strikes and sweeps on mainland Japan continued, the *FRANKLIN* was in tow out of range by a cruiser. Meanwhile, kamikaze attacks mounted inflicting damage. A destroyer was hit while refueling, and the carrier *ENTERPRISE* suffered from a bomb blast. The *NORTH CAROLINA* was part of the Task Force that covered the *FRANKLIN*'s withdrawal but switched to another Task Force for early strikes and sweeps in Okinawa. Later on, weather cut that plan short.

The *USS NORTH CAROLINA* joined a three-battleship division which bombarded the southwest end of Okinawa. Over 150 salvos provided a convincing decoy to divert attention from a landing elsewhere. Aside from anti-aircraft practice, they conducted strikes and sweeps of Ryukyu, Okinawa, Sakishima, Minami Daito Jima, and Kyushu. In addition, they supported amphibious operations around Okinawa's group of islands in the Ryukyu while a main landing commenced on Okinawa.

The first week of April 1945, they provided continuous cover for multiple Task Force assignments around Okinawa. The sixth of April turned especially demanding. Over 350 kamikaze planes attacked American forces. Their Task Force performed to perfection that day. They shot down almost 250 kamikazes with over 200 5" rounds, more than 2,600 40mm rounds and 3,200 20mm rounds. The *NORTH CAROLINA* gun crews had their work cut out for them. Three Japanese aircraft were shot down within 2,000 to 3,000 yards of the ship alone. The incredible part was, while about 25 kamikazes crashed into American vessels, none of the ships in their Task Force was hit. Innumerable near misses demonstrated constant Japanese defiance in the face of enemy supremacy. Not one Task Force crew fell short of perfect.

Events following a flawless effort, however, pointed to the internal calamities of war. Sourcing any mistake was easy enough to determine. Accepting the consequences of some mistakes was simply too difficult to tolerate. A loud bang startled John and his team. Looking around in search of its cause, he noticed several men twisting in pain and beginning to bleed. A burning, throbbing sensation in his hand drew his attention to a small piece of shrapnel lodged inside. Reaching down to pull it out, John glanced over at a sailor not far from him. His condition was far worse.

Apparently, one of their own accidentally struck them with friendly fire trying to hit a low-flying kamikaze. The 5" shell struck the Sky II director base, throwing shrapnel around the signal bridge, killing three men, wounding 44 others, and damaging the director.

The next day they buried their dead sailors at sea, twice interrupted by kamikaze attacks. This day was equally memorable for a very different reason. They again fended off kamikaze attacks off the southwestern coast of Kyushu, firing around 80 5" rounds, over 1,500 40mm rounds and more than 2,800 20mm rounds. A Japanese aircraft penetrated their defenses to strike the *HANCOCK* aircraft carrier but it could not stop her. *HANCOCK* fire fighters raced into damage control, keeping the carrier and battleship occupied, hoping to contain the chaos before it spread. Meanwhile, Japanese warships had finally been mobilized. Americans had no idea that the Japanese had dispatched the mother of all battleships, the giant *YAMATO*, and nine escorts to destroy their Task Force (TF58).

The *YAMATO* was 72,000 tons, twice the *NORTH CAROLINA*'s weight and only a little slower than the fast American battleship. In the event that the *NORTH CAROLINA* crew had to confront her alone, it is difficult to say if they could defeat the monster ship head-to-head. Furthermore, stealthy U.S. subs tracked the megaship's whereabouts, documenting and communicating the enemy ship's position and numbers to their Task Force Commander, Admiral Spruance.

The full-tilt *YAMATO* was about to position itself within range and fire upon Task Force 58 when a Task Force search plane spotted it and recommended immediate intervention. The Task Force launched an air attack, leading the *YAMATO* and its convoy to turn south toward Okinawa. Admiral Spruance sent torpedo planes, dive bombers, and fighters to attack them. It took an onslaught of this magnitude to successfully sink the *YAMATO* and five other ships. The remaining four vessels made their way back to Japan, battered or worse. Ironically, *NORTH CAROLINA* sailors could be heard expressing disappointment over not getting the chance to match wits with the *YAMATO*. John, for one, was not among them.

The *YAMATO*'s crew was more than 3,200 men. Nearly all of them, less "23 officers and 246 enlisted men went down with the ship."[41] John shook his head hearing about the fate of *YAMATO*'s crew and convoy. Ten Japanese ships may have seemed like the answer to their problems until their ships were completely overmatched. As crazy as it was to send ten ships up against a Task Force, the Japanese were known to tactically and strategically use suicide missions as if it was written in their training manual. The Imperial Japanese Navy made it a matter of honor, even in imminent defeat, to put forth an effort whether they could win or not.

With the sinking of the Yamato and several other ships, and with significant aerial forces shot down and bunkers shelled, the Japanese Navy had been reduced to long odds and pure heroics. Whether the last-ditch effort ranked as insanity or unconditional commitment remained unclear. Americans would call suicide unacceptable. The Japanese apparently would rather die in battle with honor than live with the shame of defeat or capture. That much they had proven in killing their own women and children.

During the week of April 8, the ship conducted multiple operations east of Okinawa with minimal opposition, but once again good news was impacted by bad. The good news was the U.S. military had performed brilliantly following the ambitious if ill-fated Empire of Japan's unsolicited attack against Pearl Harbor on December 7, 1941. The bad news was the compassionate President Franklin Delano Roosevelt, architect of the new America and the powerful armed forces poised and ready to claim victory against the Japanese, died on April 13, 1945.

John and his buddies discussed FDR. John related how he saw the president in a motorcade outside his aunt and uncle's house, riding through Atlanta to retrieve the man who recruited John into the Navy, Graham Jackson. It was as if FDR recruited John himself. He shared his feelings about Jackson, but the loss of Roosevelt was a great loss for all Americans. They listened intently, without any opinion one way or another.

On April 14, 1945, the *NORTH CAROLINA* gun crews were at battle stations while the air corps for Task Force carriers returned from a mission. Admiring the planes during their approach, Simpson, John's trunnion operator and plane expert, caught a serious anomaly. Mixed in with American planes was a lone Japanese kamikaze that snuck into the formation and began its descent, banking toward the *NORTH CAROLINA*. He first mentioned it to John, pointing to it, then repeated the discovery to Group Captain Clark, "There's a 'Jap Betty' up there and it's coming this way!"

While Group Captain Clark radioed the gunnery officer about the plane, Simpson cranked the gun pedestal into position for John as he had hundreds of times. John had the kamikaze locked, leading the target slightly and awaiting authorization to blast the aggressor out of the air.

When the gunnery officer gave them the order to fire, John immediately squeezed the trigger. The air-cooled automatic cannon fired at 450 rounds per minute using high-explosive, armor-piercing 70-caliber projectiles.[42] Targeting the propeller, his tracers left a trail of bending light leading to the nose of the plane. He struck the plane immediately, and he kept firing while his loader fed him fresh ammo. Everything happened so fast. By now the other gun groups had found the target and fired away. The plane faltered, breaking its arc and rendering it unable to hold its trajectory for a direct hit on the battleship.

The plane descended closer to the ship. It veered off course, narrowly missing the *NORTH CAROLINA*. The kamikaze plowed into the sea and exploded some 30 yards to starboard. As the stricken plane flew by, John could plainly see the two pilots' faces in the cockpit. They apparently carried neither guns nor a bomb, leveraging a tank of gas for both propulsion and explosion.

The event became a defining moment for John Seagraves and his anti-aircraft gun crew mates.

Simpson's expert recognition and John's quick, accurate trigger response preserved the ship and saved dozens if not hundreds of lives. They had drilled over and over for moments like this. A black gun crew spotted and shot down the kamikaze that slipped by dozens of American planes and every spotter protecting the *NORTH CAROLINA*. What mattered most was the ship's legacy of good fortune could safely continue.

For a brief period, the ship seemed deafeningly silent. Those who knew what happened and could see the plane's crash spot wanted to catch a glimpse of the fuselage before it sank. Simpson patted John on the shoulder in casual acknowledgement that they did it. John hit the mark. He was numb. It wasn't the close brush with death that rattled him. What shook him up was he finally proved himself worthy when it mattered most. He was now a gunner, no different than any other gunner.

Ship saved: John Seagraves and his gun crew spotted and fired on kamikaze first, which crashed just 30 yards away, narrowly saving the ship and its crew from disaster (April 14, 1945) – Courtesy of Battleship NORTH CAROLINA

Aside from the lone wolf attacker, American planes landed on nearby carriers. The skies cleared of activity and turned quiet. Shell casings and packing material lay strewn around the deck. Group Captain Clark knew John was required to go back and forth between the gun and the kitchen, so the captain sent him back down to the kitchen to prepare lunch, as one of the cooks had fallen ill. His gun crew was still on battle stations and the loader jumped into the harness.

John entered the galley thinking about what had happened. He wanted to tell someone he had just shot down a Japanese kamikaze, but duties called his attention. Busying himself, his mind drifted to the understanding that life and death could easily be separated by nothing more than an instant. He remembered thinking how fast things happened when he first joined the service and to keep things in perspective.

About fifteen or twenty minutes after he arrived in the kitchen, one of the black crew members on deck came to the kitchen and conveyed a request for him to return to battle stations for a photograph. When he arrived, the shell casings had been cleaned up and a photographer was staging the event, arranging the group captain and both gun crews around their guns.

The photographer seemed impatient waiting for John's return to the main deck and hastily positioned him behind the 20mm gun without recreating all the positions as they happened. John's team loader stayed in the gun harness while Simpson and Marshawn remained in their normal positions. His next instruction was to reenact the event from when Group Captain Clark first pointed to the Japanese plane. Then he directed them to "hold their positions," and the sound of the camera flash exploded.

John Seagraves (middle, smiling) and his gun crew after kamikaze was shot down (April 14, 1945) – Courtesy of Battleship NORTH CAROLINA

At the time the picture was taken, John didn't care who sat in the gun harness. He and his crew got their photo taken. To him, any kind of notoriety had significance in an environment in which nothing was officially celebrated except a change of command. He didn't know who gave the order to take the photograph.

Returning to the galley, John thought he'd get a copy of that photo one day. Shooting down the kamikaze took a giant step toward defeating the Japanese by keeping America's most proficient battleship in the war. Yet the war was far from over.

CHAPTER 18

PRICE OF FREEDOM

"Once you choose hope, anything's possible."
Christopher Reeve

Adrenaline made John faster without the usual side effects of the jitters. He didn't fear bodily harm; he feared judgment from underachievement. That's where his motivation came from. As a result, the fear that impacted most other people rarely influenced him. That gave him an advantage over other gunners.

Shooting a plane down was not a matter of being afraid he would fail. He and his gun crew did what they were trained to do. John finally proved to himself and many others that he could do the job as a gunner. Understanding the fine line between life and death was in his vocabulary now, but he still had difficulty articulating his insights to anyone. Few other black sailors on board knew what he was trying to say. More than ever he appreciated

Commander Stryker's approach to war. Stryker's preparation gave him the control he needed to be effective, widening the gap between life and death in the instant that it mattered.

Taking Okinawa had long been essential to U.S. military plans, and the Japanese dedicated whatever they had left to staving off the Americans. The *NORTH CAROLINA* and its crew rejoined a previous Task Force on April 15 to ready themselves for a new offensive. Their Task Force stayed east of Okinawa, fighting off swarming kamikaze attacks on the 16th. Their gun crews were responsible for firing over 300 rounds of 5" shells, over 1,400 rounds of 40mm shells, and over 1,800 rounds of 20mm shells.

On April 17, *USS NORTH CAROLINA* gun groups were busier than ever firing ammunition against the kamikaze threat all day. Their gun crews fired over 200 5" shells, and more than 1,400 40mm shells were expended as well as about 4,000 20mm shells. Three confirmed kills were recorded by *USS NORTH CAROLINA* anti-aircraft gun crews. Unconfirmed planes shot down had to be in the dozens on the single busiest anti-aircraft effort of the war.

After that day, John was all too thrilled to get a day off from the guns and spend more time in the kitchen. He got that opportunity because over the next couple of days they changed locations, refueled, regrouped, and fired about 200 16" salvos into southeast Okinawa supporting a landing operation.

John heard that they lost a man trying to recover the Kingfisher. He didn't know the pilot personally and likely they would not have had words, but John had grown to appreciate the camaraderie underscoring the ship's success. The sailors onboard had to understand their extraordinary fortune being on this particular battleship because they hardly ever lost a man.

For the next ten days, the gunners did little in the way of anti-aircraft activity except practice. If they were not refueling, they were hopping from Task Force to Task Force until final redirection to Ulithi. Without notice, on May 1 the ship announced it was heading to Pearl Harbor. Ship and crew arrived there on May 9. On the 25th, after sitting in port for two weeks, the ship dry docked for repairs on the damaged director at the hands of the erroneous and costly friendly fire April 6 at Okinawa.

On June 4, 1945, the ship pulled out of dry dock. In preparation for the next operation, the *NORTH CAROLINA* sat in port for a week. A day later they loaded up with ammunition, and the day after that, on June 15, they took the opportunity to change COs again.

This time Captain Byron H. Hanlon relieved Admiral Oswald S. Colclough as Commanding Officer. By now it was no secret that if a captain did his time as commander of a battleship during wartime, he left the battleship as an admiral. In the meantime, Rear Admiral Cooley shifted his command to the *NORTH CAROLINA* from the *WASHINGTON* (BB 56). Other than an exclusive passenger on board to keep the officers sharp, John did not think it meant anything to the sailors.

With new COs assuming command, the pattern had been to conduct weapons training to get them acquainted with the ship's leaders, personnel, technology, armaments, and maneuverability. Logically, the most convenient location for the new CO to sit in the driver's seat was the Hawaiian Islands. Crew members impressed him for a few days, then the ship docked in Pearl Harbor. For John, kitchen duty meant a few special meals for their special guest. As of June 28, they were back at sea headed for Eniwetok.

They entered into Eniwetok lagoon, Marshall Islands, on July 5, 1945, John's 19th legal birthday. He was now an experienced sailor in the U.S. Navy with considerable anti-aircraft experience shooting down kamikazes with 20mm weaponry and cooking for the officers at meal times. Celebrating birthdays didn't happen much, and very few people cared. Eat, sleep, duty, and minimal downtime took all 24 hours from each day. The plan was for the ship to rendezvous with a Task Force.

On July 10, the *NORTH CAROLINA* reached its launch point for Third Fleet Operations, intending to conduct strikes on Tokyo all day, mainly attacking air fields in the Tokyo area. Gunners stood at battle stations, expecting kamikaze activity. Little came their way. Moving their Task Force east, the ship sat and refueled for a dawn offensive. Bad weather canceled the launch until the next day.

Unexpectedly clear weather greeted the Task Force the next day, seemingly approving the plan to safely launch strikes on northern Honshu and southern Hokkaido. The following day, strikes included air facilities as well as industrial and shipping targets. After gassing up, Task Force command directed their attention toward attacking more air facilities in Tokyo. A British Task Force joined the fray, doubling the effort. John wasn't sure why all of a sudden the Brits were fighting with them. Despite the timing of their involvement, they formed quite a bombardment force against a Hitachi industrial complex in Honshu. Their contribution was almost 270 16" salvos.

Gun crews were forewarned to be on the lookout for "high-speed suicide boats" to protect "six major industrial plants producing arms, steel, electrical machinery and copper products."[43] Over the coming days, the ship and Task Force resupplied, rearmed, and regrouped for air training exercises. Always prepared, the *NORTH CAROLINA* was primed for offensives against air facilities and shipping in the Kure area along with airfields in Shikoku and southern Honshu. Assaults continued with aggressive systematic denial of airfields and shipping lanes in Kure. A couple of days later, they used the same approach on targets in the Tokyo and Nagoya areas.

In paradoxical contrast to the persistent shelling of Japanese assets was the natural splendor of a sunset over Mt. Fujiyama, the dormant, snow-capped Japanese volcano. John understood the necessity for war. Perhaps it was the juxtaposition of destruction that made the beauty of its backdrop completely breathtaking.

During bombardments, anti-aircraft activity had stopped. Salvos stirred no further resistance. The Task Force met no opposition whatsoever. Many Task Force commanders found this hard to believe. Factoring their easy successes compared to any Japanese attacks against them to this point, not one of them believed the battle or the war was over. Yet satisfied that the worst was over and seeing no further reason for John to pull double duty, his gunnery officer relieved him of gunner duties. On August 1, 1945, he earned a permanent reassignment from his 20mm gun crew. The kitchen was now his full-time responsibility.

The war was not over, but the heavy lifting was for now. There were wild rumors about why the Japanese were so quiet. The crew heard that the Japanese had thousands of planes and crew in training. Supposedly they were ramping up for a new offensive in November that could cost millions of American lives in such a brutal struggle for control of the Japanese mainland that new U.S. President Harry Truman considered dropping atomic bombs.

After being on the front line, John was both relieved to stay below and curious about what was happening topside. The officers knew the job John did to defend the ship, though they would never say it. He did not expect them to. All agreed he earned their respect far beyond what he could do for them in any kitchen. John at most times listened for news, but inquired less and less as the urgency of battle wound down.

A typhoon forced the Task Force south, later returning to Honshu. They were told to cancel their morning strikes and head east. The following two days they headed northeast. With all their Task Force movements, he did not think much about what they were doing. The excessive movement may have had significance. That happened a lot. But what happened next made no sense at all.

On August 6, 1945, the rumor circulated throughout the ship that President Truman had given the executive order to drop an atomic bomb on Hiroshima. The nuclear weapon had a name. It was called "Little Boy." President Truman decided the only way to prevent a prolonged engagement with the Japanese was to make a "presidential" decision to end the war without any more politically unpopular American casualties.

John had mixed feelings about the action. The American military had destroyed virtually every Japanese military asset they could possibly use to make war. With few military targets remaining, Truman just opted to kill thousands of civilians. For what? Public justification wanted to force the Japanese surrender, of course. However, the loss of life went unjustified in John's mind. The action struck him as excessive and barbaric, potentially a war crime against humanity.

By the time the dust settled on the A-bomb, the ship refueled one day later, canceled strikes a second day due to weather, and seemed to be waiting. In a very strange twist, Russia declared war on Japan that day. The timing of this move felt even more peculiar than the late entry by Great Britain. As allies to the United States, the British had their reasons, not that he knew or understood them and he definitely did not care.

But now that America had brought Japan to its knees, why had Russia declared war on Japan? The Russians had no one to fight. Then again, wasn't that the point? The Japanese were unable to fight the Russians, leading to a political snafu to take advantage of a defeated nation. The move provided free license for the Russians to feast on Japanese holdings with nominal resistance.

On August 9, the U.S. Navy carried out strikes on targets in northern Honshu all day. Then they got the news that a second A-bomb had been dropped on Nagasaki. This bomb was named "Fat Man." John still did not understand the excessive use of force Truman authorized. The Imperial Japanese Navy appeared to be out of business, and not much could have been left of the entire military. Obviously he made those decisions to end the war, but with casualties almost exclusively civilian, the body count had to be tragically high.

Strikes on northern Honshu continued. Word came down that the ship was making a downed pilot rescue attempt near Mutsu Kaiwan. The first rescue attempt by one Kingfisher seaplane failed, leading to a second Kingfisher dispatched. The second effort rescued both pilots. While that problem was being resolved, they received news that the Japanese government had made an "unconditional conditional" offer of surrender. Such an illogical position began to point to the stubbornness of the Japanese Emperor, who refused to give up despite a devastated Navy and depleted Air Force. It's fair to assume the offer was not accepted, because a few days later the ship was conducting strikes on Tokyo targets. Enemy aircraft were shot down.

John had early kitchen duty before pre-dawn strikes against Tokyo area targets on August 15. That effort ended with a cease fire order, and the Japanese finally accepted the Allied terms of surrender. Preceding events did not prevent "Bull" Halsey from an order downing five Japanese aircraft approaching the Task Force. His specific language read that "any Japanese planes approaching the [Task Force] were to be shot down, not vindictively, but in a friendly fashion."

In typical Halsey fashion, he wanted to be the Navy enforcer in complete control of the situation. John heard the growing debate among officers about a budding competition for who would be credited with winning the war in the Pacific just as much as in Europe. The race for glory was just as important as winning the war to those old titans. Grandstanding aside, the cease fire became official.

The Task Force headed toward Tokyo Bay, first for photographs, then to transfer their small Marine detachment for occupation duties in Japan. Other ships also contributed personnel to staff the landing infrastructure. The British aircraft carrier *INDEFATIGABLE* and their escorts joined the Task Force.

Once again the *NORTH CAROLINA* dodged a typhoon, heading eastward of Amami Gunto and Okinawa. Third Fleet units entered Sagami Wan, native Japanese home waters. They watched as aircraft sweeps of Tokyo Bay were conducted in preparation for the arrivals of members of the U.S. fleet coming the next day. Over the coming few days, surveillance and photo patrols combed over Japanese airfields and POW camps.

By September 1, the U.S. fleet was not taking any chances of a Japanese double-cross. If the Japanese were playing possum, Task Force participants were going to find out and squash any threat of surprise. A deal wasn't a deal until it was final. That meant shoot down anything that moved, keep an eye on every known installation, protect the brass up to the last minute, and be ready for anything. On September 2, the *NORTH CAROLINA* was still screening flight operations at sea when the formal surrender of the Japanese was signed on the deck of the *MISSOURI* in Tokyo Bay.

The *NORTH CAROLINA* returned to Tokyo Bay on September 5 to pick up the small Marine detachment. They climbed on board the next day and the ship was off to Okinawa with another Task Force. Entering Buckner Bay, Okinawa, on the 9th, the battleship gassed up, restocked, picked up passengers to transport, and headed toward Pearl Harbor. The ship entered Pearl Harbor channel

September 20. On the 25th, they set out for Boston via the Panama Canal.

On October 1, they departed for the Panama Canal accompanied by a small Task Force. On the 8th, they arrived at Balboa, CZ (Canal Zone), where Rear Admiral Cooley transferred his command back to the *WASHINGTON*.

Because they were passing through the Panama Canal, Mess Officer Slaborda instructed the chief cook and the storekeeper to reduce their meat inventory. They had too much old meat on board, particularly old lamb. The canal, being shark-infested, was the easiest way to dispose of the meat without leaving any evidence behind. So when they said toss the meat overboard, that was a direct order for John to toss the excess inventory.

The officers and crew liked chicken, pork, and seafood more than lamb. Lamb was very gamey meat, which was why the officers did not care for it very much. When they had been moored in Ulithi more than a month earlier, they loaded so much lamb onboard they couldn't eat sufficient quantities before everyone grew tired of lamb. The galley crew worked below to get their inventory straightened out while sailors on the main deck threw their hats to a cheering audience lined up along the canal.

On October 11 they completed their passage through the Panama Canal. On October 15 they broke away from their Task Force and headed to Boston, Massachusetts. A couple of days later, on October 17, they were pulling into port at the South Boston Annex to bands playing and a hero's welcome. Even a "Welcome Home" tugboat hovered in the harbor.

"No vessel of America's World War II battleship fleet served as long in combat or with greater distinction than the USS NORTH CAROLINA, from Guadalcanal to Tokyo Bay. The whole nation was proud of her."
– Harry S. Truman, President of the United States

The ship remained docked in Boston for two weeks before departing for New York on October 31, 1945.

The *USS NORTH CAROLINA* arrived and was moored in New York for a month. During this time, the USO took them for a tour of Radio City, introducing them to the latest in television technology, and Symphony Hall with Arturo Toscanini. Toscanini was a famous Italian conductor and one of the most acclaimed musicians of the late 19th and 20th century. During the month of partial duty, Mess Officer Slaborda asked John to stay in the service and offered him a Petty Officer 3rd Class rating for staying because the officers liked his cooking so much. They proposed to raise his pay from $60 per month to $90 per month. John respectfully declined. He did not want to be in the service anymore. Regardless of his employment prospects, he preferred to take his chances.

But before he accepted his honorable discharge, he asked about the food poisoning he received in Jacksonville, Florida, and his back problem after falling down the steep ladder stairs when he first got on the ship. He didn't think those incidents were ever recorded in his medical history. Navy Medical Records told him if he wanted his medical benefits to cover those injuries he had to stay 30 days for his healthcare results before being discharged. He decided against waiting and left the Navy.

In hindsight, leaving the Navy was one of the worst decisions he ever made. For one thing, what was another 30 days compared to a lifetime of medical benefits? Second, there was no work when he got out. Third, he had no plan so, frankly, he should have stayed in. But he was young and willful. Impulse overruled his best judgment.

John Seagraves was officially and honorably discharged in Florida on December 19, 1945. He wanted to return to Georgia and see his mother despite his decision that the South was no longer his home. After shore leave in '44, he wasn't sure he would ever revisit Atlanta, not that he had anywhere else to go. At least there he had his family.

He wasn't thinking about it at the time, but he should have considered himself fortunate that he received letters from his mother occasionally. A lot of guys never heard from home and didn't go home after the war. Many had nothing to go back to. Some men did not have a bed to sleep in before they entered any branch of service during WWII. At least the Navy pulled some of them out of bad situations and gave them a new life to build on. In that regard, John also had a new life now and he wanted to make the most of it.

Americans fought for freedom from tyranny. The price was steep. Too many soldiers and civilians died during the Pacific War of World War II, some necessary, some completely unnecessary. The price of freedom wasn't just trading lives to overcome oppression abroad. The real price of freedom came from the necessities of change at home, facing the contradictions of segregation, a two-class social system, and what social subjugation did to the U.S. Armed Forces domestically and abroad. Freedom from a two-class system at home was just the beginning. John wanted the right to choose the quality of life he wanted for himself. He left the South, and now the Navy, to make that dream a reality.

Joining the Navy gave John that choice. Fighting the Japanese as an American continued to offer John that choice. After the war was over, John would have to confront old southern ways and his right to freedom of choice. His experience in the Navy and being an American changed somewhat once he left American soil. Upon his return, he would have to move past the old ways once again to fight for freedom of choice in America.

Some things about John would never change and some things would never be the same. John was a courageous and brave youngster, always willing to take his chances for his family. He would never be rid of his need to prove himself. That burning desire to overcome a fourth-grade education never changed. John still did not care for the judgments people made about the color of his skin. What he could not change became his fuel. By his will, he set his mind in motion and he fought the Navy's expectations, setting instead much higher standards—extraordinary achievements—he was able to reach.

On the other hand, the world changed dramatically for him after experiencing war from the deck of a battleship. He had outgrown his old southern roots, looking beyond current civilian standards to a time of equality. Yet his greatest victory would be forever preserved in a photograph commemorating a moment when the ship almost got blindsided. His buddy Simpson caught a crafty kamikaze sneaking into position to attack, and John shot the plane down, potentially saving the lives of hundreds. His refusal to do domestic work resulted in this significant contribution to the legacy of the most decorated and celebrated battleship in U.S. Navy history. That "defining moment" set the course of his life forever.

He was grateful for the opportunity the Navy gave him. The service taught him important new skills and values. John had no idea what he would do with his life outside the service. But like most postwar personnel, he wanted the freedom to make his own way. Now it was up to him to make good on his potential. As always, he liked taking his chances.

CHAPTER 19

BITTERSWEET HOMECOMING

*"Start with what is right
rather than what is acceptable."*

Peter F. Drucker

John was excited to be out of the Navy. Despite his enthusiasm, he had mixed feelings about returning to civilian life. Segregation dictated boundaries differently between naval and civilian cultures, explaining why, no matter how difficult conditions were on a naval vessel, John often preferred that over the social climate in the old South. For this reason, choosing to leave the Navy might not have been the best thing for him. As he discovered, if he wanted something bad enough, people in the Navy worked with him – even against unwritten rules.

The Navy had practical rules and order, unlike civilian standards. John learned the glass ceiling for black Navy personnel still allowed him to reach a level of mutual respect among white sailors whether they liked him or not. Everyone had pride, discipline, and a sense of purpose when the difference between life and death was an instant. John could derive great personal pride from being a Navy man fighting for his country when it needed him most because his actions saved lives. He learned Stryker's methods of cross-training, preparation, and drilling until performance became automatic to get the most from people in pressure situations.

In exchange for his dedication, the Navy showed him the world.

Despite all the positive reasons he should have stayed in the Navy, John bid the military farewell with an honorable discharge. He needed to know what he could do outside the protective walls of military service. In order for him to reach his potential, he first had to become a civilian and remove the glass ceiling. The Navy gave him more confidence, taught him how to apply his work ethic, provided a new skill level, and values needed for a successful life. That's what he wanted. After being exposed to such limited circumstances growing up in the South, he wanted and needed to take his chances, win, lose, or draw. His time invested paid off. If he learned nothing else from the Japanese, he admired them for keeping up the fight against long odds. It was easy to say he made his decision prematurely. But, like the optimistic anticipation he experienced joining the service, leaving felt like the right thing to do, too.

After his discharge in Florida, John rode the train to Atlanta. The first thing he wanted to do was share his accomplishments with his family, particularly his mother. He would also get to meet the latest addition to the family, little stepbrother Robert who arrived earlier in the year while John was away. As he headed to Smyrna on the streetcar, John knew what he was getting into by returning to Georgia.

Not much had changed just because he saw the world or wore the uniform. It made him angry, and things like this gave him insight into what his father put up with all those years. The fact that John had just fought for the freedom of all Americans and allied nations around the world did not matter to the people who did not want change in their own back yard. History told him hateful people would hate him no matter what he did.

He walked in the door of his mother's house all dressed up in his decorated Navy uniform and toting his duffle. Mom and the family carried on like John was a celebrity, just like during shore leave. It felt good to him to be appreciated by someone in civilian life. It was great to hear the surprise in everyone's voices. He tried to explain what it was like, but he ran out of words to describe his experience during wartime. So he ended up not saying very much.

After seeing his mother, John decided to visit family down in Griffin, Georgia, including Sara, his stepmother. He exchanged his uniforms for street clothes and thought to throw the uniforms away until his mother insisted on keeping them. To get to Griffin, he learned he could take the Greyhound bus service from downtown. He took the streetcar into town and found the bus station. The wait for a Greyhound bus was long; standing in line felt even longer. The bus filled up to capacity by the time his turn came. That put him in front of the line for the next bus.

When that bus arrived, the driver looked at him and told him to go to the back of the line. John told him, "No way, I'm not going to the back of the line. I've been standing here a long time." John's first thought was, "I'm not going anywhere!" And then he thought, "To hell with this. I'll just get my money back."

Returning to the clerk's window, the man told John that he could not get his money back right then and they would have to send it to him in the mail. He knew he wasn't getting his money back nor did he get to Griffin.

To the bottom of his heart, he was sick and tired of Jim Crow restrictions and the people who took it upon themselves to enforce them to their advantage. Walking back to his mother's house became yet another kind of defining moment. No more. As soon as John walked in the door he told his mother he was leaving Georgia. Without question either he was going to kill somebody or somebody was going to kill him. Either way, somebody was going to die, and clearly John wanted no part of it.

The bittersweet homecoming came to an inevitable end. The U.S. Navy taught him to raise his expectations and he did so successfully. Thanks to an expanded revision of his future, he had no plans to live according to the dictates of a post-civil-war ideology, a 19th-century segregationist named Jim Crow, or the murderers who took it upon themselves to enforce his laws. Times had changed for him.

On the day after Christmas 1945, he caught a train to New York City. He remembered the last visit only the year before when he left thinking he would never return and he was about to tell himself the same thing all over again. After the ship returned from the war and docked in New

York City, John enjoyed New York courtesy of the USO and was treated with respect. Maybe it was the uniform. Perhaps New York City was nothing like the South.

So many immigrants braved the journey to America for the promise of success and prosperity that they didn't care what color the man in uniform was. An American soldier or sailor fought for the unalienable right of all people who sang the praises of democracy. If those same immigrant citizens were back in their native country celebrating the wonderful taste of freedom from tyranny with the help of the allies, they might have hugged a black soldier because of the uniform he was wearing alone. America had become a symbol of freedom. Those immigrants would have known that an American soldier was willing to die for them even if he didn't understand their language. Logically, a soldier defending democracy spoke the international language, "freedom." That was the language John spoke.

He went with his gut feelings a lot. His emotional compass pointed to *the* truth, not just his truth. The truth was black military personnel fought in WWII for the right to a better life in America. Southern civilians and some military personnel didn't think that way. Southerners resented losing their right to own slaves after the civil war. That was why they treated black people so badly, and they were never going to change, at least not in the 1940s. He knew they lynched black servicemen out of spite. In New York, black men in uniform owned some measure of respect.

The moment he set foot on New York soil, John became a free man. He enjoyed the freedom from the South, the military, even the choices his family members made that he did not agree with. He arrived days before New Year's Eve. John immediately called his cousin Edwina and her mother. They welcomed him with open arms and offered him a place to stay.

Cousin Edwina lived at 148th and Amsterdam. New York was fast, but he figured he could handle it. John got dressed up and went out at night. Everywhere he turned, he ran into pimps, gangsters, hustlers, and con artists. John had been halfway around the world but he was still a 19-year-old teenager from Georgia. He didn't know how to change that let alone figure out why he attracted these people.

John did not know what to do and turned to Edwina for advice. She was like a big sister to him. When John told her about his predicament, she looked at him with the biggest grin and burst into laughter. Having a chuckle at his expense, she said, "You were wearing a zoot suit! Every hustler in New York could spot you a mile away, and we've got the best hustlers in the world here. Hustlers are like vultures. They know you are not from here, probably figured you were either slow or stupid. Don't make it so easy on them." They both laughed. John shook his head and threw his hands up, saying, "What do I know about New York fashion?"

She took him under her wing and helped him get his act together. They went shopping and John got a suit, some straight leg pants, and a hat. Now he was in style. She ribbed him about it afterward and told him now he could fit in with the city slickers.

One of Edwina's girlfriends named Emily was famous for her house parties. Emily was a true New Yorker who loved the night life and the night life loved her. Edwina told John she would get him an invite, but she gave him fair warning. He had better get plenty of rest before going out because he would be up late. New York never slept. Emily's crowd partied until 3 a.m. on weekdays and weekends. Edwina told John about Harry Belafonte and Tony Curtis stopping by Emily's place fairly frequently when they were in town. John made a point to attend hoping one day he would meet them, and lo and behold they showed up. "Those guys are smooth," he told Edwina later.

The real shocker to John was that these people went to work the next day. John hated nothing more than partying all night and then working all of the next day. He had enough challenges to deal with in trying to support himself. He refused to blow all his money trying to keep up with the party set. They were not going anywhere in life and he wanted to do better. That was one thing John learned in the Navy: "Do what has to be done because it has to be done." What separated him from the people he met was that John took pride in his work ethic while the party people were more proud of their night life conquests.

Despite John's intentions, work options did not pan out the way he had planned it. He thought he could find a job as a projectionist working in a theater like back at the Peachtree Theater. All John could find were odd jobs, some in kitchens around midtown. Needing money, he did not let his pride get in the way. He took what he could find, though none of them would ever be long term.

At Roman Art Embroidery John picked up dresses by dressmakers who wanted custom embroidery added to gowns, dresses, and formalwear for their rich clients. Then he worked at Hamburger Heaven flipping burgers. After that he worked at Arthur Maisel's Steakhouse on Broadway near Times Square. Times Square held a special place in John's heart, and he got genuinely excited to go there.

Only a few months before, on August 14, 1945, Alfred Eisenstaedt photographed an American sailor kissing a young nurse in a white dress. It was called *V-J Day in Times Square.* Just like the photo of Graham Jackson playing at his friend FDR's funeral, *Life* magazine published that photo and photos from many other celebrations from around the country in a feature story called "Victory." Times Square was where the post-war victory celebration took place in New York City, making it a national landmark. John became nostalgic every day he went to work at Maisel's, walking to 145th and St Nicholas, going downstairs to the subway, and catching the train to Times Square. The route meant something to him because he did his part to help create that moment. But John was so full of grease every day when he left that job he told himself enough and quit.

In the end he decided New York was not for him. The big city was too big, the lifestyle was too fast, and he consistently found more distractions than opportunities. John really felt like he needed a better situation. He struggled during six trying months of New York City until the summer of 1946 when, shortly after he turned twenty, John called Uncle James.

Uncle James and Aunt Fannie agreed to let him stay with them and give him a chance to get on his feet. From Aunt Fannie's prodding, Uncle James made it clear the stay could only be until John found a job. John was deeply fond of Uncle James, who was always there for his mother and her kids when John was young. Uncle James left one of Atlanta's finest hotels, the Biltmore Hotel, in 1942 to take a job as a Pullman Porter on the New Haven Railroad. Friends of his got him the job, and the railroad company relocated him to Boston. Uncle James was a good man. He worked hard, took care of his family, and was a very good role model. More than anything, he was the example John wanted to follow.

John stayed with his aunt and uncle for a few weeks. Uncle James respected him for joining the service. John spoke of the war with Uncle James but he was careful not to wear out his welcome with Aunt Fannie. She kept asking him what his plans were. He did not have very much money so he got the idea to do the same thing he did in Chicago when he needed emergency funds. He went to the Red Cross in Boston for help. The great news was they gave him $25 to get him started. John put that together with the $30 or $40 he already had in his pocket and found a room at a little boarding house on Rutland Street for $10 a week. It was not much but John found a home for a while.

The landlady at the rooming house was very good to him. A middle-aged black woman, the surrogate mother took a liking to John, which he appreciated a great deal. She made it a practice to look after the young man, baking and cooking to make him feel at home and be sure he had at least one good meal most days. Then one day someone threatened that bond.

The owner of the rooming house, an older black man, came in and saw her giving John a pie. John did not know what her relationship was with the older man but he got into an argument with her. The man knocked her around a little, then went upstairs.

John knew it was not any of his business, but that was wrong. He got so angry that he went after the man, chasing him upstairs. The man ran into a room and locked the door, climbing out the window as John kicked the door open. John was determined to catch him and climbed out the window after him, proceeding to chase him down the alley into the street. He finally caught up with the older man on Tremont Street, and John threw him to the ground.

At 20 and in tip-top condition, John had not broken a sweat though he was pumped full of adrenaline. Neither breathing hard nor afraid of the consequences, he roughed up the old man for his inappropriate behavior. He recognized in this man the same self-absorbed indifference and cruelty he witnessed in his father. John was not only old enough to do something about it but this time he also felt obligated and determined to teach the man the lesson that men did not hit women. His mind was singularly trained on exacting justice from that old man's hide.

The elder fellow tried to stand up when he saw a policeman walking his beat across the street. John pushed him back down, which the policeman must have seen because he immediately crossed the street, rushing toward them. The white policeman came over and wanted to know what the ruckus was about. The offender started pointing his finger at John, telling the officer that John attacked him without telling the whole truth.

John knew the man had something coming to him and offered no explanation for his actions. He planned to make this guy pay for beating on a defenseless and generous woman. But rather than address the officer's search for facts, John ignored his opportunity to tell his side. He appeared to be out of character and out of his element. Instead, he only sought to punish the old man. Without further ado the policeman arrested John on the spot.

The policeman called the paddy wagon, put John in handcuffs, and took him off to jail. John had seen the inside of a brig before but never a local lockup. The next morning he had to call his aunt and uncle to bail him out. Aunt Fannie was so upset that she would not speak with him. He knew "if looks could kill he would have been dead and buried under the jail." Her disappointment was the last thing John wanted.

Speaking privately with his uncle, he just didn't know how to explain to the cop that the man hitting that woman was completely wrong. His vigilance was based on doing what had to be done and, from what he saw, he was just doing the right thing. When the time came for him to answer to the judge, John offered a detailed description of what happened. Unsympathetically, the judge fined him $25. Uncle James paid the fine and that was the end of it.

A doctor might have said John was having difficulty adjusting to civilian life or he needed to deal with an anger problem, but John simply saw that he was not the type to sit around and let a man hit a woman like that. Too many things had happened in his young life to not know right from wrong, and John didn't waste any time identifying or reacting to it. The painful lesson, however, was that doing the wrong thing for the right reasons was still wrong.

After all that, he vowed he would never get locked in a cell ever again. Sleeping on a concrete slab overnight for his trouble was the easy part of his teaching. Far worse was Aunt Fannie disowning him.

John lost sleep knowing he needed to make amends with her if only because Aunt Fannie and Uncle James were his only real family in Boston and he did not want her to judge him as she once did his grandmother Lizzy. Aunt Fannie despised Lizzy, calling her "too loud and country." So he asked his uncle what to do, and Uncle James coached him on how to make it up to her. John made a point to stop by their house as often as he could to help out with the chores and did little things around the house. Aunt Fannie's approval was important to him. He knew he was not the person she thought he was, but he was going to have to prove it.

CHAPTER 20

NEW FAMILY INFLUENCES

*"Those who wish to sing,
always find a song."*

Swedish Proverb

Aunt Fannie kept emphasizing that if John wanted to be productive with his time and his life, he needed to find positive influences. She recommended he get involved in church and the community. Because her husband was a role model to him and he really respected them both, John gave a lot of thought to this. Though he was willing to work hard at whatever he did, he could not get excited about hanging around a church. At the same time, he struggled to meet other people who could make a positive impact on him. He did his best to get on track, do the right things, and make good decisions.

The Shaw House, a community variety playhouse, was located on Hammond Street in Roxbury, very close to where Uncle James and Aunt Fannie lived. John had a good voice and enjoyed singing. If he took lessons and received proper training, perhaps he could make a career of singing. John started hanging out there, getting involved with their musical activities. Darnley Corbin, who produced musical plays, was the brother of Elma Lewis, a well-known local figure who taught dance, drama, and speech therapy to young people in the Roxbury and Dorchester areas. John earned one of the leading singing roles in "Carmen Jones," a popular dramatic play.

He was rehearsing one day when Mildred Johnson walked through the door. She made an indelible impression on him as the kind of girl he wanted in his life. Entering with her sister Phyllis, she seemed to know her way around. Mildred and two of her sisters were members of the Shaw House Chorus and regularly involved in the activities of the Shaw House Chorus singing group. Mildred proudly studied piano at the Boston Conservatory in the Fenway, and Phyllis demonstrated great potential taking voice lessons. All four of the sisters sang in the choir at Boylston Congregational in Jamaica Plain every Sunday. Their father was a professional singer of religious and spiritual music who had traveled throughout New England and performed in churches and colleges for many years. They were quite a musical family.

After seeing Mildred around the center, John finally gathered the courage to ask her out. She really made him work for her attention. The afternoon they chose to go out, John arrived at her house and learned she had gone out with her sister Phyllis. She actually stood him up. Confused but undaunted, John saw her the next time he visited the center and asked her "What happened?" Boy,

New Family Influences

was she distant at first, but John wasn't about to give up that easily. He asked her for another date.

She told him she was going to a park for a picnic and agreed to let him come along. At first John did not think it was a great idea because he had to meet the whole family on their first date. The question that nagged at him was, "What if we didn't get along?" Then John would end up meeting the whole family for nothing. But he went through with it, thinking to himself, "How bad could it be?" He took a chance with nothing to lose. Ultimately, he really enjoyed himself with her family.

She actually told him she was not sure about him in the beginning. Apparently she and her sisters did not care for Army guys, but they liked Navy men. She told him the story of several ships returning from the Pacific, anchored in Boston Harbor, and open to the public one October day in 1945. As it would happen, Mildred and her sister Phyllis were among a group of curious visitors seeking a tour of the *NORTH CAROLINA* but were turned away, informed that the ship was off limits. They ended up touring the older battleship *USS NEW MEXICO*. John's chest stuck out a little when he heard her confession. From that point on they got along fine.

Her family apparently approved of him, at least her mother Ethel and her siblings did. Mildred was the middle child of five girls and two boys. John got along very well with younger brothers, "Ernie," short for Ernest Jr., and "Rolie," nicknamed for Roland. Her father frequently traveled out of town on business, and the time of the picnic was no exception. The more John thought about it, he realized meeting the family early could help him later.

He would be the "good guy" in case her father did not like him.

Mildred's mother invited John to join them one Friday night for cod fishcakes, homemade Boston baked beans, and fresh-baked bread, an authentic, New England-style selection. He'd never had fishcakes before and appreciated the invitation.

Although the meal was pleasant, John was not especially impressed. He thought it best to praise the hostess for serving a "delicious meal" rather than tell the truth. John thought more highly of southern seasoning, realizing northern cooking tasted much too bland. He never let on to Mildred or her family what he knew about cooking, his background in food prep in the Navy, or any other cooking jobs before the service. He kept his secret, not wanting to offend the family and get off to a bad start.

Looking back at his fascination with cooking, John knew his interest during his Navy years stemmed from his experiences around food with his mother, grandmother, and father. He clearly took an interest in food when he was a child baking with his mother. He never chose to work in Navy kitchens because someone deemed domestic and kitchen work acceptable for black sailors. His comfort around food and dislike for boredom led him to kitchens at every stop throughout his tour of duty. John loved food, food prep, seasonings, the process of cooking, and especially positive feedback on his handiwork.

Both his mother and grandmother knew a lot about seasoning with what little food he had growing up. He also learned secrets to seasoning food from working in his father's café. During the Depression, nobody made money in the food business unless the food was good. The Navy may not have been big on seasonings, but John learned even more during that time.

John may not have known where his next meal was coming from sometimes, but he had all the confidence in the world about what to do in the kitchen. He still had not found any success finding work cooking, so for the moment his knack for the craft would have to wait as little more than a hobby.

The new couple began making plans for a cozy lunch somewhere on their own without the rest of the family. John reminisced about the exotic island beach fun he had during the war. Caught up in the moment, he easily convinced Mildred that the beach was the ideal destination for a picnic. Mildred volunteered to cook. If John had had someplace to cook he would have saved her the trouble, but the rooming house did not have cooking privileges. So, without a kitchen to work with, John let her do the cooking. She told him to bring a chicken over and she would fry it up for their first picnic.

John appreciated that she wanted to impress him and graciously accepted her offer. On an expert search mission, he went out of his way to find a freshly-killed bird in Chinatown. Quartered and ready to fry, he dropped off the chicken, telling her he would pick her up the next day. John assumed Mildred's mother did not have a talent for cooking, which probably meant Mildred would not either. Regardless, he stayed with the arrangement.

The picnic idea was a great way to get out of the city, eat some food, and have some fun. Discovering how much they both loved the water, they settled on Lynn Beach up on the North Shore. Mildred really liked the idea of fried chicken and potato salad at the beach. John wasn't sure if she could swim, but he could worry about that when they got there. They had a great plan laid out for their Saturday afternoon excursion.

The next morning John swung by the house to pick Mildred up. Judging from her anxiety levels, he speculated that she must have worked on the food until late Friday night and got up early Saturday morning to finish on time. Everything was ready, and they headed out to the beach. John did not have a car. Their means of transportation would be a train and two buses.

After a long ride, they found a comfortable spot on the beach. John spread the blanket and arranged their classic picnic fare for a romantic lunch. They both breathed a sigh of relief and admitted they were hungry. The moment of truth had come as Mildred started fixing them plates of food. He could tell she was very excited to cook for him. She handed him his plate. Her presentation was beautiful. Everything looked like she did a very good job. The chicken was golden brown, the potato salad looked delicious, and John had an appetite. Dispensing with the formalities, John began to eat.

He took one bite of a golden-brown chicken breast and blood from the chicken started to run down the side of his face. To make matters worse, the chicken desperately needed seasoning. Undercooked, unseasoned chicken made him think of the chickens he killed in Griffin for his father's café. Clearing his mind was the only way to suppress his gag reflex. Fortunately, Mildred could not see his facial expressions because she sat behind his right shoulder. When she asked him "How's the chicken?" he delayed his response to force the food down. He knew if he didn't that Mildred would get her feelings hurt and that was not a great way to celebrate her hard work. Forcing the food down, he could barely say, "Delicious." In that moment he knew if they stayed together he would have to do the cooking.

John would reveal his secret about cooking in good time. The main thing was he had a steady girl. One day he got the idea to have a studio photo taken of himself. At that time he smoked cigarettes casually. He thought it made him look handsome. When he had his photo taken, he wanted to look like a movie star, so at the last minute he grabbed a cigarette, struck a manly pose, and stared off into space with the expression of a confident young man with a bright future like the successful businessman he planned to be one day. Later he framed a copy and signed it as a gift to Mildred, "To the sweetest girl in the world, from Johnny."

A gift for Mildred in 1948: "To the sweetest girl in the world, from Johnny."

Mildred's father, Rhuben "Ernest" Johnson Sr., was a very proud and religious man. John had heard many things about him and decided he would make up his own mind about his girlfriend's father. In John's opinion, Mr.

Johnson was mainly misunderstood. He may have seemed stern, but he was not angry like everyone claimed. If anyone could understand his disciplined nature, John could.

Ernest Johnson lived by a strict code, a higher standard than other people. He worked for the Lord and he traveled in the name of the Lord. In exchange, the Lord took care of him and his family during good times and bad. Mr. Johnson journeyed throughout the Northeast, refusing to take engagements anywhere in the South. He did not care for how black people were treated down there. That was the first view point they agreed on.

Getting to know Mr. Johnson more and more, John's assessment was he lived an interesting life. He had worked for a dry cleaner as a young man. When that job ended, he followed his passion and started singing in churches. Apparently he started singing when he was 30 years old. John fully understood that this man was doing God's work and God took care of him. Mr. Johnson's faith struck John as courageous. It took a lot of guts during lean times not knowing if he would be able to feed his family and trusting that there would be enough.

Like John's family history with food, Mr. Johnson's passion for music trickled through the Johnson family. Now he knew the source of the family's musical inspiration. In fact, Mildred's father sang religious music while her Uncle Louie, his brother, played the drums and sang in a nightclub. John could not help but be impressed by someone who made a living as a professional singer. These were men to be admired for their creative expression in light of John just learning to find his own voice.

As a soloist, Mr. Johnson produced an album named "My Wonderful Lord by Ernest Johnson." On the cover of the album was a picture of this dignified man in a three-piece suit sitting with a proud smile.[44]

He bought a two-family house in Walnut Park in Roxbury where he raised the family. From what John understood, he attempted to buy that house on his own but the bank would not loan him the money. His lawyer, a smart and successful Jewish man who respected Mr. Johnson, bought the house for him, then sold the house back to him. John had never heard of anything like that before. That had to be God's work.

Aunt Fannie was a member of 12th Baptist Church in Roxbury. When she lived in Atlanta, she was a member of Ralph Abernathy's church. Aunt Fannie had met a fellow named Martin King at church. They stayed in touch after she and Uncle James moved to Boston. As it would happen, Martin attended Boston University's Doctoral Studies program in Systematic Theology. Now that she lived nearby, they had a chance to catch up.

One Sunday afternoon after church service, she invited Martin and his friend Coretta Scott to dinner at her house, 687 Shawmut Avenue in Roxbury, one of Boston's many city boroughs. Aunt Fannie and Uncle James also invited John and his young lady friend Mildred to join them for dinner. Fannie thought dinner would be an excellent opportunity to introduce John to a truly motivating future leader. Martin was quite a person. He had purpose in how he spoke, like he had a vision for the future that would affect everyone. John could see it in him.

They talked about passages in the Bible and how they applied to his studies. John knew Aunt Fannie wanted him to see an example of what he could be someday if he focused his attention inward and found a more profound purpose in life. It was funny when John reflected on the people who had crossed his path by the time he was in his 20s. As time went on, Martin chose to introduce himself using his whole name, as a sign of dignity and respect for the man after whom he was named. His name was Martin Luther King, Jr.

Soon enough Mildred and John became engaged to be married. They decided, with permission from her mother, to move into the first floor of the family home at 19 Walnut Park in Roxbury after the wedding, so they started to fix up the apartment, considering the previous tenant left the place in terrible condition. To make it habitable again, John and Mildred had to clean and repaint the entire unit. Every night they worked hard to get it ready.

The Johnson house was a large, three-story wood frame dwelling in a quiet neighborhood near the Egleston Square train and trolley station. As the first black family to own a home there, their neighbors were Greek, Italian, Jewish, and German. All along, her father never heard a peep about their plans.

One day Mr. Johnson came home from the road. Not only did he not know their intentions, but he felt they had been left alone unsupervised. The windows were all steamed up and cloudy, and he accused them of fooling around. He got very angry and told them he would not have any hanky-panky in his house. John told him, "We've been down here working. Can't you tell the difference?" The wallpaper had been stripped and progress was steady, but Mr. Johnson argued without being clear about his true complaint. Mildred's father, being the man of the house, felt he should have been consulted beforehand. In his old-fashioned way, he held the whole affair against John, as if his daughter's boyfriend was hustling his way into Mr. Johnson's domain. Obviously, John's relationship with him did not start as well as with the rest of the family, and his "good guy" strategy actually worked.

Common logic in the 1940s was that men and women did not move in together unless they planned to be married soon thereafter. In fact, people did not move in together until they got married most of the time. Of course, Mr. Johnson was a strict advocate of the principles of the Bible and wanted them to get married sooner than later, suggesting this coming June 1948. Mildred and John concurred that it would be too soon. Better to get organized before they married, they felt. They subsequently put off the date until next February 1949. Mr. Johnson informed them, "Well, unless you change the date, I am not coming to the wedding."

He meant what he said. His itinerary was made far enough in advance that he knew he could not make the wedding. Times were tough, and he had obligations to meet to keep up the mortgage on the house. John respected that as much as anybody. The young couple just needed to do what was best for them.

Meanwhile, Mr. Johnson insisted that Johnny be called "John." He spoke in his typically righteous way that John's proper name is how God knew him. Besides he would not have any man named "Johnny" in his house. That kind of name did not sound like a man of high character.

John and Mildred married in the Walnut Park house on February 22, 1949. House weddings were very common these days. Ten years after the Depression, money was still pretty tight for most people, with more debt than income to go around. If a home owner missed a payment in those days, the bank wanted to put him out on the street. Fortunately, Mr. Johnson did not owe a bank, but rather a personal friend. John knew he married into a special family because Mildred's father owned a home when few black families did. The fact that they had a place to move into together with so little money was a miracle.

However, the unfortunate reality was his new father-in-law wasn't there to give his daughter away. Mr. Johnson never told them how he felt about that. He was still a bit cool toward his new son-in-law. Once married, John gave thought to living in his father-in-law's house. With a profoundly new position in life, he had a solid foundation resulting from spiritually rich new family influences.

Wedding Day – February 22, 1949

John still felt Mr. Johnson had not accepted him fully into the family. Out of respect for the head of the household, he called his new father-in-law "Dad." For him, this was not an easy thing to do, given his history with previous fathers. That said, he had a very different opportunity for a relationship with his new father figure. As patriarchs of their respective families, John Seagraves and Ernest Johnson worked hard to manage their responsibilities with distant but mutual respect, the antithesis of what John shared with either his biological father or his stepfather. One could easily see that this was the kind of respect John longed for, though it still wasn't perfect. Because John had basically moved in with Mildred's family, they all did what they had to, with everyone contributing somehow. John was accustomed to a large family and worked very hard to feel at home.

Anyone could argue that Mr. Johnson needed all the help he could get during those uncertain times. Yes, trusting one man to oversee another man's home was a big step. It was guaranteed that another man around the house, if he was a good man, insured some financial and emotional stability in his absence. The most important thing was to maintain the roof over their heads. The furnace sometimes acted up, and John had legitimate reason to believe the house was haunted. Lots of old houses had their creeks and rattles, but what he was talking about was altogether different. Regardless, they had a place to live during long, cold, miserable winters, something for which Boston was well known.

John did not know about the finances of the house. Mildred's mother Ma struggled to keep the family fed. Her full-time job was not outside the house but at home raising all her children. Some of the kids were too young to work, anyway. The miracle was that Dad got paid at all. Twenty years after the Great Depression and Dad still did not specifically charge a fee for his singing. Each congregation passed the plate and he was paid from that. When there wasn't enough money, the church minister paid him in other ways.

Mildred and John sometimes drove to where Dad was singing. John remembered on one occasion the congregation killed a pig for him as payment for the service that day. Dad was his own agent and did his own correspondence. He ran a decent little business. Mildred explained to John how her father sat at an old typewriter typing up letters, looking for dates for his events. If he had the money, her father would hire a pianist to accompany him. When necessary, he played himself. A friend of Dad's wrote all his music. He kept himself busy on the road the best way he knew how. Sometimes the ends did not meet the need.

Mildred worked full-time as a bookkeeper at Folsom's Market on Washington Street near Northampton Station, an elevated train station. One rare day, Mildred came home from work having forgotten her key, so she rang the doorbell to the upstairs apartment. She was pregnant with their first child. Dad was upstairs, and he rushed downstairs in a huff, shouting and making a fuss over being disturbed because he spent many hours on his knees in prayer. He really gave her a hard time, and it deeply upset her.

When John arrived home from work, she told him what happened. John became so angry and concerned for her and their first baby's well being that he exploded. He stormed out the front door and rang the doorbell next door until Dad came downstairs so John could give him a piece of his mind. When Dad came to the door, John yelled, "I heard you were threatening Mildred and she was pregnant!" John continued, "Man, what was wrong with you! Are you crazy?" John could not believe a religious man, and his wife's own father, behaved that way.

Dad had quite a temper; so did John. Afterwards, Mildred revealed to John that he was the first man to ever confront her father. Everyone else was afraid of him. Conversely, Dad learned a thing or two about his ex-Navy son-in-law's toughness and commitment to his daughter from the altercation. He backed off and never did anything like that again. The fact that John stood up to him to defend his wife earned Dad's respect.

John realized that confrontation broke the ice between them. Dad began to warm up to him and treat him like family. After that, they talked all the time, sharing stories and talking about music. John told him about the war, and Dad talked about his travels and God. Dad turned out to be quite a man in John's eyes. After catching a glimpse of Dad's cross to bear, John believed his father-in-law was hard on everyone because of the times and the pressure he was under.

The strong bond between the two men proved very important to both of them. Dad was relieved to know his daughter married a man strong enough to protect her from any man, including him. And if that wasn't enough, Dad loved John's cooking.

Dad always came downstairs when John was cooking, asking him, "Seagraves, what are you cooking tonight?" John told him, "Tonight, we are having lamb chops." And he retorted, "Oh my!" with that broad, wonderful smile. Standing in the kitchen with his hands in his pants pockets, wearing a white shirt with sleeves rolled up and slacks with suspenders like he had been working in an office all day, Dad watched him cook.

They became very close. Mildred and John continued to live on Walnut Park for another year until they move to the Ruggles Street Housing Projects. John missed his bond with Dad, but the young family never had any privacy. So the time had come to move on.

CHAPTER 21

BUILDING AN EMPIRE

"Keep your dreams alive. Understand to achieve anything requires faith and belief in yourself, vision, hard work, determination, and dedication. Remember all things are possible for those who believe."

Gail Devers

After the war there were few jobs. John always thought that with naval experience finding a job would be easy. He was a Navy man who served his country and cooked for the officers of the most successful ship in the U.S. Navy. The last thing John expected to do was resort to wandering the streets of Boston in search of a cooking job with no luck at all. Employment opportunities seemed worse after the war than before he went into the service. This time John could not find any restaurant work doing anything. Struggling to find a way to make a buck, he only knew a few things that might work. If it wasn't food, maybe it was hair.

The only reason he conjured up cutting hair was because he enjoyed doing it in the service, but he had no professional training. He cut sailors' hair in the head (bathroom) of the battleship. How difficult could it be? Doing hair on the ship was just a way to make extra money until he messed up Wyatt's hair, his one and only failed attempt at styling. After that mishap, basic haircuts were the only haircuts he did on the ship. Cutting hair still made sense. John found out how to use the GI Bill to attend barber's school.

Right after graduation from barber's school John got a job at Hamp's Barber Shop. On his first day, his first customer was a drunken white fellow. He sat in the chair smelling like a whiskey bottle and said, "Give me a haircut!" John asked him, "What style would you like sir?" He blurted out, "Just give me a damn haircut!" So John draped the apron around his neck and turned to get his scissors, wondering what he should do. When he turned back around, the guy was passed out.

John did not really know what the guy wanted, so he gave him a military barber's cut. When the customer woke up, he complained that John cut off too much and refused to pay him. John blamed the customer for not being specific. Hamp blamed John for poor service, not knowing current styles, not making him money, just about everything he could think of because the customer was unhappy. So after the round-robin with the customer blaming John, John blaming the customer, and Hamp blaming John, John told both of them "to hell with them" and walked out. As ridiculously as the scenario played out, John decided cutting hair was not worth the aggravation.

Ordinarily he would not give up that easily, but he still did not know where his place was in the world. Cutting hair was a temporary solution at best; at worst, it was a waste of time compared to cooking. Satisfied with his conclusion, he still had to find a job, with very few ideas left. A movie projectionist's job was his final option. Hoping for better results he went downtown to the movie district to ask around.

Looking for projectionist positions, John knocked on several movie theater doors. Movie house managers offered him brief interviews and asked him if he had any experience. When John discussed the equipment with which he was familiar, each of them laughed at him. The technology he spoke of qualified as ancient, at least a generation or two old. "Pins falling to the floor and all that nonsense, well that's a thing of the past!" one man said. The new technology of film projection today had replaced all that antiquated junk from a few years ago. Of course, John could learn the new projection equipment if he could join the Projectionists Union of Boston, but membership was by referral only and he did not know anybody who could grant him entry. With one theater left to visit, he began to accept the improbability that he had a future as a projectionist.

His last stop was the Olympia Theater. The manager did not have any projectionist positions, telling him what he already knew about not having a union card, but he did have a night cleaning position available immediately if he wanted it. John considered his situation and the possibility of finding anything that would earn him a paycheck. Completely uninspired, John took the job. In August 1946, John started out working after hours as the night cleaner.

The owner of the Olympia Theater eventually renovated the old theater, changed the name to the Pilgrim Theater, and offered him the supervisor's job with a crew of five people in the janitorial department. John's employment with the Olympia/Pilgrim Theater lasted over three years. It was during that time that John met Mildred and married her.

He kept his eye out for cooking jobs, but prejudice was actually worse in Boston than in Atlanta. Boston neighborhoods were very ethnocentric, territorial, and bigoted with very clear boundaries. Most Boston restaurant owners were Italian or Irish and they did not like black people, leaving John no choice but to stay with the Pilgrim Theater. Unfortunately, he fell ill, developing a case of appendicitis, and required an emergency appendectomy. During his recovery, John lost his job in early September 1949.

After he healed, he was ready to go back to work. John did not see himself cleaning movie theaters anymore. At the same time he never gave up his desire to one day own his own restaurant. He knew the one thing he loved to do more than anything was cook. Every person who appreciated his culinary skills could not be wrong. Mildred was his biggest supporter. She encouraged him to set his sights on the restaurant industry. After two and a half years as a cook in the Navy, John had enough experience if anyone had a job opening.

The obvious conclusion of the times stared him in the face. The only way John was going to work in a restaurant was by opening his own. In 1950 he finally gathered sufficient resources to do just that. Back in Atlanta, his old buddy Sam Walker had gone into the Army before John went into the Navy. After the war, they met up back in Atlanta and talked about one day owning a business together. Suddenly that time had come. John tracked Sam down, told him about his idea, and asked Sam if he wanted to partner with him. Sam agreed, and they opened a small restaurant on Shawmut Avenue in Boston.

One could argue that John belonged in the restaurant business, joining a family legacy of restaurant owners. His father had his own café in Griffin. One of his stepbrothers named Buddy owned a barbeque shack located on Butler Street off Auburn Avenue, the black business center area before integration in downtown Atlanta. From his childhood in Atlanta all the way through the Navy, John was around the food business, particularly on the *NORTH CAROLINA*. Now John wanted to take his turn in the growing line of family restaurateurs.

The most definitive factor pointed to few alternatives; however, timing did not appear to be in his favor either. With a child on the way, John concluded a restaurant had a better chance to succeed than landing employment that paid him enough for him and his family to survive. Recalling his father-in-law's advice about following his heart and having faith inspired his decision.

Scraping every available dollar together to open for business, their small restaurant struggled to find customers. In need of cash flow, John received a job offer up in Maine to work at the Hillcroft Inn Seafood Restaurant in York Harbor. He accepted the position and traveled to Maine, leaving Mildred with her full-time job at Folsom's Market and Sam to handle the restaurant. John paid the landlord a month's rent in advance and told her he would send the remaining rent through Sam.

Three months later John returned from Maine and stopped by the restaurant. Approaching the front door, he saw his equipment gone and the business closed.

Stricken with grief, he was beside himself. John chased down the landlady and asked her why she shut down his business. The landlady revealed to him that she didn't get two months' rent so she confiscated all the restaurant equipment and sold it to cover the delinquent balance. If he sent money to his friend Sam, he must have run off with the rent. Moreover, she had not seen him for some time. He asked in shock, "Sam has disappeared?" She said Sam had confided in her that he was going to sell vacuum cleaners. John never heard from him again.

This could not have come at a worse possible time. Mildred and John's first daughter Patricia was born shortly thereafter, on November 3, 1950. Suddenly John was a dad with even more financial pressure. The money left over from Maine and Mildred's full-time position left them a little money set aside, so they were making it all right, but John wanted to go back to cooking in the face of a cooking job shortage all over again. He ended up right back where he started. Understandably, his faith was tested as frustration and anger got the best of him.

Lacking inspiration or hope, and unable to risk another investment in a new restaurant, pushed John to the end of his rope. He needed employment with good pay and flexible hours, and he needed it immediately. Mildred being pregnant with their second child forced John to eliminate most regular job options. Walking across the street, he nearly got clipped by a taxi cab. Desperately in need of a miracle, the taxi cab idea almost ran him over as well. In September 1951 John started driving a Checker Cab. It wasn't fancy, but it solved his problem.

John and Mildred's second daughter Linda was born on December 27, 1951. Every day while driving, he thought about what he could have done differently to save his restaurant. Every day he asked the question until he finally concluded – accepted – that Sam ripped him off. John drove a cab for almost five years.

Despite his obligations, John just wanted to cook. With two young mouths to feed, he kept driving with one eye on the road and the other on *The Boston Globe* newspaper. During the late summer of 1956 he was looking through the *Globe* when he found an Italian restaurant in Dedham named the Coronet Restaurant looking for a cook. Dedham was an upscale area way across town and as prejudiced against black people as anywhere. John did not care. He was going to the interview no matter how far away it was. Dad decided to ride to the appointment with him.

When they arrived, Dad told John he was going to get hired that day and he started praying as John went inside. John met with a Sicilian man named Don. Don had been in the service himself and he talked to John about the war. He mentioned a black buddy in the service whom he never forgot and how after the war he wondered about his buddy every day for months. Of course, Don never heard from his friend again, but he sympathized with his war pal, John too. He respected John for coming so far to meet with him.

Don's father was a first-generation Sicilian immigrant from the old school who did not want his son to hire John, but John's war history meant something to Don. He knew black men had a hard way to go, like his father's generation did. That appeared to be why the old-world Italians stuck to their own and why his father wanted his son to keep it that way. Don said he wasn't like his father and he had his own mind. Don apologized for his father's behavior, gave John the job, and provided him an opportunity to learn how to cook authentic Italian cuisine.

After John had been working at the Coronet Restaurant for a while, Don's father began to appreciate John's ability to cook like an Italian. The older man's attitude toward him changed and they grew to respect each other. On Valentine's Day 1959, John's third child and first son David was born. After a few years, John decided to broaden his cooking skills and moved on. In retrospect, John swore on his life that Dad's prayers had something to do with him getting the Coronet Restaurant job. Maybe Dad had called in a favor.

For the next several years John upgraded the quality of his life. He worked in a number of restaurants, including a Greek restaurant and Newbury Steakhouse. The goal became to increase his value by diversifying his culinary knowledge across a wide spectrum of international menus. As the economy improved and jobs became more readily available to him, John first decided to move his family out of the city. He bought a home in the South Shore suburbs 20 miles outside of Boston. Then, he came to realize that while he could be flexible and varied with his cooking skills, he preferred a more stable working environment.

Growing weary of high-pressure restaurant kitchens, though he wanted to keep cooking, John filled out an application for United Servomation in Boston. In 1965 he got a call to come in for an interview, and he accepted the position when it was offered to him. "By 1965,

Servomation was a $100,000,000 public company with over 70,000 vending units in 29 states coast-to-coast."[45] With a booming vending, dining, and recreation services business, Servomation constantly grew by way of acquisitions.

John mentioned in his interview that he wanted to expand his range of cooking experiences. It turned out that the company needed someone to fill a temporary position. He welcomed the challenge and accepted a unique offer to get out of the city over the summer to work at a campground. During the summer of 1966, Servomation sent him to Camp Robinson Crusoe where John cooked for kids attending the camp. While the surroundings were new to him, the world was a better place so long as he worked in a kitchen. In this particular instance, he unexpectedly enjoyed showing children from wealthy families how to cook. When he returned, he went to work for a division of Servomation called Recording and Statistical. John worked in their kitchen from 1966-1970.

The summer of 1970 marked a new era of technology utilization to replace human resources. The vending business deemed human labor obsolete, determining machines were cheaper than people. Corporate restructuring led to a major R&S downsizing from 450 employees to 100. Massive layoffs affected every department, including his. The time had come once again for John to consider going out on his own.

Mildred and John agreed that it was time to open another restaurant. They found a burned out furniture store on Blue Hill Avenue in Dorchester and renovated the location. In the process, they created J & S Caterers Restaurant and Function Room. John and his half-brother

Bob worked day and night to remodel the upstairs area, which included the dining area, kitchen, function room, and bar. They had to pump water out of the flooded basement, which eventually became completely redecorated office and storage space. When it came to plumbing, electrical, and all kinds of necessary repairs, they remodeled everything themselves.

The day J & S Caterers opened validated a lifelong dream for John. A grand opening marked proof that persistence and passion would eventually pay off. The restaurant specialized in southern and American cuisine, while the catering service offered an international menu. The function room was equipped to host all types of social and political events.

John handled the food, customers, and promotion. Mildred handled all the bookkeeping and banking responsibilities. Their enterprise built a nice reputation, though no one foresaw John's gift for cooking to seed building an empire. Among those who visited their restaurant and function room were Mayor Kevin White, State Representative Royal Bolling, U.S. Senator Edward Brooks, and presidential candidates U.S. Senator Ted Kennedy and Governor Michael Dukakis, to name some of the most accomplished public officials.

The business expanded to include three U.S. Navy contracts through the SBA's 8(a) program – the Winter Harbor Naval Air Station in Maine, the Brunswick Naval Air Station in Maine, and the South Weymouth Naval Air Station in South Weymouth, Massachusetts. They also ran a cafeteria food station and catering service at the University of Massachusetts at Columbia Point and Park Square in Boston.

Things were going so well that John was asked to demonstrate how to cook a Chinese dish on television. He was doing a demonstration with one of his employees at a local school on how to cook a Chinese food dish when someone from WBZ-TV 4 saw him. John found it humorous that a black man would be asked to give a Chinese food cooking demonstration on local TV, but good fortune had many faces.

Business was very good, and people loved the food. In addition, they managed food and beverage services at the Fulton Mental Health Center on Harrison Avenue in Boston. Then they opened an additional restaurant on Warren Street in Roxbury. Their catering business expanded to include Harvard University, Emerson College on Beacon Street in Boston, and an NAACP Anniversary Banquet in Boston which hosted 2,500 guests.

CHAPTER 22

THE NEW SOUTH

""When work, commitment, and pleasure all become one and you reach that deep well where passion lives, nothing is impossible."

Nancy Coey

Slavery in the "Old South" made plantation owners rich. Of course, the Old South fought to preserve slavery. Cheap labor was good for business. Money distributed to state level influencers and a motion to declare slavery a birthright of southern gentlemen backed by the legal system was written into law as an "entitlement." Entitlement was defined as "the state or condition of being; a right to benefits specified especially by law or contract; …the belief that one [was] deserving of or entitled to certain privileges."[46]

Defended by the common folk on behalf of their employers and high-ranking business and political leaders, any white man was thereby included and may believe himself above any slave to enforce the laws that supported entitlement for the gentlemen writing law. Thus even a commoner believed he was entitled. When northerners who built their legal system on the rights of free men heard of this unfair advantage and disagreed, a war broke out over this presumptuous claim called entitlement.

Although Lincoln dispatched his Union Army to break southern entitlement to own slaves, he would turn over in his grave if he would have learned the incremental compromise that later occurred. A dozen years after defeating the Confederate Army, the United States enacted Jim Crow laws legalizing "separate but equal status for black Americans" from 1876 to 1965, segregating public schools, places, and transportation between whites and blacks. It was proved on a Navy ship during the Pacific War that segregation was only an interim solution if the nation were ever to be truly united as its name suggested.

Northern and southern cultures handled this division very differently. The North respected some rights of men of color, whereas the South indignantly refused. To enforce their right to a two-class system, the Old South resorted to common thuggery, extortion, and lies by men wearing hoods and using brutality in response to cries for equality. All the nooses, mobs, and unmarked graves made the need for civil rights more important. But that was not John's war.

Like many black men, he left Georgia for military service, specifically the Navy on June 27, 1943, with a plan: to escape Georgia's legacy and to change his future. On December 26, 1945, after returning from the Pacific War, John thought better of southern trends and left Georgia a second time without a legitimate plan except to fulfill his destiny. He chose the Northeast as the start of a new life and succeeded in establishing a solid foundation.

Marriage, children, and a strong, faith-based family afforded him the chance to achieve his dreams. Elements of a two-class system up north only existed in the form of ethnic separatism without lynchings, burnings, torture, or terror. The only form of segregation he experienced was not lethal, but social and economic. But his potential seemed far greater and rightfully so.

Despite his preference to leave the South, he always wanted his northern family to know his southern family roots. From 1954 until the early 1970s, John drove Mildred and the kids from Boston down to Georgia to see their relatives. They didn't drive every year, but they did many at least. In the early years, night driving in particular was the only affordable means to travel, but each time the journey offered great danger.

The family could not go anyplace to eat. Even Krystal's hamburger drive-through was dicey. They cooked on the road with a Coleman camping stove. John remembered once after filling up with gasoline he asked the gas station attendant for a toilet the kids could use. The attendant told him to go around back. Hopeful yet suspicious, John walked back to inspect the conditions of the facilities the man recommended. The toilet he was referring to was utterly disgusting – a blotchy, brownish color reeking of urine with no toilet seat and grass growing out of the hole in the bottom. Hanging over the seat a sign read "Colored." John returned to the front and told the attendant, "I'll just pay for the gas and no thanks!"

On another trip, two cars drove to Georgia. John had introduced his sister Helen to Joe Battle, who once got John a job when he was a kid. Joe and Helen had married years before, also moving to Boston afterward. They were following John south to see the family with their children. The idea of safety in numbers was not true when women and children were involved. They stopped at a diner in North Carolina and walked in the front door. Getting a cup of coffee required them going to the back. John never accepted those terms, opting instead to refuse the coffee and drive away.

Some guys sitting in a booth in the diner saw what happened and decided to make it their business to enforce Jim Crow's doctrine. So they came out and followed the two families in an old pickup truck. Being mindful of the threat, John pulled into a well-lighted public parking lot and watched the truck go by. With children to protect, journeying to the Old South left a great deal to be desired.

By 1974, new leadership moved into Atlanta city government and took over. City Hall suddenly looked very different. Initiatives designed to support blacks replaced the "good old boy network." History was being rewritten, making room at prosperity's table for black business owners to feast. The Old South did not like it but could do little to stop a major shift in power. Atlanta became the hub of "The New South." The product Atlanta had become was rebranded as "Hot-lanta, The Golden City." The "golden city" nickname was derived from the state capital building's newly-refinished gold dome symbolizing a new beginning.

Naturally the "golden city" had to have its "golden boy," who was Maynard Jackson. This revolutionary leader was a Democrat, the first black man to serve as mayor of a major southern city for not one term but two (from 1974 to 1982) and the grandson of civil rights leader John Wesley Dobbs. Jackson leveled the playing field for black business owners and dramatically increased contract awards to minority-owned businesses; those precious contracts had been previously the exclusive right of white business owners.

Maynard Jackson's contributions to Atlanta were virtually incalculable as an ambassador of good will and equality in a city in desperate need of both. Meeting the mayor was quite similar to meeting a king or an emperor. He was the visionary who changed Atlanta in the way that FDR shifted the direction of America. Both put a new brand, reputation, and agenda in place which promised to cure the long-standing ills of bias, favoritism, and separatism within their domains, regarding all phases: social, financial, and commercial. In a very progressive new world, Jackson wasn't just at the top of the food chain, he *was* the top of the food chain. He not only reinvented the chain of command, Jackson also completely rewrote supply chain resource management throughout the city of Atlanta.

In the winter of 1978, John flew from Boston to Atlanta for a visit with his mother and the family. Business was booming back in Boston, but he could not return due to a New England blizzard shutting down area airports for nearly a week. Meanwhile, Atlanta was sunny, warm, and open for business, as if Georgia's lost sons were being called home. On the way back to Boston John made up his mind. Riding home in the car with Mildred, he felt good about saying, "The weather in Georgia was nice! I'm tired of this terrible weather here. But the mind-blower is how much opportunity is down there. I want to go back to Atlanta."

In 1979 John made a number of contacts that some might describe as a baptism, starting with a man named Jim Brown. "Big Jim" was a tall, round fellow who would have been called a carpetbagger during the Civil War. To his credit, Jim's black book was up-to-date, and he peddled his connections. He liked John and decided to open some doors, introducing John to a city councilman. At this introduction John explained what he could bring to the table, and the city councilman recommended that he meet the Atlanta City Council President Marvin Arrington.

Mr. Arrington was a very influential man who could do many things to help John move up the ladder. As John's lawyer and contract advisor, Arrington introduced him to influential cronies, informing them that one of Atlanta's native sons wanted to return. A potent résumé certainly helped in trumpeting his northern successes. The ceremonious overtures that followed ushered John straight into the inner circle. Among the names with which Mr. Arrington initiated discussions on John's behalf was Shirley Franklin, the Commissioner of Cultural Affairs, also in charge of the Atlanta Civic Center. John met several other city council people and networked his way into position to bid on a big city contract.

The Atlanta Civic Center was a good place to start. It gave him access to the big players in City Hall, show and theater production heads, corporate contacts, major vendors, and the catering business, and enabled a smooth transition back after almost 35 years in Boston. John and Mildred parlayed a strong track record into the most qualified bidder for the food and beverage contract. Once they won the contract, they moved in and went to work in September 1980.

The Atlanta Civic Center became an overnight game-changer across the board. The critical venue offered immediate cash flow and job opportunities for about thirty Bostonian friends and family who relocated with or because of them. After all the hard work and determination, the Atlanta transition was the ultimate reward and just the tip of the iceberg. John reflected on his return to Atlanta, feeling a major emotional obstacle had been removed. He really was returning home. Unknowingly, this was what he had dreamed of. He found himself among the city's new and ambitious leaders. The food business gave him both a basis and a vehicle for measuring new heights of achievement.

John's arrival marked a turning point by his growing status among the new players at the table of prosperity. His job was to make a name for himself in his field of endeavor. As a key official food and beverage contractor for the city, his was the face of a major public relations port in a surging metropolis. Behind the scenes, he brought fresh energy and a can-do attitude that no job was too big or too small as an ambassador to major corporate clients seeking a bridge to Atlanta for any number of reasons. In many ways, the Civic Center served as a gateway to City of Atlanta diplomatic relations with in- and out-of-state businesses, inviting the many events coming through the dynamic convention city to use its facility.

The location consisted of an auditorium at one end and a large exhibit hall at the other, office space, ample parking, access directly to Piedmont Avenue and only a block from Peachtree Street, between downtown and Midtown. It was one of the few stages for big shows, concerts, and large conventions. John catered events for Coca Cola, Kraft Foods, Ford Motor Company, and the Salvation Army not to mention Governor Miller, Andrew Young, other dignitaries, musicians, and actors. The list seemed endless. The Civic Center was a cash-machine that created more revenue than some of their best Boston contracts combined, without the overhead. This was an opportunity too good to pass up.

The culture of Atlanta was new and exciting. Mildred and John decided to buy a house in up-and-coming southwest Atlanta before they left Boston. Their subdivision was built and previously occupied by Delta Air Lines pilots. The house they purchased was a California ranch adjacent to the airport along the burgeoning Camp Creek corridor. In a sunny delightful area, the house sat on a quiet, lush, tranquil street full of gorgeous mid-level homes lightly shaded by one-hundred-foot Georgia pines and finished with simple, attractive landscaping. Relocation also required phasing out their business operations in Boston and selling their South Shore suburban Boston residence in the fall of 1980.

′ As well as everything went in Atlanta, the sale of the restaurant and function room in Boston did not go as planned. As a gesture of good faith, John sold the business and property to a friend and ex-employee for $229,000. The man, unfortunately, could only qualify for a $180,000 loan. Because John wanted him to buy it, he gave the man a second mortgage for $49,000. After expenses, John and

Mildred took $19,000 to Atlanta with the second mortgage for $49,000 pending.

Their trusted friend defaulted on the debt from the beginning, telling increasingly more inflammatory lies to postpone the settlement. Commuting back and forth several times between Atlanta and Boston, John met with lawyers and attempted to settle the debt the man owed him. In 1987, John and Mildred finally sued their friend.

Evidently, with his reputation less than stellar, the man lost the business John had built and fell on hard times. Things got worse for him. His wife passed away, and he learned his drug-afflicted son was stealing from him. Before the lawyers could put a lien on his house, he moved his assets into his son's name, an ill-fated move that temporarily sheltered what little he had left. Closure to an empty promise came when the man closed the business. John never recovered a penny.

Good or bad, John believed that "what goes around comes around." John always tried to do right by people. Privately, he admitted to his mistakes with the best of intentions. Many times he believed God helped him get up after being knocked down, if only because of his commitment to meet his obligations with an open heart. Resigned to take the loss, John accepted that his old friend paid a far greater price than the debt he owed. The tragedies that descended upon John's friend could not be reconciled. John reluctantly had to move on.

John and Mildred's bustling food operation included the Civic Center and the Atlanta City Hall Cafeteria. They were also the City of Atlanta's exclusive caterer from 1980 until 1988. During that time John opened a restaurant called Captain John's Seafood in East Point, which doubled as a commissary, storage, food prep, and cooking facility for Civic Center events.

Diplomacy became the quintessential prerequisite to dealing with so many celebrity personalities and their representatives. Exposure to glamour had an unexpected price. Wonderful as it seemed to shake hands with some of the biggest names in business and entertainment, the hidden price John paid was catering to inflated egos. Mingling with City Hall incumbents and regulars allowed him to ingratiate himself to an expanding circle of power players and decision makers, a formula for success which required the same skill set that satisfied the most discriminating, even overly persnickety, tastes. Even though John's penchant for diplomacy stirred talks of a political career, he showed neither interest in politics nor a desire to play that game. Life was much easier feeding people, seeing their smiling faces, and counting the money.

After eight years at the Civic Center and when their contract with the city expired, they decided to downsize their operation. On June 15, 1989, The Rouse Company, a major national commercial contractor, transformed Underground Atlanta, a poorly-conceived enterprise that constantly lost money, into an indoor-outdoor mega retail shopping mall experience in the heart of downtown. John's company was among 140 tenants, which included well-known to little-known retail franchises, restaurants, mom and pops, novelty shops, and push carts.

From the get go, this deal should be wildly successful.

CHAPTER 23

TESTED

"Infinitely more important than sharing one's material wealth is sharing the wealth of ourselves—our time and energy, our passion and commitment, and, above all, our love."
William E. Simon

John's son David came up with the catchy business name Southern Vittles and, as they say, John was off to the races. Crowning him an immediate favorite overlooked the anatomy of perfect supply and demand. Along with the competitive advantage of being open for business while the project was under construction, John had an exclusive clientele for months before the facility was open to the public. Even sweeter was the "hand-in-glove" fit that combined a southern menu with a southern construction crew daily for breakfast, lunch, and dinner over that period. Before long, the staffers began calling the regulars by name. Every day the laughter of happy customers emanated from the service area as if friends dropped by to say hello.

Following the grand opening of the Underground, John saw his co-vendors almost every day as well. He had become a popular figure around the facility, not just because his food was good or because he had a head start, but because John had connections with the partners, City Hall, and The Rouse Company. Other vendors took note and decided John should become their spokesperson and represent vendor grievances to the partners.

Unexpectedly, a very bright future turned very dark. Behind closed doors, John's success bred contempt from a criminal source. The Rouse Company assigned John to a silent investor-partner who played professional basketball in Europe. The ballplayer's ambitious sister and business consultant supposedly safeguarded his interests in his absence. Seeing the traffic at the Southern Vittles operation, they became enthralled with the notion that they could steal the business. The two conjured up a scheme complete with bogus legal paperwork, forged John's signature, assumed control of his business, and had John escorted from his own restaurant.

Forged documents implied that John signed over rights to his part. Business checking accounts were instantly cleaned out, indicating the thieves had planned nothing other than a robbery mired in legal paperwork that would take months to sort out. While the culprits escaped, the fact that they thought they could evade the long arm of federal justice was beyond anyone's imagination. At any rate, their foolish plot prevailed while The Rouse Company conducted its own preliminary investigation. Were it not for some peculiar instinct to take one of the bank deposits with him the morning of the Southern Vittles lock-out, John wouldn't have had any money at all.

By the time The Rouse Company made sense of the scam, the fraudulent paperwork, and misdirection, the thieves had left town with a paper trail pointing toward their escape route. John and his pro ball player-partner lost everything invested in the Southern Vittles venture. All other assets were frozen. The thieves remained at large, running from the FBI over a few thousand dollars. When the truth emerged, John and Mildred were left with no recourse.

If John had needed to learn some profound life lesson from the recent events, he did not have a clue what that might possibly be. In times like these, nearly anyone would immediately flash back to similar situations reminding them when they swore they'd never do it again. Giving second chances had taught John a harsh and painful lesson, only to find himself disappointed again. John revisited his first business closure at the hands of his old friend Sam Walker in 1950, followed by losing $49,000 to another old friend in the 1987 sale of J&S Caterers. John had had enough of partnerships.

John and Mildred were sick, grief stricken beyond words. They had just sold their Atlanta home and closed on another down in Boca Raton, Florida, as the first step in their retirement strategy. In the transition, only a limited reserve of funds remained, amounting virtually to pocket money. Suddenly John and Mildred's plan crumbled from a promising downsize to grand larceny with no immediate legal remedy. John felt despondent, angry, frustrated, and on the verge of a nervous breakdown. All his success came down to this. To rebuild again would be enormous pressure.

John tried to console Mildred, who was so upset John feared for her wellbeing. She took a few days to adapt to the crisis and began to pack up their brand-new house in Boca while John drove the streets of Atlanta searching for a solution.

Devoid of answers, John looked back at how both Dad and his mother had taught him to believe in God and there was a plan. John could not see the Lord's plan in the bad things that happened. Nevertheless, he never let that stop him before. This was different. He had done the right things in life, or so he thought. What did this mean? What could he do? Is Mildred okay? How would he solve this? Who could he turn to when everyone counted on him? John's heart was broken, and he needed to be strong. He needed to figure this out. John needed to think.

He went to the cemetery to visit his mother's grave. She had died in February of 1980, the year John relocated his family and friends to Atlanta. Throughout her life, Rhunette gave John hope and encouraged him to press on no matter what. All his visits to Atlanta over the years began with seeing her, and it broke his heart to see her buried. Even from the grave, her presence comforted him in his darkest moments.

He had no choice but to move on; he knew that. But where? Standing in front of his mother's headstone, John asked God for direction. He learned, when things got really bad, to ask for help. Religion came in the form of periodic visits to one or two churches in the area, but he could not recite the Bible chapter and verse. That was Dad's thing. But John certainly believed in God during the war. Men could die instantly, any moment, any day. During the war, they all believed. John had never said it before, but he never missed a chaplain service while on the ship. He apologized to God for not always making it to church every Sunday after the war, reminding Him that he did everything in his life with good intentions.

The next day John had meetings downtown. Still no trace of the criminals. Lost in thought, he drove the car south on the back roads. Numb and still recovering from shock, all he wanted to do was detach himself from everything. He wasn't really going anywhere in particular. If he could quiet his mind for ten minutes, he would be happy.

John kept driving to calm himself. Without warning, he heard his mother speak to him. He could hear her voice as clear as day. She told him, "I want you to get on Jonesboro Road and just keep driving. You're going to find a business there."

John was speechless. His first reaction was to pull over, but he reasoned he could manage. Pausing to make sense of it, he acknowledged he had heard her voice. He had not gone crazy or anything. Whatever was on Jonesboro Road, he needed to find it.

Hearing her voice, it was almost like she was sitting in the passenger's seat right there, referring to the tucked fabric seat on the other side of his armrest. Driving along, he replayed her voice over and over in his head. John did as she said. He got on Jonesboro Road and just kept going. Normally when navigating this route, he would automatically take a right turn onto the ramp to Interstate 285 and drive to his daughter Patricia's house. But this time he crossed I-285 and kept driving along Jonesboro

Road. About a mile south of the interstate, near the top of the hill, John saw a sign that read "Building for Lease."

The building was once a small one-story steakhouse with parking on three sides and an eighty-foot-high dirt wall directly behind the building. John thought that it "looked like a good building to start my restaurant and catering business." As amazed as he was encouraged, he called Mildred first to tell her what was happening. They both needed some good news. He did not know how he was going to do anything about this place yet but nothing, NOTHING was going to stop him.

Then John called the phone number on the sign. The owner of the building met him in the parking lot in front of the building. The owner got out of the car, seemed a bit cool toward John, and acted as though he did not want to lease the building to him. When John asked him what the problem was, he replied that the last two people he had rented the building to were black men and one gave him a bum check. When he tried to get the tenant to move out of the building, the tenant set off the fire protection system just for spite. White foam covered the entire interior of the building and left a mess. Because this was still fresh in his mind, the owner said he had a problem dealing with black people.

This location was John's solution. Before anger engulfed him, John caught himself, thought very clearly about the situation, and did not want to appear desperate even though he was. He contemplated what the Navy taught him about life and death. Japanese kamikazes killed Americans, not blacks or whites. For some reason that calmed him down. Having tamed his initial response long enough to speak clearly, John told him, "I'm not a black person. I am an individual. You cannot classify me with whoever was in this building before. I refuse to accept that." The man looked at John and said, "Let me think about it."

John called him back two days later and talked to him. The owner of the property made arrangements to meet him at the building again. Standing in front of the tired steakhouse, the man said to John, "You know, I like what you said to me that you didn't want to be classified as a black person but as an individual. That made me stop and think. I'm going to rent the building to you after all."

Once again, with his half-brother Bob, John renovated a building. This one was smaller than the old furniture store on Blue Hill Avenue in Dorchester, but a lot of work had to be done anyway. Actually, everything had to be done, and the Clayton County Board checklist was extensive. They started with infrastructural components like the roof, flooring, windows, and bathrooms. Once the building was waterproof, they could focus on the plumbing, electrical, grease traps, ventilation, fire system, and security system. When the building passed a fire inspection, they allowed installation of refrigeration, Fryolators, ovens, steam tables, and soft drink pumps. Cosmetic concerns, which included storage, ceiling fans, counters, tables and chairs, were last.

Yes, the punch list turned out to be exhausting, but it was the price of opening a restaurant. For most other people, the work would have been too much to do for two people. John and Bob had not only been down this road before but they also collaborated well as a team and addressed the logistics to satisfy county inspectors. They finished and got the doors open on October 27, 1988.

John's new landlord told him, "I'm going to come in here on opening day and I'm going to see what you could do." On opening day, John gave him a call and he came over for lunch. He walked in, looked around, and liked what he saw. John did find it odd but took it as a good omen that he kept coming back to the restaurant to eat. If the landlord was concerned or curious about how John was doing, he needed only stop by, but it was clear he also liked the food. Maybe John was surprised his landlord supported the business or took an interest in his success. As a matter of fact, the property owner invited John to his house for dinner with him and his daughter. They became friends.

Days went by without much traffic. John sat in his new restaurant with no customers. He could not afford employees. Again John prayed to God and asked for help.

Later that day a stranger walked in the door. The man was a local minister who noticed a new business and stopped by for lunch to try it out. The lone white visitor liked the food so much he told John he would recommend the restaurant to his congregation.

Word of mouth was the only kind of advertising John could afford because it was free. The big-hearted pastor supported the struggling proprietor whose home cooking so impressed him that he looked forward to his next visit. He also kept his promise and spread the word. John's business flourished from then on. He provided free food to the minister's church many times in thanks, ever grateful for the man's kindness.

Years later, when his landlord became deathly ill, the dying man told his daughter, "I want to sell the building to John." He wanted it all made official and written in his will that his daughter would sell John the building for a specific price, no more no less. The man's daughter told John. They wrote it up, and John and Mildred happily paid his purchase price for the building that was now John's Fine Food at 4161 Jonesboro Road in Forest Park.

They had since expanded with storage, large freezer, outdoor barbeque grille, added advertising in either direction of their exit along I-285, and many upgrades too numerous to mention. Property improvements combined would never take away John's "hole-in-the-wall" charm. They had been at this location since late October 1988 serving the area's white-collar and blue-collar workers, from executives to truck drivers, church folks to residents, all nationalities, in state, out of state, from over a 100-mile radius in all directions. John was proud of what he had been able to accomplish, what his staff had been able to do, what John and Mildred had built yet again.

John believed they were known and respected by patrons and competitors because no matter what happened to the economy, local businesses, plant closings, customer migrations to new competitors, they thrived from plain, old-fashioned word of mouth, one customer at a time since their first customer, John's original landlord. Whatever his lesson plan entailed, John stood on strong footing, feeling strongly that God had been good to them now for 24 years and counting...

CHAPTER 24

WORLD TRAVELER

*"The wise man belongs to all countries,
for the home of a great soul is the whole world."*
Democritus

Growing up in the Great Depression, John did not have hobbies. He did not think many people could afford to have hobbies back then. There wasn't extra money for luxuries when his daily treasure hunt might include his next meal. In the Navy, though, John developed a few hobbies in his spare time.

Waiting - it should have been written into the job description for military personnel. There wasn't much to do when not performing one's duties, exactly the reason why John favored work. Time passed much easier when working. He never thought much about it at the time, but he was shown at a very young age the benefits of work. He'd admit he did not always work hard, but he loved to work. He loved putting his mind to things, creating things, doing things that mattered to him. Seventy-five years later he still thought that way.

As he looked back, John learned three "hobbies" he still loved today: cooking, playing cards, and traveling. He turned 85 years young on July 5, 2011. From an objective perspective, John's 85 stood up against another man's 65 or 70 for zest and enthusiasm. Over the years, many had called him very lucky for being able to call cooking his favorite hobby as well as his career. The term "work" was irrelevant because it was basically effortless. In the early years, John had to find ways to get kitchen duty, especially in the Navy. No one gave him anything he did not work for, and yet cooking was and remained at the top of his list.

Sometimes he cooked when he traveled, though most times when he was not cooking, he was either traveling or playing cards. Playing cards relaxed him yet kept his mind active. Of course, he loved to win and he had the discipline to walk away before giving back his winnings, a special gift separating him from less disciplined players. He could go out to play cards in the same way some people went to the movies or attended a ball game. On the one hand, playing cards was pure entertainment; on the other hand, he liked figuring out what other players had in their hands by the way they played. Style, aptitude, and experience distinguished the winners from the losers and good players from bad. Observers could compare his gambling approach to how a good chess player formulated counter strategies against his opponent.

Traveling was very different. The day John enlisted in the service sparked an insatiable wanderlust to see the world. Call it the never-ending adventure to open a new and exciting chapter in a book whenever he packed his bags. That desire grew even stronger following the Pacific War. Creating a new life with a family and a career in Boston took all of John's resources until he could continue. More than two decades later, he began to travel again.

When Dad, John's father-in-law, came to visit he would joke, "I've traveled all around the world... reading National Geographic!" The family used to chuckle about that. The irony was that Dad had set the tone years before, living out of a suitcase as a traveling singer, song writer, and evangelist.

The couple began traveling in the early 1970s. Packing their bags for the next adventure kept John and Mildred going for forty-something years. Cruising became their chosen reward for the hard work they put in as entrepreneurs. To balance their grueling responsibilities as food service business owners, they required an effective, repeatable release. The only healthy way they could get away from the phone calls, clients, vendors, banks, bills, and employees was to shift strategic breaks to a regular and mandatory diet of escapism.

Residing in suburban South Shore Boston, John worked together with Mildred's brothers Rolie and Ernie to form a club called "The King's Men." They came up with a clever system that subsidized some part of their cruises. Mildred and John had barbeque parties and sold food on Pond Street, then continued when they moved around the corner to Weymouth Street. The Weymouth Street house was a superior layout. Their new home was much bigger with a more substantial yard, a big circular driveway for parking, a barbeque pit made of brick in the yard, and a big deck for entertaining, music, the works.

The group plan was to start with a bunch of people together, get them excited about a trip, set an itinerary, and encourage people to commit to taking the trip. Sometimes, as they got better at it, they would party at the restaurant function room and have meetings to get people signed up. This was a much more elaborate promotion, similar to a catered fundraiser. The deal with the travel agency was the bigger the group, the better the discount. Having parties was cheaper than paying for cruises. Their best year saw 67 people take one trip. Included were two chartered busses to New York where they boarded the ship.

Mildred got out her sewing machine and made the most exotic dresses. The same way women's hats became the highlight of the Kentucky Derby, colorful cruise attire made every trip unique and special. John and Mildred alone packed six or seven pieces of luggage full of outfits. With Mildred's mother Ma babysitting the kids during trips, the vibrant couple had it all figured out. They built a reputation for great trips and they had a ball.

Trekking was such a joyful experience to John that the latter years saw a dramatic increase in travel, often collaborating with Mildred to plan two trips concurrently. They benefitted from multi-port cruises and complex itineraries which included several cities, planes, ships, buses, and tours. On any given trip, they might have found information about another trip and a few timeshares that sounded exciting enough to book or buy. Anticipation recharged their batteries because they both loved it that much.

John's propensity for staying busy had been well documented. He only slowed down when he was too tired to keep going, and that was temporary. Friends and family speculated that work kept him young inside, yet his true fountain of youth called for getting on a plane, taking a cruise, or staying in a hotel somewhere in the world. Neither an insomniac nor a hyperactive person, John regarded rest as a last resort.

After they moved to Georgia, the formula changed some. Mildred and John did not have a cruise club following anymore, resulting in them packing up and going on their own. Business was good without the need for promotion. They just announced trips and asked how many friends wanted to go.

In the early years, their favorite travel companions were Jimmy and Norma, Harry and Betty, and Cass and Ophelia. In time, Harry's health failed him, ending their travel plans. Then Cass's health deteriorated. Pretty soon it was just Jimmy and Norma who became John and Mildred's constant companions on the road, earning the near-inseparable couples the well deserved title "road warriors." The joke among family and friends was, "Where were the road warriors headed now?"

They logged so many trips together that Jimmy and Norma became honorary members of the family, attending graduations, buying adjoining timeshares, and taking road trips. They eventually retired in Georgia as well, making their travels together more convenient and consistent. The result was plain and simple.

Occasionally Mildred and John's children accompanied them on family holidays or "just because" trips. Then the family would vote to broaden the party, inviting extended family to come along. But mostly it was Jimmy, Norma, Mildred, and John. These serial travel junkies booked typically six trips annually for over 20 years. Unscheduled trips served as special occasions.

The most memorable sight John could ever recall was of picturesque Mt. Fujiyama as the sun set over the peak in a brilliant burst of orange. The brutal Pacific War against the majestic landscape had left a lifelong impression. Modern times saw Mount Fuji as a major Japanese attraction, standing 12,389 feet high and resting near central Honshu just west of Tokyo.

Visiting Okinawa brought back sobering memories of the legions of Marines who gave their lives to secure those beachheads. During the war, John never dreamed that he would someday visit Okinawa again. He and Mildred went to Okinawa where they were wined, dined, and treated royally. It was a booming metropolis in the modern era, burgeoning with population and skyscrapers. That was one heck of a cruise. With so much to appreciate, the world travelers had much more to see.

During their travels, John and Mildred took a cruise from Florida across the Caribbean Sea down to South America, Venezuela, and Panama. They visited all the islands, including Puerto Rico, Jamaica, and Barbados. A series of cruises toured throughout Europe – Spain, France, Germany, Italy, Sweden, and England. During a Pacific travel tour, they enjoyed Seattle and Vancouver as launch cities but surprisingly enjoyed the Alaskan coast and South Africa most. The South Africa trip featured stays in Johannesburg and Cape Town while sailing up the coast to Namibia and taking a sleep-safari on a big game preserve.

They passed the equator a couple of times. India, Vietnam, Singapore, Thailand, Hong Kong, and China were truly amazing, but the Vatican and Egypt stood out as some of the world's most sacred historical sites. At the Vatican, Mildred and John caught a rare glimpse of the Pope, got to visit St. Peter's Basilica, and marveled at Michelangelo's ceiling masterpiece. As they craned their necks staring at the ceiling, they could only wonder how in the world such a timeless work of art could have been accomplished.

On a cruise through the Suez Canal, tour management warned them of the distinct possibility that the ship might be attacked. Military personnel stood armed with rifles drawn and lined up along the shore of the Suez Canal in

John Seagraves still enjoying life at sea with wife Mildred; one of more than 100 cruises over four decades."

addition to troops positioned in the ports. While it was a frightening experience, they wanted to see the state of the world as it actually was, not as a commercialized safe zone.

Egypt was very exciting, also dangerous. Their cruise ship sailed up the Nile River under warnings from the Egyptian government that pirates had been attacking tour buses. The Egyptian authorities tried to keep it quiet, but they eventually had to tell everyone, culminating in a tour announcement. Passengers could either choose to dock and take buses to Cairo or continue up the river. Every passenger, including many seniors, spoke openly that they had come a long way to see the pyramids and monuments. Maybe there was a fine line between bravery and stupidity, but all of them were willing to take their chances to see the real world. They simply refused to be afraid.

A great many American and European tourists loaded up in buses. Armed guards positioned themselves on each bus. Soldiers again stood with rifles all the way from portside to the monuments. Nerve-wracked tourists sat on edge as the buses headed into the city. The visitors went into the city plaza to shop and really enjoyed the people of Egypt. Regardless of the risks, not a single vacationer missed a tour or a port. It turned out to be a remarkable cruise, one they would never forget.

They acquired a few timeshares in cities they had frequented for well over 30 years, Old San Juan, Puerto Rico for example. They loved it there. Other timeshares took them to Las Vegas, Honolulu, and Lake Tahoe, and when they got tired of them, they put the trip back into the bank and selected another trip. At their peak, they were packing their bags six or eight times a year.

A recent sojourn entailed an Asian cruise following a tsunami catastrophe that devastated parts of Japan and several nuclear plants. This was a long-awaited itinerary originally delayed by John's triple bypass heart surgery a few years prior and further postponed by Mildred's near-identical procedure the following year almost to the day. The flight took them to Singapore where they embarked on an ocean liner to Asian points in Ko Samui and Bangkok (Laem Chabang), Thailand; Ho Chi Minh City (Phu My) and Nha Trang, Vietnam; Hong Kong, and Shanghai, China; Nagasaki, Japan; and lastly Dalian and Beijing (Tianjin), China. The return flight had to be rerouted away from Nagasaki to South Korea for the sake of avoiding the toxic air. Asian terrain and urban culture were strange and beautiful, inviting and unforgiving, ancient and, in some cases, brand new. John and Mildred summarized the amazing trip as "worth every penny."

The seasoned couple continued to enjoy seeing the world. Firsthand experience had no equal. In John's opinion, an airline ticket was a small price to pay to see the wonders of a planet. At his age, he was considered by his friends to be living the dream, hopping about to and from mysterious ports of call while his family found him *the* most impossible man to shop for because he already had everything. No doubt for every life there was a unique lesson. When people adjusted their sights enough, they would recognize theirs. For him who had the misfortune to be born poor, he needed only turn to the world to find wealth and the richest of pleasures.

CHAPTER 25

REUNION

*"No man can tell whether he is rich or poor by turning to his ledger.
It is the heart that makes a man rich. He is rich according to what he is,
not according to what he has."*

Henry Ward Beecher

A short time before the "2009 *USS NORTH CAROLINA* Former Crew Member Reunion," John had just returned home to Phoenix from a business trip. As he sat at the kitchen table opening mail, he noticed a small yellow package addressed to him. He picked it up and he proceeded to open the package with no idea what could be enclosed. Pulling out some bubble wrapped items and a receipt, he read the receipt with the curiosity and anticipation of opening the card before the gift.

The tape refused to separate from the bubble wrap, causing him to cut the cumbersome layer off. As he unrolled the wrapping, he recognized something he had not seen since he gave his originals to his son when he was a boy, perhaps four decades before. The package contained his original decorations for honorable time served in the Navy. His children thought it was a good idea to get new ones made. David located the website, completed the paperwork, and submitted a reproduction request. Weeks later produced a most unexpected surprise. So many emotions rushed into his chest that John's hands began to shake.

Words could not express the depth of his emotions recalling the days when the military required a 16 year old boy to become a man. Touching the medals helped him put his finger on moments that changed him forever. Many good and bad things happened. John came up in a time in American history when many too young grew up too fast because the world was a dangerous place, both for black Americans during the Jim Crow era and anyone who participated in World War II. John had been to the *USS NORTH CAROLINA* before, but not to a reunion.

He had not thought much about going before. Suddenly, it became important for him to go see the ship and the men who were a part of it. John admitted he did not know what to expect, and it made him apprehensive.

Come May 2009, Mildred and John went aboard the battleship for the reunion. While it was the first time he had been back in many years, John was surprised that many people he encountered knew about his ship experience. They knew about the 20mm gun photo and they wanted to know more about how the black sailors lived on the ship.

John told them how he and 65 other black sailors lived and how they were treated by 2,600 white sailors. He mentioned how he refused to shine shoes or perform standard duties required of steward's mates and mess attendants. He reflected how some people were cut out to make beds, shine shoes, or iron clothing. He had nothing against the many black men who did what they were told to survive a hostile environment, but coming from nothing, he had nothing to lose. Those actions were not for him, and he forced the Navy to reconsider the utilization of some of its black personnel.

From the first time he entered the King and Prince Hotel on St. Simons Island until he disembarked the *NORTH CAROLINA* with an honorable discharge, he refused to do largely what steward's training expected him to do. John added that he joined the Navy to be a sailor, not a flunky. He was proud of his defiance in expecting more of the Navy. He had never been afraid of hard work. He just knew there were more important things he could do to serve his country, and that was what he did. Credit the Navy, particularly Executive Officer Stryker, for allowing John to find his natural gifts in the Navy as a cook and a gunner.

Museum Services Director Kim Robinson Sincox and Curator of Collections Mary Ames Booker, the principal organizers for the *USS NORTH CAROLINA* Battleship Museum events, wanted him to take a group picture with the remaining crew members. The harsh memories of treatment during the 1940s returned with a vengeance. Every ex-sailor participated in the social norms of racial bias in those days. At first John quietly replied, "They did not want to sit with me on the ship. Why would I want to have a picture taken with them now?" His heart pained him from the crystal-clear recollections of a youngster on a Navy battleship during the Jim Crow era. The buffet-style reunion dinner was served as the others mingled freely. John was not free among them. He could not sit with the others or pretend as though everything was forgotten. After all, the last time he saw them collectively, few if any of them had a kind word for him.

John sat with his wife and daughter at a table by themselves. The only one who approached and asked to join them was an Italian man, also a member of the crew. He had been there back then. He had witnessed the cruelty directed at black sailors. He did not like it then and he had no respect for it now. Seeing the other crew members at the dinner keeping up their old separatist ways infuriated him. He said he would never attend another reunion. The incensed crew member said candidly that he would not tolerate the hypocrisy. Fully in agreement with him, John and his family opted to make the best of it.

Confronted with his emotions, John wanted to withdraw with his family as his old wounds refused to heal. The suffering could not be directed at anyone in particular, which made him feel even more unsettled. Yet the overwhelming generosity of Kim and Mary Ames soothed an aching heart with their genuine interest, attention, and care. John's bitterness softened as the ship's staff did everything they could to make him and his family comfortable. The staff had a number of activities planned to keep the crew members and their families busy throughout their visit. While mingling with a few members of the crew, John found the men and their families open and friendly. In the meantime, staff members asked him to do interviews and photo sessions. They described to him another former *USS NORTH CAROLINA* crew member who served on board before John, a fellow black sailor named

Roosevelt Flenard. He apparently attended several reunions and wrote a book about his time on the ship. Kim and Mary Ames encouraged John to do the same and tell his story if he was interested.

John remembered calling his son to tell him about the festivities and interest in his experiences on board. When the reunion ended and everyone headed home, John began to think even more about his recollections, good and bad. In the end, the reunion was a rewarding undertaking. Kim's and Mary Ames's inquiries encouraged him to record his thoughts in a book, everything before, during, and after his time in the Navy. John considered himself very fortunate to still have his health, mobility, and a life in which the Navy taught him so many things about how to live his life to the fullest, with pride, dignity, and purpose.

After the reunion, John returned to his Atlanta restaurant to get a few things done and head back to his Phoenix residence. More than a week had passed at the restaurant as John rode to the airport following a routine he had repeated many times before. He had not yet considered who to approach about writing his story as he walked through Atlanta's Hartsfield-Jackson International airport en route to his concourse.

A Delta Air Lines pilot stopped him as he walked through Concourse A. John happened to be wearing his *USS NORTH CAROLINA* hat. The pilot and several of the pilot's colleagues circled John, wondering what war he was in. When John told them he was in the Pacific War during World War II, they found his admission to be unlikely. In fact, they ribbed him about it, implying he was too young to be a World War II veteran. Flattered and amused, he dug out his driver's license to confirm that he was 83 years old at that time.

When they realized he was telling them truth, they insisted that he join them in the Delta Air Lines Military Lounge for a holiday supper where several young Marines were eating their last stateside meal before deploying in Afghanistan. The lounge contained servicemen from the Korean War, Vietnam War, and Iraq War, but nobody from World War II. Several Marines who learned of his background wanted to take a picture with him and asked him about the war in the Pacific with sincere interest. The soldiers congratulated him for his service to their country, as a survivor and hero of that historic war. Without warning, these young men saluted him. A shock of emotion fell over him as John smiled with a profound sense of appreciation. Pride welled up inside of him in that moment, validating the life he'd lived.

As the time neared for him to depart for his gate John began to worry that he would not make the plane on time. Unbeknownst to everyone involved, he had exceeded his window of opportunity to make his scheduled flight. Without hesitation, the pilots summoned a cart, called ahead to the gate to notify the attendant that John was coming, and insisted that the flight crew hold the plane. Moreover, a pilot marshaled a cart and two men drove him through the airport to make certain he got on that flight.

John was both impressed by their concern and grateful for their respect. The men waited to see him off as he prepared to board the plane. He turned and, with a single hand raised to wave, he extended his heartfelt thanks to them for everything. Then he walked down the ramp to the plane. Sitting down in his seat, John reflected on an extraordinary happening. There were times when he had been humbled by something, but never, never before had he known a moment like this one. An entire life honored in a single act. As the airplane doors closed, tears well up in his eyes.

This had not been an easy life. He was not a fighter, but he fought for what he thought was right. There had been times through the years when he had been hard-headed or hot tempered. Even to this day John ran his business firmly. Quality control and service meant everything to his restaurant's reputation, and he protected that vehemently. He believed he treated his staff fairly, albeit with military discipline and ill temperament at times.

He may not have been an expert at a lot of things, yet he did his best work cooking food and firing a weapon, and he certainly learned to appreciate some of the finer things life had to offer. John had made mistakes, missed opportunities, and reacted badly in many situations during his days. He felt the awkwardness of a misdirected tirade or making a mistake. Some of his words he knew he could never take back.

His biggest regret was wishing he could have prevented some of the losses he and his wife sustained over sixty-plus years of marriage. Things happened. But as God was his witness, he knew he played the hand he was dealt the best way he knew how.

Japan awakened the United States of America when they attacked the U.S. Naval fleet in Pearl Harbor. For a short time, at least, they unified a divided nation into the America that won the Pacific War and ultimately the European theater. No matter which side of the color line an enlisted person was on, each man or woman was an

American committed to defeating imperialism and the tyranny of oppression.

As an individual, John was part of a history that included Graham Jackson's recruitment of many black sailors into the Navy. He broke through a color barrier the Navy constructed to prevent black sailors from being gunners on their ship, and he excelled. The officers liked his cooking enough to ask him to re-enlist even after the war was over. He was extremely proud to have served on the most decorated, influential battleship in Navy history. And after more than 65 years as a veteran of the United States Navy, John was finally acknowledged for being a Navy man.

John Seagraves learned to live his life the way the Navy taught him to live during wartime, with duty and pride. He believed he had lived his life honorably with courage and dignity. John did what he needed to do. Like the sailors before him and those that followed, he believed he learned the right way, the wrong way, and the Navy way.

To this day, John's favorite vacation itineraries include a cruise ship, and his most vivid adventures begin with the quality of the food.

Black or white, rich or poor, red-blooded or blue-blooded, what summarizes the man with a fourth grade education, who has worked every year since age ten, who at eighty-five years still owns and runs his beloved restaurant, who has seen most of the world, who has everything he could ask for? One word: courage.

The life of this uncommon hero most aptly describes how poverty inexplicably made him rich.

Epilogue

An inherent design of all creation puts man and woman together to complement each other. Should a person know himself well enough, he might recognize the right partner when she comes along.

It was John's good fortune the day he first saw Mildred Johnson at The Shaw House in 1947. She came from a close family and served as a positive influence, exactly the kind of woman his Aunt Fannie approved of. Fortunately for John, Mildred liked the idea of dating a Navy man. As the years went on, she even helped him balance his fiery temperament in support of his entrepreneurial spirit. The perfect match implies that they are equally resilient to the challenges they would face.

John was a willful child who turned poverty into passion, creating a very successful food and beverage business. His future wife grew from a sickly child once impacted by tuberculosis into a strong, able and majestic woman with a quick, analytical mind, and solid business accounting credentials. Between the two of them, they enjoyed the good life together.

This couple confronted the cruel teachings of life experience, fraught with many twists and turns, seeing numerous highs and lows. Despite the difficult times, they chose to respond with as much enthusiasm for the future as they could muster. For them, and those who counted on them, there was always hope. Mildred could count on John to do what he had to do, and he could count on her to back him up.

The war gave John the ideal theater to demonstrate his desire and capacity to excel under fire. It takes a rare individual to see a challenge as an opportunity. His untimely appendectomy sent him from cleaning theaters indirectly to his first restaurant. When that did not work out, he drove a cab until he could cook again, knowing with perfect clarity that cooking was the goal. When Recording & Statistical changed its business model and significantly reduced its staff, he seized his chance to open J&S Caterers and Function Room. John's vision for his own life played out quite well as Boston served its purpose, giving way to a timely return home to Atlanta.

Atlanta's City Hall contracts, including the Atlanta Civic Center and the Atlanta Underground, became stepping stones toward his final professional legacy, a refurbished, modest little steakhouse in Forest Park, Georgia.

To watch the progression of a life from a bird's eye view is to objectively catch a glimpse of the equation $E + R = O$ in action. John, and eventually Mildred's experiences, generated responses to bravely step forward into their future as a family, which yielded financial windfalls and joyous outcomes for decades. John's determination propelled his tireless force of will to succeed, while his passion for cooking kept him on a laser focused course. His plan remained simple and he stayed with it, modifying his approach to suit the obstacle. One might say he learned to work with change, staying in flow with events as they occurred, learning to master outcomes.

The money he earned taught him that riches come and go. Therefore, the love of the activity which created the money became a continuous source of abundance and pleasure for over 63 years of marriage, and nearly that many years as a restaurateur. Money alone was never the goal; the quality of life he could afford from cooking, traveling, enjoying friends and family – that was the goal. In turn, Mildred and John's marriage has resembled something closer to art or fine wine. They got better with age.

To this day, John still believes marrying Mildred Johnson in 1949 was the best decision he ever made.

Afterword

In the final analysis, poverty can teach a man a simple thing about attaining riches. Nothing in the world can replace courage, passion, and determination. No matter where you begin, the most successful potential outcome requires your commitment and love for an activity.

Like it or not, life is one big classroom full of trial and error. We are constantly tested to determine whether or not we can see our challenges as opportunities. If we can't, we remain stuck, likely to have the same challenges repeat themselves over and over again because we have not learned our lessons. As with schooling, we suffer punishments for not overcoming our limitations in favor of embracing our far greater capacity.

Mediocrity is the most painful punishment of all. It tells us we did not discover a passion worthy of terminal devotion, and if we did, we did not translate that devoted activity into a sellable commodity. Should that product or service make thousands of people happy, just watch as transactional commerce converts your activities into riches, as lead into gold.

For many people, success eludes them because they chase money. Aside from the obvious value of money in exchange for a higher quality of life, the meaning of money is often misunderstood. Actions speak volumes about the character of the person wielding its value. In the same vein, money is neither good nor bad; it is, instead, what a man does with his money that makes it either. Conspicuous consumption is an opportunity for indulgence, more self-serving than magnanimous. Yet the same enthusiasm for spending can also bring many rewards in contribution with one's time, money, interest, effort, and focus.

The world we live in has been dominated by societal dictates creating visions for us of what we should want, what others aspire to, what we should all believe is good, better, and best. But the most successful people in the world leave that to others while they pioneer new roads to the future. They continuously show ordinary people what they do and how they do things in clear messages that are frequently overlooked. Often a less successful person is looking to the left when he should be looking to the right, or up when he would be better served looking down.

The truth is, poverty made John Seagraves rich because he wanted success more than anything and he consistently took actions in alignment with his passion to be the best that he could possibly be at the one thing he obsesses over to this day. He approached his life with honorable rebellion, saying no to anyone who had a plan for him when he had plans for himself. John never stopped learning. He chose cooking as his passage to wealth because it brings him joy beyond anything else in life. What activity gives you that level of pleasure? If you enjoyed something that much, wouldn't it become easy to master?

Have a plan and adapt, refine, change if necessary. But start with something. We get better over time at adjusting to the changes in life. Walls go up and we tell ourselves we can't. Reject that thinking. Unless your desires are life-threatening or harmful to others, the challenges you face are a test to see what you can and will do to live your dreams. The lazy one, the weaker one, the less-determined one will not succeed. Anything worth having *is* worth working for. Making boatloads of other people happy is your ticket to riches. Doing it with passion and joy is true abundance. The inevitable result is mental, emotional, spiritual, physical, and enormous financial wealth.

Follow the details of John's life in further detail, as an eBook outlines the many gold nuggets leading to his profound learning experiences and the critical decisions that anyone could be confronted with at some point in their lives. Use the information as a motivational reference guide, observe the circumstances impartially while seeing similarities in your own life, enjoy the quotes and messages that come to us every day if we only take the time to see and hear them. Above all, make your life a masterpiece and place a high value, not on the quantity, but on the quality of time and money spent. Embrace change as inevitable and enter life in flow. Either we are growing, or we are dying. We never stay the same.

What happens is not always within your control. How you respond to it, however, determines your outcome, and ultimately, the manifestation of riches in your life.

ABOUT THE AUTHOR

DAVID SEAGRAVES is a small business owner and retired financial planner who became an author when the opportunity presented itself. A third-generation entrepreneur, he has dedicated himself to professional writing, self-publishing, Internet marketing, and publicity. David avidly enjoys movies, reading, travel, and coastal living with his wife Tanja and their dog Belinda near Malibu, California. He began his collegiate career at Princeton University, later transferring to Colorado College where he graduated in 1983 with a Bachelor of Arts in English. David is originally from suburban Boston, Massachusetts.

BIBLIOGRAPHY

Books:

Black, Conrad. *Franklin Delano Roosevelt: Champion of Freedom.* New York: PublicAffairs, 2003.

Blee, Ben W., Capt. USN, Ret. *Battleship North Carolina.* USS North Carolina Battleship Commission, 2005.

Blee, Ben W., Capt. USN, Ret. *Battleship North Carolina.* USS North Carolina Battleship Commission, 1982.

Calhoun, C. Raymond, Capt. USN, Ret. *Typhoon: The Other Enemy.* Annapolis: Naval Institute Press, 1998, © 1981.

MacGregor, Morris J, Jr., *Defense Studies Series: Integration of the Armed Forces 1940-1965.* U.S. Army Center of Military History Publications, 1985, © 1981.

Miller, Richard E. *The Messman Chronicles: African Americans in the U.S. Navy, 1932-1943.* Annapolis: Naval Institute Press, 2004.

Simmons, Charles A. *The African American Press: With Special Reference to Four Newspapers, 1827-1965.* Jefferson, N.C.: McFarland & Co., 2005, ©1998

Van der Vat, Dan. *The Pacific Campaign: The U.S.-Japanese Naval War 1941-1945.* New York: Touchstone/Simon & Schuster, 1992, © 1991.

Music:

Austin, Wayne G. *My Wonderful Lord by Ernest Johnson.* Brandon Methodist Church, 1967.

Internet References:

Ch. 3

Henderson, H. P. (2004). Talmadge, Eugene (1884-1946). In *The New Georgia Encyclopedia.* Retrieved from http://www.georgiaencyclopedia.org/nge/Article.jsp?id=h-1393

Ch. 5

Jim Crow. (n.d.). In *Spartacus Educational Encyclopedia online*. Retrieved from http://www.spartacus.schoolnet.co.uk/USAjimcrow.htm

Hattie McDaniel. (2011). In *Encyclopedia of World Biography*. Retrieved from http://www.notablebiographies.com/Ma-Mo/McDaniel-Hattie.html

Ch. 6

Inventory of the Graham W. Jackson, Sr. Papers. (2011). Digital Library of Georgia. Retrieved from http://dlg.galileo.usg.edu/aafa/print/aafa_aarl89-004.html

MacGregor, Morris J, Jr. (1985) *Defense Studies Series: Integration of the Armed Forces 1940-1965*. Retrieved from http://www.history.army.mil/books/integration/IAF-03.htm

Ch. 8

The Coastal Georgia Experience. (2003-2012). The St. Simons Island Experience. *History – St. Simons Island: The Plantations*. Retrieved from http://www.stsimonsislandexperience.com/site/539680/page/123261

Stroud, Mike. (2008). *S.S. Oklahoma and Esso Baton Rouge Attacked by U-123*. Retrieved from The Historical Marker Database. http://www.hmdb.org/marker.asp?marker=15609 (currently listed: http://www.glynncounty.com/cgi-bin/oaktree.pl?dbf=data.txt&ID=00012846)

MacGregor, Morris J, Jr. (1985) *Defense Studies Series: Integration of the Armed Forces 1940-1965*. Retrieved from http://www.history.army.mil/books/integration/IAF-03.htm

Ch. 9

Matson, Lowell. (1954). Theatre for the Armed Forces in World War II. *Educational Theatre Journal, Vol. 6, No. 1.* Retrieved from http://www.jstor.org/pss/3204158

NNDB.com. (2012). *Lena Horne.* Retrieved from
http://www.nndb.com/people/842/000024770/

Pics-Celeb.com. (2010). *Lena Horne.* Retrieved from http://www.pics-celeb.com/2010/01/lena-horne.html

Karoly, Steve. (1998). Seabee Log #4. *Brown Grass and Rolling Hills: Camp Parks Continues its Military Training Mission.* Retrieved from
http://www.armed-guard.com/ag83.html

Department of the Navy – Naval Historical Center. (n.d.) *USS General John Pope (AP-110), 1943-.* Retrieved from http://www.history.navy.mil/photos/sh-usn/usnsh-g/ap110.htm

International Dateline. (2011) In *World Atlas online.* Retrieved from
http://www.worldatlas.com/aatlas/infopage/dateline.htm

Ch. 10

Noumea. (2011) In *Encyclopedia Britannica.* Retrieved from http://www.britannica.com/EBchecked/topic/420844/Noumea

New-Caledonia. (2011) In *Encyclopedia Britannica.* Retrieved from
http://www.britannica.com/EBchecked/topic/411221/New-Caledonia

Hickman, Kennedy. (n.d.). *World War II Pacific: Advancing Across the Pacific – Island Hopping.* Retrieved from About.com–Military History.
http://militaryhistory.about.com/od/worldwarii/a/wwiipacishop.htm

Hickman, Kennedy. (2007). *World War II: Island Hopping to Victory.* Retrieved from About.com–Military History. http://militaryhistory.about.com/b/2007/10/12/world-war-ii-island-hopping-to-victory.htm

Commander U.S. 7th Fleet. (2007) *USS Stethem honors WWII veterans during New Caledonia visit.* Retrieved from http://www.c7f.navy.mil/news/2007/07-july/33.htm

Tropical-cyclone. (2011) In *Encyclopedia Britannica.* Retrieved from http://www.britannica.com/EBchecked/topic/606551/tropical-cyclone

Ch. 11

Courtesy Battleship NORTH CAROLINA, (n.d.). In *War Diary.* Retrieved from a source no longer available to the general public

Honolulu. (2011) In *Encyclopedia Britannica.* Retrieved from http://www.britannica.com/EBchecked/topic/271062/Honolulu

USS North Carolina (2011) In *Facebook.* Retrieved from http://www.facebook.com/pages/USS-North-Carolina/113328105347265?sk=info

Ch. 12

Courtesy Battleship NORTH CAROLINA, (n.d.). In *War Diary.* Retrieved from a source no longer available to the general public

Ch. 13

Courtesy Battleship NORTH CAROLINA, (n.d.). In *War Diary.* Retrieved from a source no longer available to the general public

Pike, John. (2011). *Rota – Marianas Islands.* Retrieved from http://www.globalsecurity.org/military/facility/rota-cnmi.htm

McDonald, Jason. (2011). The Battle of the Philippine Sea June 18 - 20, 1944. Retrieved from http://www.worldwar2database.com/html/marianas.htm

Ch. 14

Courtesy Battleship NORTH CAROLINA, (n.d.). In *War Diary*. Retrieved from a source no longer available to the general public

Herold, Robert. (2010). *The Old Navy Way.* Retrieved from http://www.inlander.com/spokane/article-14994-the-old-navy-way.html

Snyder and Short Enterprises. (n.d.). *USN Camouflage 1941-1945.* Retrieved from http://www.shipcamouflage.com/measures.htm

Ch. 15

Courtesy Battleship NORTH CAROLINA, (n.d.). In *War Diary*. Retrieved from a source no longer available to the general public

Naval History & Heritage - Command. (n.d.). *Cook Third Class Doris Miller, USN.* Retrieved from http://www.history.navy.mil/faqs/faq57-4.htm

Ch. 16

Courtesy Battleship NORTH CAROLINA, (n.d.). In *War Diary*. Retrieved from a source no longer available to the general public

Ch. 17

Courtesy Battleship NORTH CAROLINA, (n.d.). In *War Diary*. Retrieved from a source no longer available to the general public

Maloney, Bill. (2006). *Destroyer Escort Slater - 20mm Oerlikon Anti Aircraft Guns.* Retrieved from http://www.williammaloney.com/Dad/WWII/DestroyerEscortSlater/20mmOerlikonGuns/index.htm

Ch. 18

Courtesy Battleship NORTH CAROLINA, (n.d.). In *War Diary*. Retrieved from a source no longer available to the general public

Chen, C. Peter. (2012). In *OS2U Kingfisher*. Retrieved from http://ww2db.com/aircraft_spec.php?aircraft_model_id=221

Ch. 21

International Directory of Company Histories. (1993). *Service America Corporation*. Retrieved from http://www.fundinguniverse.com/company-histories/Service-America-Corp-Company-History.html

Ch. 22

Entitlement. (2011). In *Merriam-Webster*. Retrieved from http://www.merriam-webster.com/dictionary/entitlement

ENDNOTES

[1] The depression's immediate impact on Georgia was much like that throughout the nation as a whole. Bank failures were common, and in small towns and communities opportunities for loans dried up. Small business owners were especially vulnerable. Less money in local circulation meant fewer paying customers; with the absence of credit and financing, these business owners quickly went under.

 Large landowners were usually able to ride the depression out; a small number of farmers who made the transition from cotton production to soybeans, peanuts, corn, livestock, and hogs had resources to fall back on. For the rest of Georgia's farmers (69 percent of the population was rural in 1930), the depression was a catastrophe.

 First, the state experienced its worst drought on record in 1930-31. As the depression wore on, the defects and negative trends of cash-crop agriculture became magnified. The typical Georgia farm family had no electricity, no running water, and no indoor privies. Diets were inadequate, consisting mainly of molasses, fatback, and cornbread. The poverty of the state's most rural counties made the support of even minimal education standards impossible. There were few rural clinics, hospitals, or health care workers. Some counties had no health facilities at all.
http://www.georgiaencyclopedia.org/nge/Article.jsp?id=h-3540

[2] For the state's African American population, as the blues singer Lonnie Johnson put it, "Hard times don't worry me / I was broke when it first started out." Condemned by Jim Crow before the depression to inferior levels of education and the lowest-paying menial jobs, blacks were

blocked from participating in the state's political system. The income of rural blacks was about half that of rural whites. In the entire state there were only four black insurance companies, one bank (Citizens Trust Bank in Atlanta), and one wholly owned newspaper. According to the 1930 U.S. census, there were 10,110 black professionals in Georgia (out of a population of 1,071,125), the majority being clergymen and teachers. Hospitals for blacks existed only in the largest urban areas. The Great Depression slowed the black migratory stream north but did not stop it entirely. In 1890 African Americans accounted for 47 percent of Georgia's population and by 1930 just 37 percent.
http://www.georgiaencyclopedia.org/nge/Article.jsp?id=h-3540

[3] http://www.georgiaencyclopedia.org/nge/Article.jsp?id=h-1393

[4] After the American Civil War [1865] most states in the South passed anti-African American legislation. These became known as Jim Crow laws. This included laws that discriminated against African Americans with concern to attendance in public schools and the use of facilities such as restaurants, theaters, hotels, cinemas and public baths. Trains and buses were also segregated and in many states marriage between whites and African American people.
http://www.spartacus.schoolnet.co.uk/USAjimcrow.htm

[5] In attendance were Clark Gable, Vivien Leigh, Leslie Howard, Olivia de Havilland and Margaret Mitchell. Margaret Mitchell wrote the book that the movie was based on in 1936. Ironically, she lived only blocks away from the theatre on Peachtree Street. The film's black actors could not attend the premiere due to the Jim Crow segregation laws.

Actress Hattie McDaniel who played "Mammy," one of the maids in the movie, received honors in Hollywood for her performance. Due to segregation she could not stay in the same hotel with the rest of the cast, nor could she sit in the theatre. She did however attend the Hollywood debut on December 28, 1939 and won the 1940 Academy Award for Best Supporting Actress. McDaniel would become the first black person to win an Oscar.
http://www.notablebiographies.com/Ma-Mo/McDaniel-Hattie.html

[6] Graham Jackson Graham W. Jackson was born in Portsmouth, Virginia in 1903. His mother was a talented vocalist and musician. Graham W. Jackson exhibited musical talent as early as age three and was recognized as a prodigy because of his ability to master virtually any instrument without instruction. Excelling on both the piano and organ, Jackson was giving concerts while in high school. With the assistance of a well-to-do patron, he had hoped to go to college to further his studies. The unexpected death of the patron, Dr. King, destroyed Jackson's hope of going to college.

Graham W. Jackson continued performing and began touring, which led him to Atlanta, Georgia, in 1923. Here he found opportunities…to perform in such places as Atlanta's Royal Theater and Bailey's "81" [Theater] In 1928, Graham W. Jackson accepted an appointment to Washington High School as head of the music department. He held this position until 1940. During these 12 years, Jackson continued performing in and out of Atlanta, often for President Franklin D. Roosevelt. Jackson enlisted in the United States Navy May 16, 1942, and was discharged September 8, 1945. He was given numerous citations for his service to our country in helping to raise over $3 million worth of bonds and for recruiting for the Navy.

In 1945, Jackson became a national symbol of the grief felt over the passing of Franklin D. Roosevelt. A picture of Jackson playing the accordion and weeping as the body of Roosevelt left the Little White House in Warm Springs, Georgia, was published in Life magazine. Throughout his lifetime, people would remember Jackson from this picture and his association with Roosevelt.

Besides performing for and being known as the favorite musician of Franklin D. Roosevelt, Graham W. Jackson, Sr. had tributes too numerous to list here. He did perform for a total of seven consecutive presidents and was designated the "Official Musician of the State of Georgia.". He was remembered by many for his performances at Johnny Reb's Dixieland and Pittypat's Porch, two Atlanta restaurants.
http://dlg.galileo.usg.edu/aafa/print/aafa_aarl89-004.html

[7] http://www.history.army.mil/books/integration/IAF-03.htm

[8] Major Pierce Butler, an ex-officer in the British Army, became a Charleston, South Carolina rice planter during the 18th century.

Eventually his crops suffered from depleted soil. He purchased seventeen hundred acres at the northern end of St. Simons Island in 1774 and called it "Hampton." Butler ran a tight ship growing hundreds of acres of Sea Island cotton, utilizing the services of nearly a thousand slaves, and earning him the reputation as one of the largest plantations in the south. With him started "the era of the great plantations" during the 1790s.

During the same decade Scotsmen John Couper and partner James Hamilton who owned the southern end and southwestern portions of St. Simons made their own contributions to St. Simons' history. Couper, owner of "Cannon's Point" plantation took credit for experimenting with Sea Island cotton seeds which ultimately improved yield as well as selling the land the lighthouse stood on at the southern tip of St. Simons to the U.S. government for one dollar. Hamilton who owned a plantation of the same name meanwhile sold live oak timber to the "fledgling U.S. Navy" in 1794 for the construction of the USS Constitution known as "Old Ironsides." Couper and Hamilton tested cotton seeds Hamilton found from around the world.

Other plantation owners included Major William Page overseer to Butler's estate who saw an adjacent plot settled by James Spalding and purchased it. He named it "Retreat" overlooking St. Simons Sound and Jekyll Island. The Retreat produced "as many as ninety-six varieties of roses, among other flower plants."

In 1798, the State Legislature prohibited the direct acquisition of slaves from Africa, relying instead on the natural increase of those already in Georgia. Rather than eliminating importation, however, the edict gave rise to a slave smuggling trade along the isolated coastal islands. Tradition has it that slaves were brought ashore on the banks of the Dunbar Creek at a spot known today as Ebos Landing. The leader of the Ebos - a proud and noble tribe of Nigeria - led his people into the waters of the creek where they drowned themselves rather than submit to slavery. For many years, the blacks on St. Simons refused to go fishing in that portion of Dunbar Creek because they believed it was haunted by the spirits of those Ebo tribesmen.

If slavery was responsible for the emergence of the great plantations of St. Simons, so it was for their demise. The culture anchored by [Sea Island] cotton, slavery and the character of the planters who shaped it didn't survive beyond its third generation.

When the Civil War came to St. Simons, the island proved to be in a strategic location. It could supply food for soldiers, serve as a base for raiders and blockade-runners and command the entrance to Brunswick Harbor. Consequently, in January of 1861, Governor Brown ordered the Jackson Artillery from Macon to occupy St. Simons Island. But after several months at Frederica, the garrison duty was so dull they asked to be removed. When the Southern coastline was blockaded by the Federal fleet, 1,500 Georgia troops manned batteries at the south end of the island, near old Fort St. Simons, as well as strong fortifications on the northern end strengthened by five batteries. There was much social interaction between Confederate officers and islanders, particularly with the King family of Retreat Plantation, on whose property the fort was built.

The enthusiasm of those early days of the war soon dispersed when Robert E. Lee ordered the evacuation of St. Simons. The Confederate troops were sent north to defend Savannah; the planters, their families and most of the slaves went inland to seek refuge from the invading Yankees. As they departed, the Confederates destroyed the lighthouse, lest it become a navigational aid to the Union blockading fleet.

Federal warships soon patrolled the coastal waters, and the U.S. Navy assumed jurisdiction of St. Simons Island.
http://www.stsimonsislandexperience.com/site/539680/page/123261

[9] http://www.stsimonsislandexperience.com/site/539680/page/123261

[10] http://www.glynncounty.com/cgi-bin/oaktree.pl?dbf=data.txt&ID=00012846

[11] In June 1940 the Navy had 4,007 black personnel, 2.3 percent of its nearly 170,000-man total. All were enlisted men, and with the exception of six regular rated seamen, lone survivors of the exclusion clause, all were steward's mates, labeled by the black press "seagoing bellhops."…

Most Negroes performed humbler duties. By mid-1944 over 38,000 black sailors were serving as mess stewards, cooks, and bakers. These jobs remained in the Negro's eyes a symbol of his second-class citizenship in the naval establishment. Under pressure to provide more stewards to serve the officers whose number multiplied in the early months of the war, recruiters had netted all the men they could for that separate duty. Often recruiters took in many as stewards who were equipped by education and training for better jobs, and when these men were immediately put into uniforms and trained on the job at local naval stations the result was often dismaying. The Navy thus received poor service as well as unwelcome publicity for maintaining a segregated servants' branch. In an effort to standardize the training of messmen, the Bureau of Naval Personnel established a stewards school in the spring of 1943 at Norfolk and later one at Bainbridge, Maryland. The change in training did little to improve the standards of the service and much to intensify the feeling of isolation among many stewards.
http://www.history.army.mil/books/integration/IAF-03.htm

[12] …fifteen black crewmen on the U.S.S. Philadelphia, which Roosevelt had commandeered for cruising on occasion, wrote to the Pittsburgh Courier, advising other African-Americans to join the navy so as not to become "sea-going bell hops, chambermaids, and dishwashers." The

signatories to this letter expressed the view that no disciplinary action could "possible surpass the mental cruelty inflicted upon us in this ship." The signers of the letter were thrown into the brig and dishonorably discharged as unfit.
Black, Conrad. *Franklin Delano Roosevelt: Champion of Freedom.* New York: PublicAffairs, 2003.

13   Simmons, Charles A. *The African American Press: A History of News Coverage During National Crises, with Special Reference to Four Black Newspapers, 1827-1965.* Jefferson, N.C.: McFarland, 1998: pp. 73-4

14   Franklin D. Roosevelt [once] said: "Entertainment is always a national asset. Invaluable in time of peace, it is indispensable in wartime. Concurrence in this belief by many of our military men from Generals George C. Marshall and Dwight D. Eisenhower on down made the theatre projects of World War II possible. Commanders in all services realized that recreation of any kind was greatly responsible in reducing AWOL [absent without leave], venereal diseases, and lawlessness."
http://www.jstor.org/pss/3204158

15   Lena Horne was a singer, dancer, actress, and activist who had a wildly successful career as a nightclub performer and recording artist. She was also a noted stage actress, but her success in Hollywood was cut short because of her outspoken activism and African-American heritage... Her first memorable movies were both made in 1943... During World War II, like many American performers, she toured Europe entertaining American troops. She became controversial, however, when she refused to sing for segregated audiences, leading to "one-night integration" for numerous military concerts, and more often performing at black-only

venues. When she was not allowed to perform on the bases, she instead sang at whatever local nightclub welcomed African-American customers.
http://www.nndb.com/people/842/000024770/

[16] Horne had her most substantial film part in Cabin in the Sky (1943), playing the temptress Georgia Brown in this all-African-American musical... In Stormy Weather (1943),... she sang the title song, which became her signature tune... During World War II, Horne became the favorite pinup girl of African-American soldiers. She was also a popular entertainer in USO tours, though she would not perform if African Americans were denied admittance to her show. At the beginning of one performance, she walked offstage when she realized that African-American troops had been seated behind German prisoners of war. The USO pulled her from its tours, so Horne began entertaining troops on tours she financed herself.
http://www.pics-celeb.com/2010/01/lena-horne.html

[17] Since late 1942, Camp Parks has been home to the Navy, Air Force and Army... [A] base for Seabees, sailors, airmen and soldiers Commissioned on January 19, 1943, as the Construction Battalion Replacement Depot, Camp Parks functioned as home for Seabees returning from the Pacific Theater of Operations. Battalions returned to the States after a year or more of arduous construction duty. They came to Camp Parks for medical treatment, military training and reorganization.

The base housed up to 20 battalions at a time. Most battalions prepared for a second tour in the Pacific. Many Seabees were hospitalized, and those no longer fit for duty received their discharge. After leave, personnel were subjected to a rigorous training schedule. The battalions were brought back up to fighting strength.

This land-locked naval base sat adjacent to the quiet Bay Area towns of Dublin, Livermore and Pleasanton... Camp Parks is located 28 miles east of Oakland, California.

East of the Seabee base, toward Livermore, Camp Shoemaker housed a Naval Hospital and Naval Training and Personnel Distribution Center. These facilities served the fleet in much the same manner as Camp Parks served the Seabees. Collectively the area was known as Fleet City.
http://www.armed-guard.com/ag83.html

[18] USS General John Pope, name ship of a class of 19,650-ton (full load displacement) transports, was built at Kearny, New Jersey, to the Maritime Commission's P2-S2-R2 design. Placed in ferry commission in July 1943, she was commissioned in full in August 1943. After shakedown and a round-trip voyage to Scotland, in late September the ship arrived at Norfolk, Virginia, where her lifeboats and davits were replaced by life rafts. She was the only ship of her class so modified. In early October 1943 General John Pope sailed for the Pacific and during the next year and a half transported troops between San Francisco, California, and the southwest Pacific.
http://www.history.navy.mil/photos/sh-usn/usnsh-g/ap110.htm

[19] The International Date Line sits on the 180° line of longitude in the middle of the Pacific Ocean, and is the imaginary line that separates two consecutive calendar days. It is not a perfectly straight line and has been moved slightly over the years to accommodate needs of varied countries in the Pacific Ocean... Immediately to the left of the International Date Line the date is always

one day ahead of the date (or day) immediately to the right of the International Date Line in the Western Hemisphere... [T]ravel east across the International Date Line results in a day, or 24 hours, being subtracted. Travel west across the International Date Line results in a day being added.
http://www.worldatlas.com/aatlas/infopage/dateline.htm

[20] Nouméa, also spelled Numea, city, port, and capital of the French overseas country of New Caledonia, southwestern Pacific Ocean, in the southwestern corner of the main island of New Caledonia. It was founded in 1854 as Port-de-France. It [was] situated on an excellent deepwater harbour protected by Nou Island and a reef. The Grand Quay has a 1,450-foot- (442-metre-) long frontage.
http://www.britannica.com/EBchecked/topic/420844/Noumea

[21] New Caledonia, French Nouvelle-Calédonie, [is a] French unique collectivity in the southwestern Pacific Ocean, about 900 miles (1,500 km) east of Australia. It includes the island of New Caledonia (the Grande Terre [Mainland]), where the capital, Nouméa, [was] located; the Loyalty Islands; the Bélep Islands; and the Île des Pins. These islands form more than 99 percent of the total land area and lie between latitudes 18° and 23° S and longitudes 163° and 169° E. New Caledonia also includes a number of far-flung uninhabited islets: Huon and Surprise islands in the D'Entrecasteaux Reefs, the atolls of the Chesterfield Islands and the Bellona Reefs, Walpole Island, Beautemps-Beaupré Atoll, and Astrolabe Reefs. France also claims Hunter and Matthew islands, but the claim [was] disputed by Vanuatu.
http://www.britannica.com/EBchecked/topic/411221/New-Caledonia

[22] http://militaryhistory.about.com/od/worldwarii/a/wwiipacishop.htm

[23] http://militaryhistory.about.com/b/2007/10/12/world-war-ii-island-hopping-to-victory.htm

[24] http://www.c7f.navy.mil/news/2007/07-july/33.htm

[25] Tropical Cyclone, also called typhoon or hurricane, an intense circular storm that originates over warm tropical oceans and [was] characterized by low atmospheric pressure, high winds, and heavy rain. Drawing energy from the sea surface and maintaining its strength as long as it remains over warm water, a tropical cyclone generates winds that exceed 119 km (74 miles) per hour. In extreme cases winds may exceed 240 km (150 miles) per hour, and gusts may surpass 320 km (200 miles) per hour. Accompanying these strong winds [were] torrential rains and a devastating phenomenon known as the storm surge, an elevation of the sea surface that can reach 6 metres (20 feet) above normal levels. Such a combination of high winds and water makes cyclones a serious hazard for coastal areas in tropical and subtropical areas of the world. Every year during the late summer months (July–September in the Northern Hemisphere and January–March in the Southern Hemisphere), cyclones strike regions as far apart as the Gulf Coast of North America, northwestern Australia, and eastern India and Bangladesh.

Tropical cyclones [were] known by various names in different parts of the world. In the North Atlantic Ocean and the eastern North Pacific they [were] called hurricanes, and in the western North Pacific around the Philippines, Japan, and China the storms [were] referred to as typhoons. In the western South Pacific and Indian Ocean they [were] variously referred to as severe tropical

cyclones, tropical cyclones, or simply cyclones. All these different names refer to the same type of storm.
http://www.britannica.com/EBchecked/topic/606551/tropical-cyclone

[26] Honolulu, capital and principal port of Hawaii, U.S., seat of Honolulu county. A modern city, it extends about 10 miles (16 km) along the southeastern shore of Oahu Island and 4 miles (6 km) inland across a plain into the foothills of the Koolau Range. It [was] the crossroads of trans-Pacific shipping and air routes, the focus of interisland services, and the commercial and industrial centre of the state. The city-county (area 597 square miles [1,545 square km]) comprise all of Oahu and some outlying islets, which [had] an area aggregate of only 3 square miles (8 square km) but extend for more than 1,300 miles (2,100 km) and constitute the Hawaiian and Pacific Islands National Wildlife Refuge [Established 1909]. It [was] administered as a single entity and [had] about 80 percent of the state's population... December 1941 the city and the adjacent Pearl Harbor naval-military complex came under Japanese aerial attack. Honolulu became a prime staging area for the remainder of World War II...
http://www.britannica.com/EBchecked/topic/271062/Honolulu

[27] http://www.facebook.com/pages/USS-North-Carolina/113328105347265?sk=info

[28] NORTH CAROLINA was designed in an era when battleships were the principal combatants of the world's great navies, their role being to "slug it out" with big guns at ranges of up to 20 miles... [The] NORTH CAROLINA... was well equipped to hold her own with the guns finally selected as her main battery. Her nine 16-inch/45-caliber rifles have an internal barrel diameter of 16 inches, and a length of 45 times that

diameter or 60 feet. Each rifle weighs 96 tons; the weight of an entire turret was over 1,400 tons.
Blee, USN (Ret) Captain Ben W., *Battleship North Carolina*, USS North Carolina Battleship Commission, 2005: p. 10-11

[29] The [armor-piercing] projectiles could penetrate more than 20 inches of the strongest hardened steel armor at ranges up to 15,000 yards and more than 10 inches at 35,000 yards. Muzzle velocity was 2,300 feet per second. Maximum range, achieved by at a gun elevation angle of 45 degrees, was 36,900 yards or 21 statute miles. When fired at a range of 10,000 yards, the projectiles had a very flat trajectory and hit the target at an angle of only 6.8 degrees from the horizontal. At a range of 35,000 yards, following a maximum ordinate (highest in-flight altitude) of 22,490 feet, the projectiles crashed down on the target like bombs with an angle of fall of 45.16 degrees.

The 1,900-pound HC (high capacity) projectiles were designed for use against unarmored surface vessels such as destroyers, tankers and troopships; or against objectives ashore such as buildings, airstrips and enemy troops. The weight of the explosive charge was 153.58 pounds. Muzzle velocity was 2,635 feet per second. Maximum range, achieved at a gun elevation angle of 45 degrees, was 40,180 yards or 23 statute miles. In a shore bombardment of HC projectile could blow a hole in the ground 20 feet deep and 50 feet in diameter.
Blee, USN (Ret) Captain Ben W., *Battleship North Carolina*, USS North Carolina Battleship Commission, 2005: p. 12

[30] Japanese optical range finders for gunfire control were superior to those of the Americans, but the IJN was far behind in the development and use of radar. Although dedicated gunfire control radar was under development in Japan late in World War II, such equipment was not

known to had been installed operationally on any IJN ships. The nearest Japanese equivalent to shipboard fire control radar was the Type 22 surface search radar mounted on YAMATO during a January-April 1944 refit. This radar, never intended for gunfire control, provided a maximum detection range on battleships of 35,000 yards, with a range accuracy of ±765 yards and a bearing accuracy of ±5 degrees. In contrast, at a range of 37,000 yards the Mark 8 main battery fire control radars mounted on U.S. battleships provided range accuracy of ±15 yards and bearing accuracy of 2 mils (a little over one-tenth of 1 degree). These wide differences meant that American battleships would possess a potentially decisive advantage over the Japanese in the event of a surface action at long range in low daytime visibility or at night.
Blee, USN (Ret) Captain Ben W., *Battleship North Carolina*, USS North Carolina Battleship Commission, 2005: p. 109

[31] ...NORTH CAROLINA rejoined Task Force 58 in early June preparatory to the invasion of Saipan and Tinian and the recovery of Guam. The latter, with its excellent harbor and airfield, was the primary naval objective; but Saipan and Tinian were needed, too, as bases for future heavy bomber operations against the mainland of Japan. As usual Task Force 58 struck first, helping clear the way for the amphibious forces and assault troops. These were to include the 2nd, 3rd and 4th Marine Divisions; the 1st Provisional Marine Brigade; plus the 27th and 77th Infantry Divisions of the U.S. Army. Initial landings on Saipan were to be carried out on June 15; on Guam, July 21; and on Tinian, July 24. The Showboat was to take part in the first of these operations, but not the latter two.

On June 13, two days prior to the assault landings on Saipan, NORTH CAROLINA and six other fast

battleships subjected the island to a preliminary bombardment. NORTH CAROLINA, WASHINGTON and INDIANA fired at ranges between 16,000 and 10,000 yards into the western side of the island, where the landings were to take place. The main purpose was to cover minesweeping operations being conducted in shallower water closer to shore, in order to make way for the amphibious force. Under cover of the battleships' guns, the minesweeping operation was successfully accomplished by ascertaining that no mines had actually been laid off the landing beaches. Ammunition expended by NORTH CAROLINA: 360 rounds of 16-inch, 2,096 of 5-inch.
Blee, USN (Ret) Captain Ben W., *Battleship North Carolina*, USS North Carolina Battleship Commission, 2005: p. 106-7

[32] The Battle of the Philippine Sea in the Marianas in June 1944 was marked by the destruction of huge numbers of Japanese with low losses to the United States Navy. The Americans had set up an extensive program, including building a carrier that had no hangar deck, to train both aircrew and deck handlers. American pilots were entering combat with some 600 hours in the air. In contrast, the Japanese were sending green pilots into combat with only 50 hours of flight time and little combat training.

In addition, the Americans had numerical and technological superiority. The Japanese were replacing their aging B5N torpedo bombers with a more advanced version, the B6N Tenzan. It still lacked self-sealing fuel tanks or crew armor. In contrast, the Americans were continually introducing new aircraft. The F4F Wildcat was in service throughout the war, but after 1942 it was used as a ground attack aircraft. It was replaced in the front line carrier squadrons with the F6F Hellcat, which had more powerful armor and could dogfight with the

Japanese Mitsubishi Type 00. The Marines were given the F4U Corsair, which was not rated for carrier duty. Flying from forward airstrips, it was very effective against Japanese aircraft.

Nevertheless, the Japanese sent 500 aircraft on the new Taiho, the *Pearl Harbor* veteran Shokaku, and the hybrid battleships Ise and Hyuga. They were all that was left of the First Air Fleet after three years of continuous operations. Ozawa's pilots did not have night landing training, and they were given a single order: sink the enemy carriers. On June 18, 1944, as the Americans were landing all over the Marianas, Ozawa's search planes discovered the American Fleet. A more aggressive commander would have advanced on the Americans, but Ozawa was not Yamamoto. Cautious and slow, he chose to launch the next day when his pilots would have light to see.

The Americans were alerted to his presence by then. During the day of June 19, 1944, 429 of Ozawa's planes were shot down for the loss of twenty-nine *US Navy* planes. The one-sided engagement was the end of Japanese carrier-based air power. The Americans called the battle the "Marianas Turkey Shoot." The coming fight for the Philippines would depend on the battleships of the Imperial Japanese Navy in a war that was defined by airpower. The Americans would have 1200 aircraft on their carriers; the Japanese would have ninety. The few optimists left in *Japan* found their faith severely shaken.
http://www.worldwar2database.com/html/marianas.htm

[33] http://www.globalsecurity.org/military/facility/rota-cnmi.htm

[34] http://www.inlander.com/spokane/article-14994-the-old-navy-way.html

[35] http://www.shipcamouflage.com/measures.htm

[36] Following the training at the Naval Training Station, Norfolk, Virginia, Miller was assigned to the ammunition ship USS PYRO (AE-1) where he served as a Mess Attendant, and on 2 January 1940 was transferred to USS WEST VIRGINIA (BB-48), where he became the ship's heavyweight boxing champion. In July of that year he had temporary duty aboard USS NEVADA (BB-36) at Secondary Battery Gunnery School. He returned to West Virginia on 3 August, and was serving in that battleship when the Japanese attacked Pearl Harbor on 7 December 1941. Miller had arisen at 6 a.m., and was collecting laundry when the alarm for General Quarters sounded. He headed for his battle station, the antiaircraft battery magazine amidship, only to discover that torpedo damage had wrecked it, so he went on deck. Because of his physical prowess, he was assigned to carry wounded fellow Sailors to places of greater safety. Then an officer ordered him to the bridge to aid the mortally wounded Captain of the ship. He subsequently manned a 50 caliber Browning antiaircraft machine gun until he ran out of ammunition and was ordered to abandon ship...

Miller was commended by the Secretary of the Navy Frank Knox on 1 April 1942, and on 27 May 1942 he received the Navy Cross, which Fleet Admiral (then Admiral) Chester W. Nimitz, the Commander in Chief, Pacific Fleet personally presented to Miller on board aircraft carrier USS Enterprise (CV-6) for his extraordinary courage in battle. Speaking of Miller, Nimitz remarked: This marks the first time in this conflict that such high tribute had been made in the Pacific Fleet to a member of his race and I'm sure that the future would see others similarly honored for brave acts.
http://www.history.navy.mil/faqs/faq57-4.htm

[37] The rapid-fire 20-mm cannons were viewed as the last resort in an air attack since they were effective only within a 2,000-yard range. Mounted on a pedestal, the air-cooled gun was trained, elevated and fired manually by a gunner strapped snugly against the shoulder rests. A "trunnion operator" raised and lowered the pedestal (trunnion) on which the gun was mounted. The "spotter" observed gunfire and changed range settings on the Mark 14 gun sight accordingly. The "loader" fed heavy drum-shaped magazines onto the gun. Each magazine held 60 rounds, providing a theoretical maximum rate of fire of 450 rounds per minute. Like the 40-mm projectiles, the 20-mm exploded on impact.
Blee, USN (Ret) Captain Ben W., *Battleship North Carolina*, USS North Carolina Battleship Commission, 2005: p. 27

[38] The Japanese word kamikaze, or "divine wind," dates from the year 1281, when Mongols under Kublai Khan attempted to invade Japan, but were thwarted by a wind said to have been sent from heaven. That wind, actually a typhoon, destroyed the invasion fleet and saved Japan. Hoping to achieve the same happy outcome in the waning months of the World War II, kamikaze operation "Ten Go" was launched in deadly earnest..."
Blee, USN (Ret) Captain Ben W., *Battleship North Carolina*, USS North Carolina Battleship Commission, 2005: p. 132

[39] http://ww2db.com/aircraft_spec.php?aircraft_model_id=221

[40] With FRANKLIN launching her second strike of the day, the enemy pilot succeeded in reaching a position above her, diving on her out of the cloud cover and dropping two bombs amidst the heavily armed and fully gassed planes crowding the carrier's flight deck. "Big Ben" immediately burst into flames fore and aft. By the hundreds, men were blown over or compelled to jump

over the side. Over 1,700 men were soon visible as a trail of bobbing heads in the wake of the stricken ship, some dead and some terribly wounded. NORTH CAROLINA, steaming at high speed directly astern of the carrier, was forced to swerve sharply to port in order to avoid plowing through these men. As the Showboat streamed past, her crew showered the sea with their own life jackets, life rafts, empty powder cases, spud crates and anything else that would float. Destroyers quickly closed in for the rescue. When the losses were finally tallied up, 724 men of FRANKLIN's crew were killed or missing, 265 wounded. This was the single worst combat disaster witnessed during the entire war from the decks of NORTH CAROLINA.
Blee, USN (Ret) Captain Ben W., *Battleship North Carolina*, USS North Carolina Battleship Commission, 2005: p. 129

[41] Blee, USN (Ret) Captain Ben W., *Battleship North Carolina*, USS North Carolina Battleship Commission, 2005: p. 136

[42] http://www.williammaloney.com/Dad/WWII/DestroyerEscortSlater/20mmOerlikonGuns/index.htm

[43] Blee, USN (Ret) Captain Ben W., *Battleship North Carolina*, USS North Carolina Battleship Commission, 2005: p. 138-9

[44] [Ernest Johnson was born in Chelsea, Massachusetts on July 18, 1895.] It had been the writer's privilege and good fortune to have known Ernest Johnson for over 35 years. During these many years he had traveled over New England, New York, parts of the middle West, and Lower Canada. Vermont had been the particular field of his services. His songs have delighted and inspired thousands of people, young and old. His songs have a peculiar spiritual quality which tend to have a cleansing effect on the hearts of his audiences. His range of songs made it possible for him to serve all kinds of helpful organizations. He often took charge of morning or evening services. Thousands of ministers and lay folks have

entertained him in their homes. These visits were never forgotten...

...For many years Ernest Johnson delighted and edified large audiences of children and teenagers in our public schools. Many times he had entertained folks in our institutions where his music had great therapeutic value.

He had never put a price on his music. His singing had been a work of faith, for his support had come from free will offerings. Now his first record at the age of 72, will continue to bring the Gospel message of our wonderful Lord to thousands of homes.

[45] http://www.fundinguniverse.com/company-histories/Service-America-Corp-Company-History.html

[46] http://www.merriam-webster.com/dictionary/entitlement

www.ingramcontent.com/pod-product-compliance
Lightning Source LLC
Chambersburg PA
CBHW060450170426
43199CB00011B/1155